Lewis' I

Christoper Ryan has been actively involved in genealogy and history for many years. He has published papers in many journals and edited *Aspects of Irish Genealogy 3*.

Lewis' Dublin

A TOPOGRAPHICAL DICTIONARY OF THE
PARISHES, TOWNS AND VILLAGES OF DUBLIN
CITY AND COUNTY

COMPILED BY
CHRISTOPHER RYAN

The Collins Press

Published in 2001 by
The Collins Press,
West Link Park,
Doughcloyne,
Wilton,
Cork

First published as part of *The Topographical Dictionary of Ireland* by S. Lewis & Co., London, 1837
Introduction © Christopher Ryan, 2001

British Library Cataloguing in Publication data.

Printed in Ireland by Wood Printcraft Group.

Typesetting by Red Barn Publishing.

ISBN: 1-898256-95-0

Samuel Lewis created a sensation with his *Topographical Dictionary of Ireland* when it was first published in 1837. It contained the statistics from the first complete census of Ireland, which had been conducted in 1831, and included a description of 3,255 places, including towns and villages of any consequence, along with civil parish divisions. It described agriculture, industry, fishing, mineral resources, buildings, schools, churches and the people, in two volumes, covering the whole of Ireland and totalling 1,400 pages. For each listing this source identified its exact location by province, county, barony, direction and distance from the nearest major town or city. It is a major source on early nineteenth-century Ireland.

Over 120 places were described for Dublin, four per cent of the total, from Artane in the north side to Williamstown in the south side. Extensive entries on Dublin – city and county – describe their origins, archaeology and history, industry, buildings, institutions, etc. This is probably the most comprehensive description of Dublin in pre-famine times.

ARTANE, otherwise Artaine, a parish in the barony of Coolock, county of Dublin, and province of Leinster, 2½ miles (N.) from the Post-Office, Dublin; containing 583 inhabitants. The village is situated on the road from Dublin to Malahide, and has a penny post. Artane castle was long the property of the Donellans of Ravensdale, and is said to have been the scene of the death of John Alen or Alan, Archbishop of Dublin, who in endeavouring to escape from the vengeance of the house of Kildare, which he had provoked by his adherence to the will and measures of Cardinal Wolsey, was shipwrecked near Clontarf; and being made prisoner by some followers of that family, was brought before Lord Thos. Fitzgerald, then posted here with the insurgent army, whom he earnestly entreated to spare his life; but, either failing in his supplications, or from the wilful reconstruction of a contemptuous expression by Fitzgerald into a sentence of death on the part of those around him, as variously alleged by different writers, he was instantly slain in the great hall of the castle, on the 28th of July, 1534. On the breaking out of hostilities in 1641, it was taken by Luke Netterville, one of the R. C. leaders, at the head of a body of royalists, and garrisoned. The parish comprises 946 statute acres, of which about 20, including roads, are untitheable and of no value. The old castle was pulled down in 1825, and on its site and with its materials was erected, by the late Matthew Boyle, Esq., uncle of the present proprietor, M. Callaghan, Esq., a handsome house, which commands a splendid view of the islands of Lambay and Ireland's Eye, the hill of Howth, and the Dublin and Wicklow mountains. The other seats are Elm Park, the residence of T. Hutton, Esq.; Thorndale, of D. H. Sherrard, Esq.; Woodville, of J. Cornwall, Esq.; Artaine House, of T. Alley, Esq.; Mount Dillon, of H. Cooper, Esq.; Kilmore House, of H. Hutton, Esq.; Belfield, of Capt. Cottingham; Artaine Cottage, of J. Cusack, Esq.; Pozzodigotto, of Mrs. Atkinson; and Stella Lodge, of M. Curwen, Esq. In its ecclesiastical concerns this is a chapelry, in the diocese of Dublin, and one of three which, with the rectory of Finglas and the curacy of St. Werburgh's, Dublin, constitute the corps of the chancellorship in the cathedral church of St. Patrick, Dublin, which is in the patronage of the Archbishop. The church is a picturesque ruin, partly covered with ivy: in the burial-ground is a tombstone to the Hollywood family, to which the manor belonged for many ages, and of which John Hollywood, a distinguished mathematician and philosopher of the 13th

1

century, was a member. In the R. C. divisions it is in the union or district of Clontarf, Coolock, and Santry. A neat school-house for boys and girls, with apartments for the master and mistress, was built near the old church by the late M. Boyle, Esq., in 1832, at an expense of more than £600, of which £150 was repaid by the National Board, which contributes £25 per annum towards the support of the school, and, in 1833, Mr. Boyle bequeathed £10 per annum for the same purpose: the number of boys on the books is 116, and of girls, 107.

BALBRIGGAN, a seaport, market, and post-town, and a chapelry, in the parish and barony of Balrothery, county of Dublin, and province of Leinster, 15 miles (N. by E.) from Dublin; containing 3016 inhabitants. According to Ware, a sanguinary conflict took place here on Whitsun-eve, 1329, between John de Bermingham, Earl of Louth, who had been elevated to the palatine dignity of that county, Richard, Lord De Malahide, and several of their kindred, in array against the partisans of the Verduns, Gernons, and Savages, who were opposed to the elevation of the earl to the palatinate of their county; and in which the former, with 60 of their English followers, were killed. After the battle of the Boyne, Wm. III. encamped at this place on the 3rd of July, 1690. The town, which is situated on the eastern coast and on the road from Dublin to the North of Ireland, owes its rise, from a small fishing village to a place of manufacturing and commercial importance, to the late Baron Hamilton, who, in 1780, introduced the cotton manufacture, for which he erected factories, and who may justly be regarded as its founder. It contains at present about 600 houses, many of which are well built; hot baths have been constructed for visitors who frequent this place during the bathing season. In the environs are several gentlemen's seats, of which the principal is Hampton Hall, the residence of G. A. Hamilton, Esq. The inhabitants are partly employed in the fishery, but principally in the cotton manufacture; there are two large factories, the machinery of which is worked by steam engines and water-wheels of the aggregate power of 84 horses, giving motion to 7500 spindles, and spinning upon the average about 7400 lb. of cotton yarn per week. More than 300 persons are employed in these factories, to which are attached blue dye-works; and in the town and neighbourhood are 942 hand-looms employed in the weaving department. The principal articles made at present are checks, jeans, calicoes, and fustians. The town is also celebrated for the manufacture of the finest cotton stockings, which has been carried on successfully since its first establishment about 40 years since; there are 60 frames employed in this trade, and the average produce is about 60 dozen per week. There are on the quay a large corn store belonging to Messrs. Frost & Co., of Chester, and some extensive salt-works; and in the town is a tanyard. The fishery, since the withdrawing of the bounty, has very much diminished: there are at present only 10 wherries or small fishing boats belonging to the port. The town carries on a tolerably brisk coasting trade: in 1833, 134 coal vessels, of the aggregate burden of 11,566 tons, and 29 coasting vessels of 1795 tons, entered inwards, and 17 coasters of 1034 tons cleared outwards, from and to ports in Great Britain. The harbour is rendered safe for vessels of 150 tons' burden by an excellent pier, completed in 1763, principally by Baron Hamilton aided by a parliamentary grant, and is a place of refuge for vessels of that burden at ¾ tide. A jetty or pier, 420 feet long from the N.W. part of the harbour, with a curve of 105 feet in a western direction, forming an inner harbour in which at high tide is 14 feet of water, and affording complete shelter from all winds, was commenced in 1826 and completed in 1829, at an expense of £2912. 7. 9, of which the late Fishery Board gave £1569, the Marquess of Lansdowne £100, and the remainder was subscribed by the late Rev. Geo. Hamilton, proprietor of the town. At the end of the old pier there is a lighthouse. The Drogheda or Grand Northern Trunk railway from Dublin, for which an act has been obtained, is intended to pass along the shore close to the town and to the east of the church. The market is on Monday, and is abundantly supplied with corn, of which great quantities are sent to Dublin and to Liverpool; and there is a market for provisions on Saturday. Fairs are held on the 29th of April and September, chiefly for cattle. A market-house was erected in 1811, partly by subscription and partly at the expense of the Hamilton family. The town is the headquarters of the constabulary police force of the county and near it is a martello tower with a coast-guard station, which is one of the nine stations within the district of Swords. Petty sessions for the north-east division of the county are held here every alternate Tuesday.

The chapelry of St. George, Balbriggan, was founded by the late Rev. G. Hamilton, of Hampton Hall, who in 1813 granted some land and settled an endowment, under the 11th and 12th of Geo. III., for the establishment of a perpetual curacy; and an augmentation of £25 per annum has been recently granted by the Ecclesiastical Commissioners from Primate Boulter's fund. In 1816 a chapel was completed, at an expense of £3018. 2. 2., of which £1400 was given by the late Board of First Fruits, £478. 15. 2. was raised by voluntary subscriptions of the inhabitants, and £1139. 7. was given by the founder and his family. This chapel, which was a handsome edifice with a square embattled tower, and contained monuments to the memory of R. Hamilton, Esq., and the Rev. G. Hamilton, was burned by accident in 1835, and the congregation assemble for divine service in a school-room till it shall be restored, for which purpose the Ecclesiastical Commissioners have lately granted £480. The living is in the patronage of G. A. Hamilton, Esq. There is a chapel belonging to the R. C. union or district of Balrothery and Balbriggan, also a place of worship for Wesleyan Methodists. The parochial school and a dispensary are in the town. —See BALROTHERY.

BALDOYLE, a parish, in the barony of Coolock, county of Dublin, and province of Leinster, 6 miles (N.E.) from Dublin; containing 1208 inhabitants, of which number, 1009 are in the village. The village is pleasantly situated on an inlet or creek of the Irish Sea, to the north of the low isthmus that connects Howth with the mainland: it comprises about 200 houses, and is much frequented in summer for sea-bathing. Some of the inhabitants are engaged in the fishery, which at the commencement of the present century employed nine wherries belonging to this place, averaging seven or eight men each; at present nearly 100 men are so engaged. Sir W. de Windsor, lord-justice of Ireland, held a parliament here in 1369. The creek is formed between the mainland and the long tract of sand on the north of Howth, at the point of which, near that port, a white buoy is placed; it is fit only for small craft. The manor was granted to the priory of All Saints, Dublin, by Diarmit, the son of Murchard, King of Leinster, who founded that house in 1166. The corporation of Dublin owns the entire parish, about two-thirds of which are arable: the system of agriculture is improving, and the general routine of crops is pursued with success. Donaghmede, the seat of Mrs. King; Talavera, of Capt. N. Furnace; and Grange Lodge, of W. Allen, Esq., are the principal seats. The village is a chief station of the constabulary police, and also a coast-guard station, forming one of the nine which constitute the district of Swords. The Drogheda or Grand Northern Trunk railway from Dublin to that town, for which an act has been obtained, is intended to pass through the grange of Baldoyle. The parish is in the diocese of Dublin, and is a curacy forming part of the union of Howth: it is tithe-free. In the R. C. divisions it is included in the union or district of Baldoyle and Howth, which comprises also the parishes of Kinsealy and Kilbarrack, and contains three chapels, situated respectively at Howth, Kinsealy, and Baldoyle, which last has been lately rebuilt by subscription, and has a portico of four Tuscan pillars surmounted by a pediment, above which rises a turret supporting a dome and cross: attached to the chapel are school-rooms, in which about 60 boys and 60 girls are taught. The parochial school-house is in the village, and there is also a hedge school in the parish, in which are 12 children. At the Grange are the picturesque ruins of the ancient church, surrounded by horse-chestnut, lime, and sycamore trees; and in the grounds of Donaghmede is a holy well, which is resorted to on St. John's eve by the peasantry.

BALDUNGAN, a parish, in the barony of Balrothery, county of Dublin, and province of Leinster, 14 miles (N.N.E.) from Dublin; containing 88 inhabitants. A strong fortress was erected here, in the 13th century, by the Barnewall family, which subsequently became the property of the Lords of Howth, and in the civil war of 1641 was defended for the parliament by Col. Fitzwilliam, but was ultimately surrendered to the royalists, by whom it was dismantled and a great portion of the building destroyed; the remains, which were very extensive, have, within the last few years, been almost wholly taken down by the tenant. Near its site are still some remains of a church, more than 80 feet in length, with a tower of ten sides, of durable materials and excellent workmanship. According to Archdall, here was a commandery of Knights Templars, dedicated to the Blessed Virgin, of which this was probably the church. The prevailing substratum of the parish is limestone; but the hill of Baldungan is chiefly composed of Lydian stone and flinty slate. The living is a rectory, in the diocese of Dublin, and in the patronage of the Earl of Howth: the tithes amount to £52. 4. The church is in ruins, and there is neither glebe-house nor glebe. In the R. C. divisions the parish forms part of the union or district of Skerries.

BALDWINSTOWN, a village in the parish of Garistown, barony of Balrothery, county of Dublin, and province of Leinster, 4 miles (N.W.) from Ashbourne; containing 35 houses and 218 inhabitants.

BALGRIFFIN – See BELGRIFFIN.

BALL'S-BRIDGE, a village, in that part of the parish of St. Mary, Donnybrook, which is within the county of the city of Dublin, in the province of Leinster, 1½ mile (S.E.) from the Post-Office, Dublin: the population is returned with the parish. This place derives its name from a bridge of three arches erected here over the Dodder, in 1791, and rebuilt in 1835. It is pleasantly situated on the high road from Dublin to Kingstown and Bray, and on the left or west bank of the river, which issues from the mountains near Rockbrook, and falls into the Liffey near Ringsend. In the immediate vicinity, and on the right of the road from Dublin, stood Baggot-rath Castle, which was seized during the night by the forces of the Marquess of Ormonde, on his meditated investiture of the city, in 1649; but soon after daybreak on the following morning, the assailants were driven out by the garrison of Dublin and pursued and completely defeated. In 1651 the castle was taken by storm by Oliver Cromwell. All remains of it have long since disappeared; and within the last few years several handsome houses have been erected on its site. Adjoining the village, on the south, and along the banks of the Dodder, are works for printing linen, calico, and cotton, established about the year 1740, and since greatly extended and improved by Messrs. Duffy and Co., who for more than 40 years have been the sole proprietors. They are at present capable of finishing 100,000 pieces annually, are worked by the water of the Dodder and by steam-engines of 40-horse power, and afford constant employment to more than 400 persons. Near the village are the Hammersmith iron-works, established in 1834 by Mr. R. Turner: the front of this extensive establishment is 200 feet long, presenting a handsome façade towards the road; and at the back are numerous dwelling houses for the workmen, which are called the Hammersmith cottages. The road on which these works are situated has been greatly improved; wide footpaths have been formed, and the whole is lighted with gas. Nearly adjoining the works are the botanical gardens belonging to Trinity College. The village is within the jurisdiction of the Dublin Court of Conscience for the recovery of small debts, and for all criminal matters within that of the metropolitan police. In the post-office arrangements it is within the limits of the twopenny-post delivery. An infants' school, a neat building with apartments for a master and mistress, was erected chiefly at the expense of Mr. and Mrs. Patten: here is also a dispensary. —See DONNYBROOK (St Mary).

BALLYBOGHILL, a parish, in the barony of Balrothery, county of Dublin, and province of Leinster, 4 miles (N.W. by N.) from Swords, on the road from Dublin, by Naul, to Drogheda; containing 664 inhabitants, of which number, 144 are in the village, in which is a station of the constabulary police. It is a vicarage, in the diocese of Dublin, and forms part of the union and corps of the prebend of Clonmethan in the cathedral of St. Patrick, Dublin; the rectory is impropriate in the Crown. The tithes amount to £275. 15. of which £141 is payable to the crown, and, £134. 15. to the vicar. The church is in ruins. In the R. C. divisions it is in the union or district of Naul, also called Damastown; the chapel is a neat building. A schoolhouse was erected in the village by subscription, and there are two private schools in the parish.

BALLYBOUGHT, a parish, in the barony of Uppercross, county of Dublin, and province of Leinster, 2 miles (S.W.) from Ballymore-Eustace; containing 207 inhabitants. This parish is situated on the road from Ballymore to Hollywood, and is chiefly under an improving system of tillage and pasturage; it forms part of the lordship and manor of Ballymore. White Lays is the seat of J. M. Lynch, Esq. It is a vicarage, in the diocese of Dublin, and is one of four which constitute the union of Ballymore; the rectory is appropriate to the treasurership in the cathedral of St. Patrick, Dublin. The tithes amount to £41. 3. 1., of which £11. 18. 9. is payable to the treasurer, and £29. 4. 4. to the vicar. The church is in ruins; and there is neither glebe nor glebe-house. In the R. C. divisions also it is included in the union or district of Ballymore. Near Broad Lays is a rath or moat, in which, on its being opened a few years since, was discovered, about twenty feet from the surface, a large circular flagstone placed over several compartments, each having a small flag at the top and containing ashes and burnt bones. Near

White Lays there is a circle of large blocks of granite, which must have been brought hither, as there is no granite in the parish; in the centre were several upright stones, which have been removed; it is supposed to be a druidical relic.

BALLYCOOLANE, or CLOGHRAN-HIDART, a parish, in the barony of Castleknock, county of Dublin, and province of Leinster, 4 miles (N.) from Dublin; containing 72 inhabitants. This place, which originally belonged to the priory of All Saints, passed, on the dissolution of that house, with its other possessions, to the mayor and corporation of Dublin. The gentlemen's seats are Haighfield, the residence of J. Martin, Esq., and Yellow Walls, that of W. Finn, Esq., both commanding fine views of the Dublin and Wicklow mountains, with the country adjacent. Here is a constabulary police station. The living is an impropriate curacy, in the diocese of Dublin, held with the vicarage of Finglass, and in the patronage of the Archbishop; the rectory is impropriate in the corporation of Dublin. There is no church, but the churchyard is still used as a burial-place. In the R. C. divisions the parish forms part of the union or district of Castleknock. There are two pay schools, in which are about 50 children.

BALLYFERMOT, a parish. in the barony of Newcastle, county of Dublin, and province of Leinster, 3 miles (W. by S.) from Dublin; containing 402 inhabitants. It is intersected on the south side by the Grand Canal, and comprises 1178 statute acres, as applotted under the tithe act, and valued at £3214 per annum. Ballyfermot Castle, an ancient building, is now the residence of Capt. Lamplin; the other seats are Johnstown, the residence of T. Daly, Esq., and Johnstown Lodge, of — Place, Esq. An extensive paper-manufactory, belonging to Messrs McDonnel and Sons, in which from 70 to 80 persons are generally employed, is carried on at Killeen: the principal kinds made are bank-note paper for the Bank of Ireland, and printing paper for the Dublin newspapers. Within the enclosure of this establishment, which resembles a small town, are dwelling-houses for the workmen and their families: the house of the proprietor is pleasantly situated in some tastefully ornamented grounds. There is also in the parish a small manufacture of glue and parchment. It is a rectory, in the diocese of Dublin, and is part of the union of Chapelizod: the tithes amount to £130. The church is in ruins. In the R. C. divisions it is included in the union or district of Lucan, Palmerstown, and Clondalkin.

BALLYMADUN, or BALLYMODUM, a parish, in the barony of Balrothery, county of Dublin, and province of Leinster, 1½ mile (N.) from Ashbourne; containing 795 inhabitants, of which number 73 are in the village. This parish is situated on the road from Balbriggan to Ratoath: it was anciently the residence of a hermitess, who had a cell here, and claimed a small rent-charge from the prioress of Grace-Dieu at Lusk; the ruins of an ancient church may still be traced. Part of the bog of Corragh is within its limits, and white marl is found in great abundance; there is also a very fine quarry of calp in the village. Borranstown, the residence of W. P. Segrave, Esq., is a handsome mansion with an elegant Ionic portico of four columns supporting a cornice and pediment in the principal front; it occupies an elevated site commanding extensive views of the surrounding country. Nutstown, the residence of M. Curtis, Esq., is also in the parish. It is a vicarage, in the diocese of Dublin, and is part of the union and corps of the prebend of Clonmethan in the cathedral of St. Patrick, Dublin; the rectory is impropriate in Robert William Netterville, Esq. The tithes amount to £162. 9. 3., the whole of which is payable to the impropriator. The church is in ruins. The glebe comprises 31a. 3r., statute measure. In the R. C. divisions it is included in the union or district of Garristown and Ballymadun; the chapel is a neat building, and was enlarged by the addition of a gallery in 1833. The horns of an elk, measuring 11f. 8in. from tip to tip, were dug up in 1823, and are now in the possession of F. Savage, Esq., one of the principal proprietors of the parish.

BALLYMORE, or BALLYMORE-EUSTACE, a market-town and parish, in the barony of Uppercross, county of Dublin, and province of Leinster, 18 miles (S.W.) from Dublin; containing 2085 inhabitants, of which number, 841 are in the town. This town derives its name, signifying "the great town of Eustace," from its foundation by that family, a branch of the Fitzgeralds, who also erected here a castle of great strength, the ruins of which have been lately entirely removed. It is situated on the river Liffey, over which is a handsome stone bridge of six arches, and consists of one principal and three smaller streets: there is a penny post to Naas. The great southern road formerly passed through it, but has been diverted through the village of Kilcullen by the construction of a new line, and the town has since considerably decayed. A large manufactory, in which every description of cloth is made, was erected in the vicinity by Mr. Christopher Dromgoole, in 1802 and, when in full work, employs about 700 persons. The market, granted by Jas.I. to the Archbishop of Dublin, having fallen into disuse, was revived about seven years since; it is held on Wednesday and is well supplied with grain. Fairs are held on Easter-Monday, June 24th, Aug. 26th, Oct. 28th, and Dec. 21st, principally for cattle, pigs, and sheep. Here is a station of the constabulary police. The parish is the head of a lordship and manor belonging to the Archbishop of Dublin, and comprising the parishes of Ballymore, Ballybought, Cotlandstown, Yagoe, Tipperkevin, and Tubber, in the county of Dublin, and of Milltown and Tornant, and part of Rathsallagh, in the county of Wicklow. The system of agriculture is improving. Mount-Cashell Lodge, the property of the Earl of Mount-Cashell, is pleasantly situated, and is in the occupation of Mr. Dromgoole. The other principal residences are Ardenode, that of E. Homan, Esq.; Season, of Mrs. O'Brien; and Willfield, of R. Doyle, Esq. The living is a vicarage, in the diocese of Dublin and Glendalough, with those of Ballybought, Cotlandstown, and Yagoe episcopally united time immemorially, forming the union of Ballymore, in the patronage of the Archbishop: the rectory is partly appropriate to the economy estate of the cathedral of St. Patrick, Dublin, and partly united to those of Boystown and Luske, which together constitute the corps of the treasurership in that cathedral. The tithes amount to £145. 11. 1., of which £27. 10. 7. is payable to the lessee of the dean and chapter, £39. 2. 7. to the lessee of the treasurer, and £78. 17. 11. to the vicar; and the gross tithes of the benefice amount to £137. 2. 3. The church is a plain building with an embattled tower surmounted with pinnacles, erected in 1820 by the late Board of First Fruits, at a cost of £900: the churchyard is of great extent, and contains the remains of the old church, and numerous ancient tombstones. There is neither glebe nor glebe-house. In the R. C. divisions this parish is the head of a union or district, which comprises also the parishes of Ballybought, Cotlandstown, and Tipperkevin, in the county of Dublin, and the parish of Hollywood and part of Blessington, in that of Wicklow the chapel at Ballymore is a substantial and commodious building, and there is another at

Hollywood. The parochial school is supported by subscription; and there is another school, for which a school-house was erected by subscription in 1835, at an expense of about £400: there are also two private schools in the parish. About a mile from the town the river Liffey forms the celebrated cascade of Poul-a-Phuca, or the Demon's Hole, consisting of three successive waterfalls 150 feet in height. The chasm is only 40 feet wide, and is skirted on each side by perpendicular masses of grauwacke rock; and when the river is swollen by heavy rains the water rushes down with tumultuous impetuosity into a circular basin of the rock, worn quite smooth and of great depth, the form of which imparts to it the motion of a whirlpool, and from which the cascade derives its name. It then dashes through narrow openings in the rocks, and forms two more falls, the lowest being about 50 feet high. Immediately over the basin, on the line of the new turnpike road from Blessington to Baltinglass, is a picturesque bridge of one pointed arch springing from rock to rock, built in an antique style from a design by the late Alex. Nimmo, Esq., at an expense, including the land arches and approaches, of £4074. 15.; the span of the arch is 65 feet, the altitude of the chord above the upper fall is 47 feet, and the height of the keystone of the arch above the bed of the river is 150 feet. The late Earl of Miltown took a lively interest in this picturesque spot, which he embellished by planting one side of the glen forming part of his estate, making walks, and erecting rustic buildings in various places, besides a banqueting room, 45 feet long by 25 wide, from which there is a delightful view of the falls and the bridge, with the perpendicular rocks partly planted, and the upper moss seat appearing through the arch; but owing to the disturbances of 1798 he went abroad, and some time after sold it to Col. Aylmer, who is now the proprietor, and has appointed a person to take proper care of it, by whom accommodation has been prepared for the numerous visitors that resort hither from Dublin and elsewhere, and seats have been placed in the most advantageous situations for obtaining different views of the fall; a rustic seat above the head of the fall commands an excellent view of the cataract, bridge, lower rustic seat, and banqueting-hall, with the windings of the river.

BALROTHERY, a parish and village, in the barony of Balrothery, county of Dublin, and province of Leinster; containing, with the post-town of Balbriggan, 5078 inhabitants, of which number, 375 are in the village. This place, which gives name to the barony, was anciently annexed to that part of the church of Lusk, which in the earlier ages belonged to the archdeaconry of Dublin, and was separated from it about the year 1220 by Archbishop Henry. The village is situated on the road from Dublin to Balbriggan, from which latter it is distant about a mile, and in 1831 contained 84 houses. According to tradition, Jas. II. is said to have slept at the White Hart Inn here, before the battle of the Boyne: and the same distinction is claimed by another ancient house in the village, which was formerly an extensive inn. Fairs are held on the 6th of May and 12th of August. The parish comprises 8767 statute acres, as applotted under the tithe act: about 320 acres are woodland, principally in the demesne of G. A. Hamilton, Esq., and about 80 are bog or waste land; the remainder is arable and pasture, but is principally under tillage, and is very fertile in corn, which is the chief produce. A small portion of the bog of Ring is within the parish; and near the glebe is a reservoir of 22 acres, called the Knock, which supplies the mills of Balbriggan with water. At Curtlagh is a very fine stone quarry, and good stone for building is also obtained from the cliffs. The coast is composed of strata of transition rocks of grauwacke, grauwacke slate, clay-slate, and greenstone, with spar in small portions. The Drogheda, or Grand Northern Trunk, railway from Dublin to that town will pass through the parish, close to the shore. Hampton Hall, the seat of G. A. Hamilton, Esq., is an elegant mansion situated in a rich demesne of 500 acres, finely wooded and pleasingly diversified with hill and dale: the grounds command extensive sea views alternated with luxuriant woods, with the isles of Skerries in the foreground, and the Mourne mountains in the distance, stretching far into the sea towards the north. Ardgillan Castle, the seat of the Hon. and Rev. E. Taylor, is a handsome building in the castellated style, beautifully situated in a park finely wooded and commanding some interesting views of the sea. The other seats are Lowther Lodge, that of G. Macartney, Esq., in the grounds of which is an ancient rath; Inch House, of J. Madden, Esq., having also a rath within the demesne; Knockingin, of W. O'Reilly, Esq.; and Tankerville, of T. Swan Croker, Esq.

The living is a vicarage, in the diocese of Dublin, and in the patronage of the Rev. Fras. Baker, the present incumbent; the rectory is impropriate in the trustees of Wilson's hospital, in the county of Westmeath. The tithes amount to £530, of which £250 is payable to the impropriators, and £280 to the vicar. The church, with the exception of the tower, which is embattled and surmounted at the north-west angle with a circular turret, and at the others with small turrets, was taken down and rebuilt, by aid of a loan of £1000 from the late Board of First Fruits, in 1816. The glebe-house was built by aid of a gift of £250 and a loan of £550 from the same Board, in 1815; the glebe comprises 29¾ acres. There is a chapel of ease at Balbriggan, the living of which is a perpetual curacy, endowed by the late Rev. George Hamilton. In the R. C. divisions this parish is the head of a union or district, called the union of Balrothery and Balbriggan, and comprising also the parish of Balscadden: there are three chapels in the union, one at the village of Balrothery, another at Balbriggan, and a third in the parish of Balscadden. There is also at Balbriggan a place of worship for Wesleyan Methodists. There are three schools, in which about 205 boys and 110 girls receive instruction; also three pay schools, and a dispensary, in the town. Near the church are the remains of Balrothery castle, the date of which is unknown; the roof is covered with flag-stones of great thickness, and the general style of the building refers it to a period of considerable antiquity. Within a quarter of a mile of the town are the ruins of Bremore castle, the ancient seat of a branch of the Barnewall family, consisting of some of the out-buildings and part of a chapel, with a burial-ground, which is still used by some of the inhabitants. The skeletons of four moose deer were dug up on the glebe by the Rev. Mr. Baker. At Curtlagh there is a chalybeate spring. —See BALBRIGGAN.

BALSCADDEN, a parish, in the barony of Balrothery, county of Dublin, and province of Leinster, 2 miles (W.) from Balbriggan; containing 1011 inhabitants. This parish borders on the county of Meath, from which it is separated by the Naul river: it contains two commons, called the common of Balscadden and the bog of the Ring; and there is a quarry of good building stone on the lands of Milestown. Part of the demesne of Gormanston Castle is within its limits, but the castle itself is in the adjoining county. Winter Lodge, the residence of the late J. Woods, Esq., is not now inhabited. The living is a vicarage, in the diocese of Dublin and in the patronage of the Dean and Chapter of Christ-Church, Dublin; the rectory forms the corps of the treasurership in the cathedral of Christ-Church, in the gift of the crown. The tithes amount to £180, of which £120 is payable to the treasurer, and £60 to the vicar. There is neither church nor glebe-house, but in a burial-ground in the village are the ruins of a church: the glebe consists of 4½ acres of profitable land. In the R. C. divisions this parish forms part of the union or district of Balrothery and Balbriggan: the chapel, situated in the village, is a neat structure, built by subscription in 1819, at an expense of more than £500. There is a school on the common of Balscadden, in which about 80 boys and 70 girls are taught: the school-house was built in 1832, when 3½ acres of the common were enclosed and attached to it; and it is in contemplation to erect a house for the master and mistress. There are also two private pay schools in the parish. Local tradition states that a battle was fought near the village, at a place called Cross Malin, where a small mound has been raised and a wooden cross erected on its summit; and it is said that there was an encampment on the common. The well of Tubbersoole was formerly resorted to from an opinion of its efficacy in healing diseases of the eye.

BELGRIFFIN, or BALGRIFFIN, a parish, in the barony of Coolock, county of Dublin, and province of Leinster, 5 miles (N.E.) from Dublin; containing 259 inhabitants. This place formerly belonged to the ancient family of the De Burgos, who held the manor in the 14th century, and by whom the castle was erected. It afterwards became the property of the O'Neills and De Bathes, and the castle was for some time the residence of Richard, Duke of Tyrconnel, Lord Deputy of Ireland under Jas. II. The parish is situated on the turnpike road from Dublin to Malahide: the lands are chiefly under tillage; the system of agriculture is improving, and the parish generally is noted as a corn district. Belgriffin Park, the seat of the Rev. T. F. Walker is pleasantly situated; the mansion is built with the materials of the ancient castle, of which there are now no remains. The other seats are Bellcamp, the property of J. J. Baggot, Esq.; Clare Grove, of General Cuppage; Airfield, of Alderman Sir Edmund Nugent; and Sea View, of T. Franklyn, Esq. The living is a rectory and vicarage, in the diocese of Dublin; the rectory is united to that of Drumshallen and to the half rectories of Kilcullen and Glasnevin, together forming the corps of the precentorship in the cathedral of Christ-Church, Dublin, in the patronage of the Crown; and the vicarage is part of the union of St. Doulogh's, in the patronage of the Precentor. The lands in this parish belonging to the precentor comprise 29*a*. 2*r*. 3*p*., let on lease for £3. 13. 4. per annum, and an annual renewal fine of, £18. 9. 2¼; and the lands of the union comprise altogether 680*a*. 3*r*. 21*p*., let on lease for £95. 19. 5. per annum, and annual renewal fines of £114. 9. 2.; making the gross income of the precentorship, including the tithes, £484. 9. 6¼. per annum. In the R. C. divisions the parish forms part of the union or district of Baldoyle and Howth. In 1580, Mr. John Bathe left a piece of land at Chapelizod for the support of an hospital for four poor men of this parish. There are some remains of the old church.

BLACKROCK, a village, in the parish of Monkstown, half-barony of Rathdown, county of Dublin, and province of Leinster, 4 miles (S.E.) from Dublin Castle; containing 2050 inhabitants. This place, which is situated on the southern shore of Dublin bay, consists of one principal street extending along the road from Dublin to the head of the village, and continued along the two roads which meet there from Kingstown, also of several minor streets and avenues, containing altogether 308 houses irregularly built, of which some are in pleasant and retired situations. The village itself possesses few pleasing features, but the country around it is beautifully diversified, and the immediate vicinity is embellished with numerous detached villas surrounded with pleasure grounds disposed with much taste. Maritimo, the marine villa of Lord Cloncurry, and Blackrock House, the residence of the Rev. Sir Harcourt Lees, Bart., are beautifully situated; the Dublin and Kingstown railway passes through the grounds of both these seats. Carysfort House, the villa of the Right Hon. W. Saurin, commands a fine view of the sea and of the mountains in the neighbourhood; Newtown House, belonging to W. Hodgens, Esq., is finely situated, and from the rear is a noble view of the bay of Dublin. The other principal seats are Montpelier House, that of J. Duckett, Esq.; Mount Temple, of E. Brewster, Esq.; Frescati Lodge, of H. Cole, Esq.; Field Villa, of H. C. Field, Esq.; and Laurel Hill, of the Rev. Hugh White. Frescati, formerly the seat of the Fitzgerald family, a spacious mansion erected by the mother of Lord Thomas Fitzgerald, called "Silken Thomas," is now divided into four separate dwellings, and occupied by respectable families. The facilities for sea-bathing render this a place of great resort during the summer months; several respectable boarding-houses have been opened for the accommodation of visitors; and an excellent hotel, called Seapoint House, has been built and fitted up for the reception of families. Baths have been constructed by the Dublin and Kingstown Railway Company, on the side of the railway embankment, which passes along the sea-shore close to the village, and to these access is obtained by a handsome foot-bridge from the high ground. An elegant bridge has been built over the railway, which passes close under Seapoint House, affording the inmates a facility of access to a boat pier on the opposite side. In the centre of the village is a large block of granite, on which are the remains of an ancient cross; to this spot, which is the southern extremity of the city of Dublin, the lord mayor, with the civic authorities, proceeds when perambulating the boundaries of his jurisdiction. The twopenny post has three deliveries daily from the metropolis; and in addition to the constant railway communication with the city, numerous cars are stationed here, plying in all directions. There is an Episcopal chapel in Carysfort avenue; it was formerly a dissenting place of worship, but was purchased a few years since, and endowed with £1000 from a fund bequeathed by Lord Powerscourt; the chaplain is appointed by the trustees. In the R. C. divisions this place forms part of the union of Booterstown; the chapel, situated in the village, was built in 1822, by subscription, at an expense of £750. A nunnery of Carmelite sisters was established in 1822, consisting of a superior, 20 professed nuns, and three lay sisters; the ladies of this convent support a school for the gratuitous instruction of 120 girls, who are also clothed annually at Christmas. A school for boys was built in 1822, by subscription, and is supported by collections at charity sermons; and a girls' school was erected in 1827, chiefly at the expense of the Rev. J. McCormick, R. C. clergyman, by whom it is partly supported. A savings' bank has been established. —See MONKSTOWN.

BLANCHARDSTOWN, a village, in the parish and barony of Castleknock, county of Dublin, and province of Leinster, 4 miles (N.W.) from Dublin, on the road to Navan; containing 57 houses and 342 inhabitants. It is within the limits of the Dublin twopenny post delivery; and a constabulary police station has been established, in the barrack of which petty sessions for the district are held the second

Monday in every month. The R. C. parochial chapel is situated here; also the Cabra nunnery, in which a school of 200 girls is maintained by the nuns, a few of the children paying a penny weekly merely to ensure their attendance; there is also a school for children of both sexes. —See CASTLEKNOCK.

BOOTERSTOWN, a parish, in the half-barony of Rathdown, county of Dublin, and province of Leinster, 3¼ miles (S.E.) from Dublin; containing 2875 inhabitants. This place is situated on the road from Dublin to Kingstown and Bray, and on the southern coast of Dublin bay, the shores of which here assume a most interesting and beautifully picturesque appearance. On the opposite side are the finely wooded lands of Clontarf, the mountainous ridge of Howth connected with the main land by a low sandy isthmus, and the islands of Ireland's Eye and Lambay. Of the other side the land swells into the romantic hill of Mount Anville, with slopes richly wooded and embellished with numerous handsome seats, and to the east are the projecting high grounds of the Blackrock covered to the water's edge with trees. The parish comprises 450 statute acres, as applotted under the tithe act, and valued at £1589 per annum; the substratum is chiefly limestone and limestone gravel. Of the numerous handsome seats and villas, many of which are delightfully situated in highly embellished demesnes, commanding beautiful views of the bay of Dublin and of the mountains, the principal are Seamount, that of the Rt. Hon. J. Doherty, Chief Justice of the Court of Common Pleas; Sans Souci, of the late R. Roe, Esq.; Willow Park, of J. Ferrier, Esq.; Colognes, of I. M. D'Olier, Esq.; Rosemount, of C. Smith, Esq.; Rockville, of W. Murphy, Esq.; Sion Hill, of H. Lanauze, Esq.; Rockville House, of C. Hope, Esq.; Hermitage, of W. F. Mostyn, Esq.; Clareville, of Sir Ross Mahon, Bart.; Lota, of O'Gorman Mahon, Esq.; Chesterfield, of the Rev. W. Betty; Belleview, of J. Gillman, Esq.; Church View, of H. Higinbotham, Esq.; Arbutus Lodge, of W. Cullen, Esq.; South Hill, of A. Beytagh, Esq.; Mount Merrion, of H. Staines, Esq.; Woodview, of Lady Waller; Marino, of the Rev. R. H. Nixon; Brook Lawn, of J. McCullagh, Esq.; Graceville, of J. Woods, Esq.; Albion Cottage, of J. C. Bacon, Esq.; Baymount, of Capt. Cockburn; Mereview, of T. Clinch, Esq.; Woodbine Cottage, of Capt. McNaghton; and Waltham, of A. Ormsby, Esq. The village, with those of Williamstown and Blackrock, nearly forms a continuous extent of town; and within the parish are the avenues of Merrion, Cross, Sydney and Williamstown, in each of which are rows of neat houses, with numerous detached villas. This place is much frequented during the summer season on account of its facilities for sea-bathing and its fine strand of smooth sand; numerous lodging-houses have been prepared for the accommodation of visitors; and a cross embankment communicating with the railway, which is carried on an embankment through the sea in front of the town, at a short distance from high water mark, has been constructed for their convenience. The twopenny post has three deliveries daily from the metropolis, and a constant and rapid communication with the city is maintained by the railway and by cars, which ply in both directions.

The living is a perpetual curacy, in the diocese of Dublin, erected out of the parish of Donnybrook by act of council in 1821, and in the patronage of the Archdeacon of Dublin; the rectory forms part of the corps of the archdeaconry. The tithes amount to £65. 0. 2., the whole of which is payable to the archdeacon, who allows the perpetual curate £16 per annum; the curacy was also endowed by the late Earl of Pembroke with £1000, since invested in ground rents now producing £73.16.10. The church is a handsome structure, in the later English style, with a square embattled tower with crocketed pinnacles at the angles, and surmounted by a lofty spire; the walls are strengthened with buttresses terminating in pinnacles, and crowned with an embattled parapet. It was erected in 1824, on a piece of ground given by the late Earl of Pembroke in Cross Avenue, at an expense of £5000, of which sum, £2700 was a gift from the late Board of First Fruits; and contains neat monuments to James Digges Latouche and Richard Verschoyle, Esqrs. In the R. C. divisions this parish forms the head of a union or district including also parts of the parishes of Donnybrook, Kill, Monkstown, Rathfarnham, Stillorgan, and Taney. The chapel is a spacious and handsome edifice, erected at the sole expense of the late Earl Fitzwilliam; there are also chapels at Blackrock and Dundrum. A neat parochial school-house, with apartments for a master and mistress, was built in 1826, near the church, at an expense of £600, defrayed by subscription; and an infants' school was built adjoining the former in 1833, in which is kept a parochial lending library; these schools are supported by subscription and collections at charity sermons. In connection with the R. C. chapel is a girls' school, to which

Mrs. Verschoyle contributes £20 per annum. Here is a dispensary; and a Dorcas Society is supported by subscription and collections at charity sermons.

BULLOCK, BLOYKE, or BULLOG, a village, in the parish of Monkstown, half-barony of Rathdown, county of Dublin, and province of Leinster, 6¾ miles (S.E.) from Dublin: the population is returned with the parish. This place, which is now only a small fishing village, situated close to the southern shore of Dublin bay, was formerly defended by a castle of considerable extent. The period of its erection is unknown, though it is supposed to be co-eval with those of Dalkey; it is an octangular building, having but few windows and surmounted by a graduated parapet. Near it is a neat residence occupied by Capt. Hutchinson; and in the vicinity is Perrin Castle, the residence of Alderman Perrin, a handsome building in the castellated style, beautifully situated in grounds tastefully laid out and commanding some fine mountain and sea views. The Ballast Board of Dublin have a small quay here for shipping granite, with which this neighbourhood abounds. On blasting the rocks, a large quantity of silver coins was found a few years since. The fishery, at the commencement of the present century, employed several yawls in taking whiting, pollock, and herrings; at present there are about tea yawls belonging to the village. —See MONKSTOWN.

CABINTEELY, a village, partly in the parish of Killiney, but chiefly in that of Tully, half-barony of Rathdown, county of Dublin, and province of Leinster, 6¼ miles (S.S.E.) from Dublin: the population is returned with the respective parishes. This place, which is situated on the road from Dublin to Bray, is a constabulary police station, and has a twopenny post to Dublin: it comprises a number of small irregularly built houses, and a R. C. chapel for the union or district of Kingstown. In the vicinity are several handsome seats, the principal of which is Cabinteely House, the residence of the Misses Byrne, descended from the O'Byrne dynasty of Wicklow: the house forms three sides of a square, commanding extensive views of the bays of Dublin and Killiney, with the beautiful adjacent country; and the demesne is adorned with thriving plantations and presents many natural beauties. Among the other seats are Brenanstown House, the admired residence of G. Pim, Esq.; and Glen-Druid, of Mrs. Barrington. Near Loughlin-stown, on the right of the road leading to Bray, is the site of an extensive encampment, held there in 1797 and for several years after the disturbances in 1798. At Glen-Druid there is a very perfect cromlech, consisting of six upright stones supporting one of 14 feet by 12, which is supposed to weigh about 25 tons.

CALLIAGHSTOWN, a parish, in the barony of Newcastle, county of Dublin, and province of Leinster, contiguous to the post-town of Rathcoole; containing 67 inhabitants. It is situated on the road from Dublin to Naas, and comprises about 972 statute acres of arable and pasture land. For all civil purposes it is considered a townland in the parish of Rathcoole, and even in ecclesiastical affairs is regarded only as a chapelry in that parish. It is a rectory and vicarage, in the diocese of Dublin, forming part of the union of Rathcoole, in which its tithes are included.

CARRICKMINES, a village, in the parish of Tully, half-barony of Rathdown, county of Dublin, and province of Leinster, 7 miles (S.S.E.) from Dublin. Fairs are held on Jan. 12th, April 14th, June 24th, and Oct. 14th; here are the remains of an old castle.

CASTLANE. —see WHITECHURCH.

CASTLEKNOCK, a parish, in the barony of Castleknock, county of Dublin, and province of Leinster, 3¾ miles (N.W.) from Dublin; containing 4251 inhabitants, of which number, 188 are in the village. Tradition says that this was a royal residence of the Danes, and that, in 1167 Roderick O'Connor encamped here with his Connaught forces, when he led a numerous army to Dublin, where he was solemnly inaugurated King of Ireland, and engaged the Danish residents in his pay. The castle was given by Earl Strongbow to his friend, Hugh de Tyrrell, who was styled Baron of Castleknock. It was taken by Edward Bruce in 1316, and Hugh de Tyrrell and his lady made prisoners, but released on the payment of a large ransom. In June, 1642, the castle was taken for the parliament by Col. Monk, afterwards Duke of Alber-marle, who slew in the assault 80 of its defenders, and subsequently hanged many more; but in November, 1647, Owen Roe O'Nial, and

Sir Thomas Esmonde, Bart., at the head of a royalist force, retook it. The Marquess of Ormonde encamped here in 1649, when he threatened to besiege Dublin; and after the Restoration it fell into decay.

The parish is situated on the road from Dublin to Navan, and is intersected by the Royal Canal: it contains 6627 statute acres, the whole of which is arable land. Here are extensive limestone quarries, in which fossil remains are frequently found. On the Liffey are three woollen mills, where friezes, kerseys, lambskins, and Petershams, are manufactured; they have been established nearly a century, and employ above 60 persons during the winter. A factory for worsted and worsted yarn has been recently established at Blanchardstown, which employs between 80 and 100 persons; there are also on the Liffey a mustard and two flourmills, and at Cardiff Bridge is a small iron-foundry. The parish is within the Dublin twopenny post delivery. Petty sessions are held every alternate Monday at Blanchardstown, where there is a constabulary police station. The scenery on the banks of the Liffey, towards Lucan, is very beautiful, and the northern side of the valley is celebrated for strawberries. In addition to the vice-regal lodge, and the chief and under secretaries' residences, the parish contains many seats commanding delightful views: the principal seats are Sheep-hill, the residence of J. H. Hamilton, Esq., situated in a demesne of 500 acres; Farmley, of Charles Trench, Esq.; Knockmaroon, of Col. Colby; Park View, of A. Ferrier, Esq.; Mountsackville, of J. Hawkins, Esq.; Diswellstown, of C. O'Keeffe, Esq.; Airfield, of R. Manders, Esq.; Hybla, of the Rev. G. O'Connor; Scripplestown, of W. Rathborne Esq.; Dunsinea, of H. Rathborne, Esq.; Scribblestown, of A. Holmes, Esq.; Ashtown, of J. Dunne, Esq.; Elm Green, of F. Dwyer, Esq.; Oatlands, of J. Godley, Esq.; Haymount, of Dr. Marsh; Bellville, of J. Murphy, Esq.; Ashfield, of W. Oldham Esq.; Cabra, of J. Plunkett, Esq.; and Huntstown, of O. Coghlan, Esq.

The parish is divided into the northern and southern portions, each of which is subdivided into smaller parts: the prebendal or northern part furnishes an endowment for the two prebends of Mullahidart, or *"Castrum Knoc ex parte decani,"* and Castleknock, or *"Castrum Knoc ex parte precentoris,"* in the cathedral church of St. Patrick, Dublin. In 1219, the great tithes were appropriated by Archbishop Henry to the priory of Malvern, in Worcestershire, on condition that they should add five monks to their number; and in 1225 the prior and monks granted to the uses of the economy fund of St. Patrick's cathedral a moiety of the tithes of the manor of Castleknock, renouncing to the archbishop all right to the vicarage and its small tithes and oblations. During the prelacy of Archbishop Luke, a new division of the tithes was made, by which, of the four parts into which they were divided, one was assigned to the prebendary of Mullahidart, one to the prebendary of Castleknock, one to the economy estate of St. Patrick's cathedral, and one to the priory of Malvern, which transferred its interest to the abbot and convent of St. Mary, near Dublin, in 1468. This last portion having become impropriate on the dissolution of the religious houses, and forfeited by the rebellion of the impropriator, was granted as an augmentation of the vicar's means: and this division of the tithes still exists. The living is consequently a vicarage, in the diocese of Dublin, endowed with a portion of the great tithes, and united to the prebend of Castleknock and the rectory of Clonsillagh and curacy of Mullahidart, with cure of souls: it is in the patronage of the Bishop. The tithes amount to £560, of which £220 is payable to the economy estate, £140 to the prebendary of Mullahidart, and £200 to the prebendary of Castleknock. There are two churches in the vicarial union, one at Castleknock, the other at Clonsillagh; the former was rebuilt by a loan of £1000 from the late Board of First Fruits, and large subscriptions, in 1810, replacing one that had been built, in 1609, on the site of an Augustinian abbey for Canons Regular, founded in the 13th century by Richard Tyrrell, and dedicated to St. Bridget. There is a glebe-house; and the glebe, in two parcels, comprises 19a. 1r. 5p., besides 8 acres which have been taken into the Phoenix Park and for which, and also for the tithes of the park, the vicar receives £50.15. per ann. late currency, from Government. In the R. C. divisions this parish is the head of a union or district, comprising the parishes of Castleknock, Chapelizod, Clonsillagh, Cloghranhidart, and Mullahidart; and containing three chapels, one at Blanchardstown, one at Porterstown (in Clonsillagh), and one at Chapelizod. At Cabra is a nunnery of the order of St. Dominick: the society removed hither from Clontarf about 1820, and consists of a chaplain, prioress, and nuns, besides lay-sisters; it is a respectable ladies' school, and the sisterhood also instruct from 150 to 200 poor children, who are partly clothed. The nunnery is surrounded with grounds tastefully laid out, and has a neat chapel and dwelling-house for the chaplain. There is another nunnery at Blanchardstown, in which more than 200 poor children are taught. In addition to the parochial school, there are two by the side of the canal, one for boys, maintained by a bequest from the late Mr. Morgan; and the other supported out of the produce of lands devised by a lady named Mercer, and yielding a rent of more than £750 per ann., vested in trustees, by whom 50 girls are maintained, clothed, and educated. A school for boys and girls at Abbotstown is supported solely by J. H. Hamilton, Esq., of Sheep-hill, by whom the children are also partly clothed; at Blanchardstown is a national school for both sexes; and a free school was built by Luke White, Esq. The late Mr. Tisdal bequeathed a large sum to the parochial schools, which is to be paid after his widow's death. There are a savings' bank and a dispensary. The remains of the ancient fortress of Castleknock occupy the summit of a lofty hill. In Knockbrush Hill, which is situated near the Ashbourne road, are occasionally found bones of men and horses, military weapons, and coins. Part of this hill is evidently artificial, and tradition says that it was raised over those who fell on this spot, in 1014, in the widely extended battle of Clontarf. Ancient horse-shoes, spurs, and other relics, have been dug up at Scripplestown. At Abbotstown are some remains of the abbey; and there is also a well dedicated to St. Bridget.

CHAPELIZOD, a parish, in the barony of Castleknock, county of Dublin, and province of Leinster 3 miles (W.) from Dublin; containing 2181 inhabitants, of which number 1632 are in the village. This place is supposed to have derived its name from *La Belle Isode* a daughter of one of the ancient Irish kings, who had a chapel here. The lands belonging to it were granted by Hugh de Lacy, in 1173, to Hugh Tyrrell, which grant was afterwards confirmed by Hen. II. In 1176, they were given by the Tyrrells to the hospital of the Knights Templars of Kilmainham, and after the suppression of that order remained in possession of their successors, the Knights of St. John of Jerusalem, till the dissolution of the monasteries, in the reign of Hen. VIII. They subsequently passed through various hands till 1665, when the Duke of Ormonde, by command of the king, purchased the entire manor, with the mansion, from Sir Maurice Eustace, for the purpose of enclosing the Phoenix park, and the old mansion-house became the occasional residence of the Lord-Lieutenant. In 1671, Col. Lawrence obtained a grant of several houses and about 15 acres of land adjacent to the village for 41 years, at an annual rent of £42, for the purpose of establishing the linen manufacture, under the auspices of the Duke of Ormonde, who, with a view to promote its success, invited over numerous families from Brabant, Rochelle, the Isle of Rhé, and other places, who were skilled in the art of manufacturing linens, diapers, tickens, sail-cloth, and cordage, and established those manufactures here in the greatest perfection. In 1690, Gen. Douglas, on his march to Athlone, encamped for one night at this place; and soon after, King William himself, subsequently to his expedition to the south, passed several days here in issuing various orders and redressing grievances. In 1696, Lord Capel, Lord-Deputy of Ireland, died at the vice-regal residence here after a long illness, during which several important meetings of the council took place; and though the house was repaired by Primate Boulter, when Lord-Justice of Ireland, in 1726, it has never since been occupied by the lord-lieutenants: a house near the village, called the King's, is said to be that occasionally used as the vice-regal lodge. The village, which is of considerable size, and extends into the parish of Palmerstown, in the barony of Newcastle, is situated on the south-western verge of the Phoenix park, and contains 200 houses, of which 103 are in that part of it which is in the parish of Palmerstown. It is within the delivery of the Dublin twopenny post, and is chiefly remarkable for the beautiful scenery in its vicinity, especially along the banks of the Liffey, towards Lucan, and for the extensive strawberry beds which are spread over the northern side of the vale. The woollen manufacture was formerly carried on very extensively, and continued to flourish till the commencement of the present century, when there was a large factory, two fulling-mills, and an extensive corn and wash mill, which have been succeeded by a flax-mill on a very large scale, erected by Messrs. Crosthwaite, the present proprietors, and affording constant employment to more than 600 persons. There are also a bleach-green and several mills.

The living is a rectory and vicarage, in the diocese of Dublin, united at a period unknown to the rectories of Palmerstown and Ballyfermot, together forming the union of Chapelizod, in the patronage of the Archbishop: the tithes amount to £1. 19. 5½., and the gross amount for the whole benefice is £301. 19. 5½. The church is a small plain edifice, erected in the reign of Anne, and remarkable only for its tower covered with ivy, from the summit of which is an extensive and highly interesting prospect over the surrounding country. There is neither glebe-house nor glebe. In the R. C. divisions this parish forms part of the union or district of Castleknock. There is a chapel in the village; and near it is a schoolroom, erected in 1834 for a school to be placed in connection with the National Board. A school is supported by sub-scription, in which about 18 boys and 54 girls are instructed; and there are also a pay school, in which are 60 boys and 40 girls, and two Sun-day schools. A dispensary in the village is supported in the usual way. Col. Lawrence, the founder of the manufactures of this place, was the author of a well-known pamphlet, published in 1682, and entitled "The Interest of Ireland in its Trade and Wealth." The Hibernian school in the Phoenix park, described in the article on Dublin, is in this parish.

CHAPELMIDWAY, a parish, in the barony of Castleknock, county of Dublin, and province of Leinster, 7 miles (N.) from Dublin; contain-ing 335 inhabitants. The principal seats are Corrstown, the residence of H. Cosgrave, Esq., and Kilcorkin, of J. Litton, Esq. It is a rectory and vicarage, in the diocese of Dublin, forming part of the union of Kilsallaghan, with which the tithes are included. In the R. C. divisions it is part of the union or district of Finglas. The ruins of the church are situated on the old road from Dublin to the Naul.

CHURCHTOWN, county of Dublin. —See TANEY.

CLOGHRAN or CLOGHRAN-SWORDS, a parish, in the barony of Coolock, county of Dublin, and province of Leinster, 1½ mile (S.) from Swords; containing 613 inhabitants. This parish, which takes the adjunct of Swords to distinguish it from another parish of the same name south-west from Dublin, is situated on the road from Dublin to Swords. Limestone abounds, and near the church is a quarry in which various fossils are found; under this quarry are copper and lead ores, but neither has yet been profitably worked. Baskin Hill, the seat of J. Tymons, Esq., was built by the present Bishop of Dromore, who resided there while rector of St. Doulough's; and Castle Moat, the seat of J. Mac Owen, Esq., takes its name from an extensive moat, or rath, within the demesne, from which is a fine view of the country towards the village of the Man-of-War and the sea, including Lambay Island, Ireland's Eye, Howth, and the Dublin and Wicklow mountains. In 1822, some ancient silver and copper coins, Danish pipes, pikes, and musket bullets were ploughed up near the spot. The living is a rectory, in the diocese of Dublin, and in the patronage of the Crown: the tithes amount to £184. 2. 3¾. The church is a very plain and simple edifice. The glebe-house was rebuilt in 1812, by aid of a gift of £400 and a loan of £392 from the late Board of First Fruits: the glebe comprises seven acres of cultivated land. In the R. C. divisions the parish forms part of the union or district of Swords.

CLOGHRAN-HIDART. —See BALLYCOOLANE.

CLONDALKIN, a parish, in the barony of Uppercross, county of Dublin, and province of Leinster, 5 miles (S.W.) from Dublin; containing 2976 inhabitants, of which number, 374 are in the village. This place, anciently called *Cluain-Dolcan*, and by the Danes *Dun-Awley*, appears, from the evidence of its ancient round tower, still in good preservation, to have had a very remote origin. A monastery was founded here, of which St. Cronan Mochua was the first abbot; and a palace here belonging to Anlaff, or Auliffe, the Danish king of Dublin, was, in 806, destroyed by the Irish under Ciaran, the son of Ronan. The monastery was plundered and burnt in 832, 1071, and 1076, since which last date there is no further record of its history. In 1171, Roderic O'Connor, King of Leinster, with the forces of O'Ruarc and O'Carrol, Prince of Argial, marched to this place against Earl Strongbow, who was then besieging Dublin; but in order to oppose his further progress, Strongbow advanced to give him battle, and after some days' skirmishing compelled him to retreat, leaving Dublin to the mercy of the English. The village, near the entrance of which are the remains of a fortified castle consists chiefly of one irregular street, and in 1831 contained 150 houses neatly built, though small, and some neatly ornamented cottages appropriated to the uses of charitable and benevolent institutions. It is situated on the small river Camma, and the road from Dublin to Newcastle, and is a constabulary police station. In common with the parish, it is within the jurisdiction of the manor court of St. Sepulchre's Dublin. The greater portion of the parish is arable land; the soil is fertile, and the system of agriculture very much improved under the auspices of many resident gentlemen, who farm their own estates, and have established ploughing matches for prizes, which are annually distributed. There are quarries of good limestone, which is raised in abundance for agricultural and other uses. The gentlemen's seats are Newlands, the residence of P. Crotty, Esq., a handsome modern mansion, previously occupied by the late Lord Kilwarden, Chief-Justice of the King's Bench; Collinstown, of M. Mills, Esq.; Larkfield, of J. Hamilton, Esq., in the grounds of which are the ruins of an old castle covered with ivy; Corkagh, of W. Stockley, Esq.; Little Corkagh, of H. Arabin. Esq.; Moyle Park, of W. Caldbeck, Esq.; Neilstown House, of L. Rorke, Esq.; Nanger, of P. C. Rorke, Esq., formerly an old embattled castle, now modernised; Clondalkin, of Mrs. Anne Connolly; Kilcarbery, of H. Phillips, Esq.; St. Mark's, of Capt. Foss; Neilstown Lodge, of C. Brabazon, Esq.; Flora-ville, of F. Smith, Esq.; Rosebank, of W. Bayly. Esq.; Clonburrows, of M. Pearson, Esq.; Collinstown Cottage, of the Rev. Mr. O'Callaghan; and Clover Hill, of D. Kinalson, Esq. There is an oil-mill in the parish, and in the demesne of Little Corkagh are some gunpowder-mills, established a century since, but not used since 1815; one of them has been converted into a thrashing and cleaning mill, capable of preparing 100 barrels daily. The Grand Canal passes through the parish, and the Royal Canal through the northern part of the union, near the Duke of Leinster's demesne.

The living is a rectory and a vicarage, in the diocese of Dublin; the rectory is united to those of Rathcool, Esker, Kilberry, and Tallagh, together constituting the corps of the deanery of St. Patrick's Dublin, in the patronage of the Chapter; and the vicarage is united to the rectory of Kilmactalway, the vicarage of Kilbride, the curacies of Drimnagh and Kilmacrudery, and the half rectories of Donoghmore and Donocomper, together constituting the union of Clondalkin, in the patronage of the Archbishop. The tithes of Clondalkin amount to £473. 18. 11., of which £428. 2. 5¼. is payable to the dean, and £43. 0. 9¾. to the vicar. The glebe-house, a good residence in the village, was built in 1810, by aid of a gift of £100 and a loan of £450 from the late Board of First Fruits: the glebe comprises 17a. 2r. 5p. of profitable land. The church is a small modern edifice in good repair, and requires to be enlarged. In the R. C. divisions the parish forms part of the union or district of Palmerstown, Clondalkin, and Lucan; the chapel at the village of Clondalkin is a neat building. There is also a chapel attached to the monastery of Mount Joseph, which is pleasantly situated on high ground commanding extensive views, at no great distance from the mail coach road from Dublin to Naas: this establishment was founded in 1813, and consists of a prior and several brethren, with a chaplain, who support themselves by their own industry. Some of them conduct a day and boarding school for such as can afford to pay; and in connection with the monastery is a school of about 200 boys, supported by a grant of £16 per annum from the National Board, and collections at an annual charity sermon. There is another national school, and there are two others and a Sunday school, for which school-rooms have been erected at an expense of £240, towards which the Rev. Dr. Reade, the present incumbent, contributed £140, and also assigned in perpetuity to the parish the ground on which they are built; the total number in these schools is about 216 boys and 305 girls. There is also a school in the village, in which about 130 girls are instructed and 40 annually clothed; it is under the management of Mrs. Caldbeck, and supported by her, aided by collections at the R. C. chapel and the sale of the children's work. The school-room was built by subscription, in 1831, on land given by Wm. Caldbeck, Esq., who also, in 1833, gave land for the erection of a house for the R. C. clergyman, and for a dispensary. The Rev. Dr. Reade has also established almshouses for destitute widows, a poor shop, repository, Dorcas institution, and a lying-in hospital. Nearly adjacent to the present church are the almost shapeless ruins of the old conventual church of the monastery, which was afterwards the parochial church, and among them is an ancient cross of granite, nine feet high; it appears to have been a spacious structure, about 120 feet long and from 50 to 60 feet wide; and near it is the ancient round tower previously noticed. This tower is about 100 feet high and 15 feet in diameter, and is covered with a conical roof of stone; its style is of the plainest order, and it is in good preservation; the entrance is about 10 feet from the ground, and the base of the column to that height was, about 60 years since, cased with strong masonry. There are four openings looking towards the cardinal points in the upper story, in which a room has been formed by its proprietor, R. Caldbeck, Esq., having an ascent by ladders from within, and commanding a most extensive and interesting prospect over the surrounding country. At

Ballymount are extensive remains of a once strong castle, consisting principally of the enclosing walls and the keep: within the walls is a respectable farm-house, evidently built with the old materials.

CLONMETHAN, a parish, in the barony of Nethercross, county of Dublin, and province of Leinster, 4 miles (E.) from Ashbourne; containing 677 inhabitants. A great quantity of corn is grown in this parish, and it contains a limestone quarry. A cattle fair is held in the demesne of Fieldstown on Whit-Monday. The principal seats are the glebe-house, the residence of the Rev. T. Radcliff, from which is a fine view of the surrounding country; Fieldstown, the seat of P. Bourne, Esq.; Brown's Cross, of W. L. Galbraith, Esq.; and Wyanstown, of R. Rooney, Esq. The parish is in the diocese of Dublin, and with the vicarages of Ballyboghill, Ballymadun, Palmerstown, and Westpalstown, perpetually united to it by act of council in 1675, constitutes the prebend of Clonmethan in the cathedral of St. Patrick, and in the patronage of the Archbishop: the tithes amount to £270. The glebe-house was erected in 1817, by aid of a gift of £100, and a loan of £1350, from the late Board: there is a glebe of 35 acres in this parish, and one of 19 acres and 2 roods in Ballymadun; and the gross revenue of the prebend, according to the report of the Commissioners of Ecclesiastical Inquiry, is £638. A neat church was erected in 1818, by £250 parish cess, and a loan of £500 from the late Board of First Fruits, and the Ecclesiastical Commissioners have lately granted £175. 4. 11. towards its repair. The mother church of Clonmethan was dedicated to St. Mary, and the chapel of Fieldstown, which was dedicated to St. Catharine, was subordinate to it. In the R. C. divisions the parish forms part of the union or district of Rollestown, and has a chapel at Old Town, which was erected in 1827, by subscription, and cost nearly £300. Here is a private school, in which are 50 children; and at Old Town is a dispensary.

CLONSILLAGH, a parish, in the barony of Castleknock, county of Dublin, and province of Leinster, 7 miles (N.W.) from Dublin; containing 954 inhabitants, and comprising 2943 statute acres, the whole of which is arable land. There are limestone quarries in the parish, and an extensive flour-mill on the Liffey, erected on the site of a very ancient one, called "the Devil's Mill," from its having been erected, according to tradition, in one night. The Royal Canal passes through the parish. Woodlands, formerly called Luttrell's Town, and the seat of the Earls of Carhampton, is now the property and residence of Col. T. White. The demesne includes above 648 statute acres, exceedingly picturesque; the mansion is a noble building, in the castellated style, and is said to contain a room in which king John slept: that monarch granted the estate to the Luttrell family. In a glen, a stream, which is supplied from a beautiful lake in the park, of 20 acres, rolls over a rocky bed and forms a cascade about 30 feet high. The other seats are Coolmine, the residence of A. Fitzpatrick, Esq.; Clonsillagh, of R. H. French, Esq.; Broomfield, of the Rev. S. Thompson; Clonsillagh, of Ignatius Callaghan, Esq.; Hansfield, of T. Willan, Esq.; and Phibblestown, of Capt. H. Reid, R. N. The parish formerly belonged to the priory of Malvern, in Worcestershire. It is a rectory, in the diocese of Dublin, and is part of the union of Castleknock: the tithes amount to £240. The church is a small neat building. In the R. C. divisions it also forms part of the union or district of Castleknock, and has a neat chapel at Porterstown, built by the late L. White, Esq., who also built a schoolhouse, with apartments for the master and mistress: the school is supported by subscription, and there is one on the lower road, near the Liffey; they afford instruction to about 90 children.

CLONSKEA, anciently CLONSKEAGH, a small village, in that part of the parish of St. Mary, Donnybrook, which is in the half-barony of Rathdown, county of Dublin, and province of Leinster, 2 miles (S.) from the Post-Office, Dublin, on the road to Enniskerry, by way of Roebuck; the population is included in the return for the parish. It contains a dye stuff factory and iron-works; and is within the jurisdiction of the city of Dublin court of requests. ClonskeaCastlegh, the handsome residence of G. Thompson, Esq., affords fine views of the city and bay of Dublin, with the adjacent mountains; it was built by H. Jackson, who acted a prominent part in the disturbances of 1798. On digging in front of the mansion, a few years since, a layer of muscle shells, about three feet thick, and imbedded in clay, was found about eight feet below the surface. The other seats are Rich View, the residence of M. Powell, Esq., and Virge Mount, of the Rev. J. C. Crosthwaite.

CLONTARF, a parish, in the barony of Coolock, county of Dublin, and province of Leinster, on the northern shore of Dublin bay, 2½ miles (E.N.E.) from the Post-Office, Dublin; containing 3314 inhabitants, of which number, 1309 are in the village. Clontarf stands in a very richly wooded and finely cultivated country, and is distinguished in Irish history as the scene of a sanguinary battle, which put a final period to the Danish power in Ireland. But although this memorable battle takes its distinguishing name from this parish, it is probable, from the numbers of human bones discovered in excavating the ground for streets on the north side of Dublin, and at Knockbrush Hill near Finglass, that the scene of action embraced a much more extended tract of country. On the first invasion of Ireland by the English, O'Brian and O'Carrol, who came to the assistance of Roderic, the last king of all Ireland, at the siege of Dublin, took post in this vicinity. The principal lands in the parish appear to have been vested in a religious house founded here in 550, and erected into a commandery of Knights Templars in the reign of Hen. II., which, on the suppression of that order, became a preceptory of Knights Hospitallers of St. John of Jerusalem, and was one of the chief appendages of the grand priory of Kilmainham. Sir J. Rawson, the last prior, after the surrender of this house and its revenues, was created, by Hen. VIII., Viscount Clontarf, with a pension of 500 marks per annum. Since that period, the possessions of the establishment, after passing through various hands, were erected into a manor and conferred by the Crown on Admiral Vernon, whose descendant, J. E. Venables Vernon, Esq., is the present proprietor. This place was burned in 1641, by the parliamentarian general, Sir C. Coote, on the 15th of December.

The present village is of considerable extent, and is much frequented for sea-bathing by visitors from the north of Dublin; and the scenery in many parts is highly interesting. It was formerly a fishing town of some importance, and along the water's edge are still many wooden buildings, called the Clontarf sheds, formerly used for the purpose of curing the fish taken here. Several neat lodging-houses have been erected and numerous pleasant villas and ornamented cottages have been built in detached situations. Near the strand was formerly the Royal Marine charter school; the buildings now belong to Mr. Brierly, who has erected large hot and cold sea-water baths. Opposite to Dollymount is an extensive causeway stretching into the sea, erected by the Ballast Board to deepen the channel between Poolbeg, or the south wall lighthouse and the north wall light. From this causeway is a long strip of sandy ground, called the North Bull, which is partly green, extending towards the hill of Howth, and surrounded on all sides by the sea; and off the sheds is a profitable oyster bank. The parish comprises 1039 statute acres, as applotted under the tithe act, and valued at £5283 per annum. On the shore is the shaft of a lead mine, which has been opened at different times since the reign of Jas. I., and although it afforded a considerable quantity of rich ore, both of the common sulphate and cubicular kinds, the operations have invariably been unsuccessful from the influx of sea water. The Drogheda, or Grand Northern Trunk railway from Dublin to Drogheda will, when completed, pass through this parish; and there is a constabulary police station. Clontarf Castle, the seat of J. E. V. Vernon, Esq., was one of the most ancient castles within the English pale, and is supposed to have been erected either by Hugh de Lacy or by Adam de Frepo, one of his knights, to whom he granted the lordship; the old castle was taken down in 1835, and a handsome mansion in the later English style, with a tower of Norman character, is now in progress of erection, from a design by Mr. W. Morrison. There are many handsome seats and pleasant villas: the principal are Furry Park, the residence of T. Bushe, Esq.; Sybil Hill, of J. Barlow, Esq.; Clontarf House, of Mrs. Colvill; Elm View, of W. C. Colvill, Esq., formerly the seat of Lords Shannon and Southwell; Verville, of C. A. Nicholson, Esq., Convent House, of the Hon. Arthur Moore, second justice of the court of common pleas; Dollymount, of T. and L. Crosthwaite, Esqrs.; Prospect, of R. Warren, Esq.; Bellgrove, of R. Simpson, Esq.; Beachfield, of J. Tudor, Esq.; Clontarf, of B. Mitford, Esq.; Ivy House, of R. Ellis, Esq.; Danesfield, of J. Campbell, Esq.; Seafield House, of T. Gresham, Esq.; Merchamp, of E. Shaw, Esq.; Thornhill, of H. O'Reilly, Esq.; Bay View, of F. L'Estrange, Esq.; Baymount House, of J. Keily, Esq., formerly for some years the residence of Dr. Trail, Bishop of Down and Connor; Bedford Lodge, of W. I. Moore, Esq.; Rose Vale, of Sir E. Stanley, Knt.; Strandville, of Alderman Tyndall; Strandville House, of W. Minchiner, Esq.; Merville, of R. Peter, Esq.; Moira Lodge, of W. Taylor, Esq.; Fort View, of S. Morris, Esq.; Sea View, of Capt. Dundas; and Crab-lake, of W. Leckie, Esq.

The living is a rectory, in the diocese of Dublin, and in the patronage of the Crown: the tithes amount to £220. By a clause in the act of

Explanation in 1680, the tithes and altarages were settled on the incumbent and his successors, at a rent of £6. 2. 6¼. per ann. The church, dedicated to St. John the Baptist, occupies the site of the ancient monastery, and was rebuilt in 1609: it is a small neat edifice, with an elevation above the western entrance perforated for a bell, and contains several ancient monuments in good preservation. In the R. C. divisions the parish is the head of a union or district, comprising the parishes of Artane, Clontarf, Clonturk, Coolock, Glasnevin, Killester, Raheny, and Santry and at Annesley bridge; there are chapels at Clontarf, Coolock, Ballyman near Santry, Clontarf chapel was built after a design by P. Byrne and Son, on a site near the sheds, presented by Mr. Vernon; and M. Carey, Esq., bequeathed £1000 towards its erection. It is a spacious and elegant structure in the later style of English architecture, 152 feet in length and 63 feet 6 inches in breadth, and forms a striking ornament to the place. In the village is a Carmelite monastery, consisting of five laymen, who carry on their respective trades as a means of supporting the institution; among these is an extensive bakery, which supplies the neighbourhood and part of Dublin with excellent bread; attached to the establishment is a neat chapel. There was formerly a nunnery, the inmates of which removed to Cabragh about 12 years since, and the house is now occupied by the Hon. Judge Moore. In the old chapel is a male and female school, supported by the interest of accumulated receipts at charity sermons, amounting to £700, and of a bequest of £500 by M. Carey, Esq.: the average number of children is about 100. The parochial school, to which Mr. Vernon has given a house rent-free, is supported by subscription; an almshouse for 12 widows is supported by Sunday collections and charity sermons; and a loan fund was established in 1835. In making some alterations at Elm View, silver coins of Hen. II. and brass coins of Jas. I. were found; and at Danesfield a Danish sword was dug up in the garden, in 1830.

CLONTURK, or DRUMCONDRA, a parish, in the barony of Coolock, county of Dublin, and province of Leinster, 1 mile (N.) from Dublin, on the roads to Howth, Malahide, and Swords; containing 2713 inhabitants. The river Tolka bounds the parish on the south, a woollen mill on which was washed away in 1834 by a flood, but was rebuilt in 1836; there is also a brass foundry. The city police have a station on the strand. There are many beautiful seats, the chief of which is Marino, that of the Earl of Charlemont; it is entered from the Strand road, near Fair View, by an elegant semicircular gateway of hewn granite, which attracted the notice of his late Majesty, Geo.IV., who pronounced it to be the most perfect structure of the kind in his dominions. The demesne contains above 100 acres, and is well wooded. The mansion, which contains some elegant apartments, is of plain and unpretending exterior; but this want of embellishment is fully compensated by the Temple or Casino. This fine imitation of Grecian architecture crowns the summit of a gentle eminence in the centre of the demesne. It rises from a square platform, ascended on the north and south sides by broad flights of marble steps. Contiguous to the Casino, which was erected by the late Lord Charlemont, from a design by Sir W. Chambers, is an extensive pleasure ground surrounding a small but beautiful sheet of water, supplied from a copious fountain gushing from a rock-work grotto. The other residences are Belvidere House, that of Sir J. C. Coghill, Bart.; Drumcondra House, of Gen. Sir Guy Campbell, K.C.B., in whose grounds are the remains of an ancient building; Drumcondra Castle, of R. Williams, Esq.; Hampton Lodge, of Mrs. A. Williams; High Park, of G. Gray, Esq.; Hartfield, of P. Twigg, Esq.; Donnycarney, of Abel Labertouche, Esq.; Richmond Castle, of A. Williams, Esq.; Annadale, of W. Hone, Esq.; Union Lodge, of J. English, Esq.; Well Park, of W. Kirwan, Esq.; Woodbine Lodge, of H. Yeo, Esq.; Richmond House, of P. Birch, Esq.; Tokay Lodge, of M. Kerr, Esq.; Mary Ville, of J. J. Finn, Esq.; Rosemount, of W. Butler, Esq.; and Sally Park, of W. Mathews, Esq.

The living is a perpetual curacy, in the diocese of Dublin, and in the patronage of the Corporation of Dublin, in which the rectory is impropriate. The church is a small plain building, erected in the early part of the last century by the Coghill family, and was repaired and decorated by the corporation in 1833, at an expense of £500. On its north side is a large tomb, erected to the memory of Marmaduke Coghill, Chancellor of the Exchequer for Ireland, on which reclines his effigy in his official robes, with figures of Minerva and Religion below. On the south side of the churchyard are interred the remains of F. Grose, Esq., the distinguished antiquary, who died in Dublin, in May 1791 and T. Furlong, a native poet, was buried here in 1827. In the R. C. divisions the parish is in the union or district of Clontarf, and has a chapel near Annesley bridge. The parochial school is in the village of Drumcondra; and an infants' school was established in 1829, at Philipsburgh strand; there is also a girls' school at the Richmond convent. This nunnery is of the Presentation order, and is surrounded with grounds tastefully laid out, and has a chapel annexed. In the village of Drumcondra is an asylum for poor women, called the Retreat. Annesley bridge, and the causeway connected with it, were erected by act of parliament in 1796 and 1797, at an expense of about £6000: they cross a portion of ground overflowed by the tide, at the confluence of the Tolka with the Liffey. Higher up, on the left, the Tolka is crossed by the old bridge of Ballybough. Philipsburgh strand extends from one bridge to the other. To the east of Annesley bridge is a cluster of buildings, called Fair View; and beyond them, between the Malahide and Howth roads, is Marino Crescent, consisting of large handsome houses, with an enclosed lawn in front, which extends to the road bounding the strand; it commands fine views, and is very convenient for sea-bathing.

CONNAUGHT (OLD), a parish, in the half-barony of Rathdown, county of Dublin, and province of Leinster; containing, with part of the town of Bray, 1947 inhabitants. This parish, which is commonly called Old Conna or Connagh, is situated on the mail coach road from Dublin to Bray and Newtown-Mount-Kennedy. Besides the village of Old Connaught, it contains Little Bray, which forms the northern portion of the town of Bray, within the manor of which this parish is included. It is bounded on the east by the sea, and on the south by the Dargle river, over which there is a bridge that connects the counties of Wicklow and Dublin, and near which is a common of about 14 acres, that is used as a race-course. The parish, most of which belongs to Miss Roberts, contains 4050 statute acres, and is remarkable for salubrity of climate, beauty of sea and mountain prospect, and convenience of seabathing. The land is chiefly laid out in villas and ornamental plantations, and the part that is under tillage is occupied by substantial farmers. From its proximity to the sea, the Wicklow mountains, and the metropolis, with other natural advantages, this is a favourite place of residence. The principal seats are Old Connaught, the residence of the Rt. Hon. Lord Plunket; Palermo, of the Rev. Sir S. S. Hutchinson, Bart.; Cork Abbey, of the Hon. Col. Wingfield; Woodbrook, of Sir J. Ribton, Bart.; Old Connagh Hill, of

Miss Roberts; Thornhill, of F. Leigh, Esq.; Jubilee, of Miss Ryan; Oak-lawn, of W. Garde, Esq.; Ravenswell, of I. Weld, Esq.; Beauchamp, of Capt. Lovelace Stamer; Woodlawn, of W. Magan, Esq.; Moatfield Cottage, of Capt. C. Johnstone; Bray Lodge, of W. C. W. Newberry, Esq.; Crinlin Lodge, of J. Cahill, Esq.; and Wilfort, of Messrs. Toole. At the entrance to Little Bray, through which the coaches from Dublin to Wexford pass, are three handsome houses, occupied by the physician to the dispensary, the Rev. W. Purcell, and Mrs Galway. The village of Old Connaught is small and pleasant, having a flourishing plantation of horse chestnut trees in its centre: it contains several neat cottages, and the handsome residence of R. Morrison, Esq. the architect.

It is a rectory and vicarage, in the diocese of Dublin, and forms part of the union of Bray: the tithes amount to £240. Prior to 1728, the rectorial tithes formed part of the Archbishop of Dublin's mensal, but in that year, the tithes of this parish and of several others were annexed to their respective incumbencies having cure of souls. In the R. C. divisions this parish forms part of the union or district of Kingstown, and has a chapel at Crinkin. There are two schools, one for boys, aided by a collection at the church, and the other for girls, supported by voluntary subscriptions, in which are educated 100 girls and 87 boys. The poor enjoy a share of the rents of an estate in the county of Longford, bequeathed by F. Adair, Esq., to the unions of Delgany and Bray, and the parish of Powerscourt. In the grounds of Moatfield, or Wilfort, is an old rath; and in those of Ballyman are the ruins of a church, in a curiously detached churchyard. The ruins of the parish church also form a picturesque object.

COOLOCK, a parish, in the barony of Coolock, county of Dublin, and province of Leinster, 3¾ miles (N.N.E.) from Dublin, on the road to Malahide; containing, 914 inhabitants, of which number, 190 are in the village, which contains 26 houses, and is a constabulary police station. The parish comprises 1691 statute acres, as applotted under the tithe act: the soil is fertile, and well adapted for corn. Limestone abounds, and a quarry near the glebe-house is worked for agricultural and other purposes. There are numerous handsome seats and pleasant villas, from most of which are fine views of the bay and city of Dublin, with the adjacent country. Of these the principal are Beaumont, the residence of A. Guinness, Esq.; Newbrook, of E. H.

Casey, Esq.; Belcamp, of Sir H. M. J. W. Jervis, Bart.; Brookeville, of R. Law, Esq.; Coolock House, of H. Brooke, Esq.; Coolock Lodge, of T. Sherrard, Esq.; Shrubs, of W. White, Esq.; Bonnybrook, of T. W. White, Esq.; Newbury Hill, of A. Ong, Esq.; Priors Wood, of T. Cosgrave, Esq.; Gracefield, of R. Eames, Esq.; Lark Hill, of E. Hickson, Esq.; Moatfield, of M. Staunton, Esq.; Darendale, of F. Gogarty, Esq.; Clare Grove, of Gen. A. Cuppage; Airfield, of Alderman Sir E. Nugent, Knt.; and Cameron Lodge, of H. Jones Esq.

The living is a vicarage, in the diocese of Dublin, and in the patronage of the Marquess of Drogheda, in whom the rectory is impropriate: the vicarial tithes amount to £249. 4. 7½. There is a glebe-house, with a glebe comprising 17*a*. 2*r*. 25*p*. The church, dedicated to St. Brandon, a neat edifice, was partly rebuilt and enlarged, by aid of a loan of £500 from the late Board of First Fruits, in 1818. In the R. C. divisions the parish forms part of the union or district of Clontarf. The chapel was erected in 1831, at an expense of £800, raised by subscription: it is a very neat edifice, in the later English style, with a belfry over the principal entrance; the interior is very well arranged and neatly decorated. The parochial school, for which a house was built, it an expense of £300, the gift of Sir Compton Domville, Bart., is supported by subscription, and attended by 30 or 40 children. A school of 30 children, for which a handsome cottage has been built in the grounds of Beaumont, and an infants' school in connection with it, are wholly supported by Mrs. Guinness; and in connection with the R. C. chapel is a school to which W. Sweetman, Esq., gives £20 per annum. On a common near the church, which is now enclosed, a great concourse of persons connected with Emmet's insurrection was assembled, ready to march into Dublin at the appointed signal. In the grounds of Newbrook, through which flows a small stream, are the walls of a holy well, dedicated to St. Donagh; the spot is much resorted to, on St. John's Eve, by poor sick people, who, after rubbing themselves against the walls, wash in a well in the adjoining grounds of Donaghmede. In the grounds of Shrubs was anciently a nunnery, and human bones are frequently dug up there. There are ancient raths in the grounds of Bonnybrook and Moatfield.

COTLANDSTOWN, a parish, partly in the barony of Uppercross, county of Dublin, and partly in that of Upper Naas, county of Kildare, and province of Leinster, 1¼ mile (E. by N.) from Ballymore-Eustace; containing 459 inhabitants. This parish is situated on the river Liffey, and on the road from Ballymore-Eustace to Kilcullen. It comprises 1490 statute acres, partly in pasture and partly under tillage; the system of agriculture is improving, and the principal crops are barley, oats, and potatoes. The gentlemen's seats are of Stonebrook, the residence of O'Connor Henehy, Esq., in whose demesne is the ancient parochial burialground; and Mullaboden, of the Rev. H. Johnston. The Dublin part of the parish is within the jurisdiction of St. Sepulchre's Court, Dublin. The parish is partly in the diocese of Dublin, and partly in that of Kildare: the rectory of the Kildare portion is appropriate to the see, and that of the Dublin portion forms part of the corps of the treasurership of St. Patrick's cathedral; the vicarage forms part of the union of Ballymore-Eustace. The tithes amount to £69. 15. 5¼, of which £49. 7. 6¼ is payable to the Bishop of Kildare, £4. 7. 11. to the lessee of the treasurer of St. Patrick's, Dublin, and the remaining £8 to the vicar. In the R. C. divisions the parish forms part of the union or district of Ballymore-Eustace. In the Kildare part of the parish is a private school of about 20 boys and 20 girls.

CRUAGH, or CREVAGH, a parish, in the barony of Newcastle, county of Dublin, and province of Leinster, 6 miles (S.) from Dublin containing 1216 inhabitants. This parish is situated on the river Owendugher, a branch of the Dugher or Dodder river, by which it is separated from the parish of Whitechurch; and comprises 4762½ statute acres, of which 2400 are mountain, including about 400 acres of good bog. Killakee, the residence of S. White, Esq., is a spacious mansion, situated in a tastefully embellished demesne, with a well-wooded glen through which a mountain stream rushes with great force over its rocky bed; and surrounded by a winding road, several miles in circuit, commanding some magnificent views of the city and bay of Dublin, with the hill of Howth, Ireland's Eye, Lambay Island; of the mountains of Mourne in the distance, which are distinctly visible in clear weather, and of a beautiful country in the foreground. There are numerous handsome villas, with tastefully disposed grounds, commanding fine views of the city and bay of Dublin and the country adjacent. Among these are, Woodtown House, the residence of the Hon. Chief Baron Joy; Orlagh, of N. Callwell, Esq.; Rockbrook, of Mrs. Fry; Tibradon, of

J. Jones, Esq.; Cloragh, of C. Davis, Esq.; Woodbine Lodge, of T. B. Smithson, Esq.; Springfield, of R. Jones, Esq.; Woodtown, of Mrs. Collins; Air Park, of J. Delaney, Esq.; Spring Vale, of R. Sherlock, Esq.; Mount Venus House, of H. R. Armstrong, Esq.; Mount Michael, of M. Walsh, Esq.; Laurel Hill, of W. Bourk, Esq.; Summerville, of J. T. Moran, Esq.; Woodtown, of J. Dodd, Esq.; Hayfield, of W. Scott, Esq.; and Prospect Hill, of J. Dodd, Esq. There are four paper-mills, only one of which is at present at work, and employs about 60 persons. Two woollen-manufactories have been established; the chief articles are friezes, flannels, kersey, coating, and blankets, and the number of persons employed at present is 100, though a few years since, when in full work, more than 600 were engaged. The great military road commences in this parish, taking a course of 37 miles through a wild mountainous district previously deemed incapable of improvement, and opening a communication with Wicklow and with the south and west parts of the country. It is a rectory, in the diocese of Dublin, forming part of the union of Tallaght: the tithes amount to £181. 17. 6. In the R. C. divisions it forms part of the union or district of Rathfarnham. On the grounds of Mount Venus are the remains of a cromlech, the table stone of which has fallen; and of the upright stones on which it was supported, one only is standing, the others lying near it. The whole is of granite; the table stone is 19 feet long, 10 feet broad, and 5 feet thick; and the pillars are about 10 feet in height. The burial ground of the old church, now a ruin, is still much used.

CRUMLIN, or CROMLIN, a parish, in the barony of Newcastle, county of Dublin, and province of Leinster, 2¾ miles (S.W.) from the Post-Office, Dublin; containing 958 inhabitants, of which number, 544 are in the village, which consists of 115 houses. It is one of the four manors of the county anciently annexed to the Crown, and governed by a senechal, who receives £300 per annum. In 1594 the village was burned by Gerald Fitzgerald, at the head of the Wicklow insurgents. In 1690, after the victory of the Boyne, a part of William's army encamped here; and it is said to have been at this place that the king himself settled the method of granting protection, which was accordingly made public. On July 10th, he also issued hence his proclamation for stopping the currency of the brass money coined by Jas. II., except at reduced rates of valuation. It is a police station connected with the city of Dublin police. Here are extensive quarries of lime-stone, from which Dublin is chiefly supplied; and large flour-mills have for many years been in operation at Kimmage. The principal gentle-men's residences are Crumlin House, that of W. Collins, Esq.; Crumlin Lodge, of G. Oakley, Esq.; Crumlin, of R. Smith, Esq.; and the Glebe-house, of the Rev. J. Elliott: in the grounds of Mr. Smith is a moat or rath, from which is an extensive view of the beautiful scenery in the neighbourhood. The living is an impropriate curacy, in the dio-cese of Dublin, and in the patronage of the Dean and Chapter of St. Patrick's, to whom the rectory is appropriate. The tithes amount to £250: the glebe comprises only 1*a*. 36*p*. The church, which is a neat structure, was rebuilt, in 1816, by aid of a loan of £1000 from the late Board of First Fruits, but the old tower was preserved. In the R. C. divisions the parish forms part of the union or district of Rathfarn-ham: the chapel in the village is a neat building. There is a school in connection with the church, and one under the National Board of Education, in which together about 120 boys and 80 girls are edu-cated. About £70 per annum, arising from land bequeathed at a very remote period, is applied to the relief of the poor of this parish.

DALKEY, a parish, in the barony of Uppercross, county of Dublin, and province of Leinster, 6¾ miles (S.E.) from Dublin; containing 1402 inhabitants, of which number, 544 are in the village. This place, which is situated at the eastern extremity of the bay of Dublin, was formerly a town of considerable importance, and appears to have had a charter of incorporation at an early period, as, from an enrolment in the 33rd of Edw. III., dated Feb. 8th, 1358, "the provost and bailiffs in the town of Dalkey, the sheriff of Dublin, and the bailiff of Senkyl, were com-manded to allow the master of a Spanish ship arrested by them to depart." In 1414, Sir John Talbot, Lord Furneval, afterwards the celebrated Earl of Shrewsbury, landed here to take upon him the viceregal government; and, in 1558, the Earl of Sussex embarked his forces at this port to oppose the Scottish invaders at the isle of Rath-lin, on the coast of Antrim. Fairs and markets were established in 1480, for the encouragement of foreigners, who resorted hither to trade with the inhabitants; and seven strong castles were erected for their protec-tion and the security of their merchandise. The harbour was extremely favourable to the commerce of the town; vessels could lie in safety under shelter of the neighbouring island, by which they were protected from the north-east winds, and from the depth of water they could sail at any hour. The tolls of the fairs and markets were appropriated to the paving and improvement of the town, which, till the latter part of the 17th century, continued to be a place of great commercial resort, especially for the merchants of Dublin; but since that period its harbour has been abandoned for others of greater convenience, and the town has dwindled into an insignificant village. It is situated at the base of a high hill, commanding extensive views over the bay of Dublin, and in a neighbourhood abounding with picturesque and diversified scenery. Four of its ancient castles have been entirely destroyed, and the remains of three others, which have been long dismantled, convey striking indications of their former importance; one has been converted into a private dwelling-house, another is used as a store, and the third as a carpenter's shop. A twopenny post has been established, and there is a constabulary police station in the village. Here is also a station of the coast-guard, the limits of which extend from Dalkey Head to Irishtown, within which are batteries at Dalkey island, Sandy Cove, and Kingstown, and nine martello towers.

The parish comprises 444 statute acres, as applotted under the tithe act, and valued at £703. 6. 6½. per ann. A great portion of the land is open common, an extensive tract of which, adjoining the village, has, during the continuance of the public works at Kingstown harbour, been allowed to remain in the occupation of many who put themselves in possession of it, and have sold their assumed portions of it to others. At the farthest extremity of the common, on the coast opposite Dalkey island, are lead mines, which were formerly worked to some extent, but are now discontinued. On the common are the government quarries, which are worked by Messrs. Henry, Mullins and McMahon, under a contract for the completion of Kingstown Harbour. The largest blocks of granite blasted by gunpowder are lowered to the long level of the railway by three inclined planes. Dalkey common is celebrated in the old ballad of the "Kilruddery Hunt," written in 1774, by Mr. Fleming, and of which a copy was presented by the Earl of Meath to Geo. IV., on his visit to Dublin in 1821. The marine views are exceedingly beautiful, and the general scenery of the neighbourhood, which is richly diversified, is enlivened by numerous pleasing villas; the principal are Sorrento, the seat of the Rev. R. Mac

Donnell, F.T.C.D., commanding a beautiful view of the sea, with Wicklow and Bray Head, the Sugar Loaves, Djouce, Shankill, part of the Dublin mountains, and the beautiful bay of Killiney; Braganza Lodge, of — Armstrong, Esq.; Barn Hill, of Mrs. Johnston; Shamrock Lodge, of T. O'Reilly, Esq.; Charleville, of C. Brabazon, Esq.; and Coolamore, of Jeremiah Hanks, Esq., from which is an extensive view of the bay of Dublin. There are also numerous pleasant cottages, commanding fine views of the sea, which are let during the summer to respectable families. It is a perpetual curacy, in the diocese of Dublin, and is part of the union of Monkstown; the rectory forms part of the corps of the deanery of Christ-Church, Dublin. The tithes amount to £21. 9. 8., of which two-thirds are payable to the dean, and the remainder to the curate. The church is in ruins: it was situated in the village, and appears to have been originally a very spacious structure. In the R. C. divisions the parish forms part of the union or district of Kingstown. A national school is maintained by subscription, for which a good school-house was erected by subscription, in 1824; and there is also a school on the common, supported by small payments from the children aided by subscription; in these are about 190 boys and 150 girls. About the commencement of the present century, a circle of granite blocks enclosing a cromlech was standing on the common; but the cromlech and the stones surrounding it were blasted with gunpowder and carried away, to furnish materials for the erection of a martello tower on the coast. About five years since, in ploughing the grounds of Quatrebras, a stone grave was discovered, in which was a perfect skeleton; the proprietor of the estate, Capt. Nicholson, would not suffer it to be disturbed, and it still remains in the same state as when first found. Numerous ancient copper coins have been discovered in the same field.

DALKEY ISLAND, in the parish of Dalkey, barony of Uppercross, county of Dublin, and province of Leinster. This island is situated in 53° 16' 40" (N. Lat.), and 6° 5' 20" (W. Lon.), and forms the southeastern extremity of the bay of Dublin. Tradition states that the citizens of Dublin retired to it when that place was visited by the great plague, in 1575; and in modern times they have occasionally resorted hither for convivial purposes. Prior to 1798, it was the custom annually in the month of June to elect a mock king of Dalkey, with various officers of state, whose proceedings were recorded in a newspaper called the "Dalkey Gazette." The island is separated from the mainland of the parish by a channel called Dalkey Sound, about 1200 yards long, and 330 wide at its S.E., and 230 at its N.W. entrance. It was formerly considered a very safe and convenient harbour, and was the principal anchorage for ships resorting to the ancient sea-port of Dalkey. In 1815, it was surveyed as a site for an asylum harbour for the bay, and disapproved. The island contains about 25 statute acres of land, one-half of which affords good pasturage for cattle. The only inhabitants are a few artillerymen stationed at the battery, which mounts three 24 pounders, and has on its summit a martello tower, which is entered from the top. Here are the ruins of a church, dedicated to St. Benedict; and kistvaens, or stone coffins, of rude workmanship and great antiquity have been found near the shore. Near the church is a well, said to be efficacious in ophthalmic complaints; and some medicinal plants are found on the island. To the N.W. of Dalkey are the Clara, Lamb, and Maiden rocks, in the cavities of which an abundance of shell fish is found; and to the N.E. are the small islands called the Muglins.

DARGLE, LITTLE. —See WHITECHURCH, county of Dublin.

DOLPHIN'S BARN, a village, partly in the parish of St. James, barony of Newcastle, and partly in that of St. Catherine, barony of Uppercross, county of Dublin, and province of Leinster. This village, forming a suburb of the city of Dublin, consists chiefly of a long street on the road to Crumlin, partly situated between the circular road and the Grand Canal, which latter intersects the village, and is here crossed by a stone bridge. There are several tanyards, and the extensive dyeworks of Messrs. Pims, who have also dye stuff mills at Rudland; and on the Crumlin road are the dyeing and finishing works of Mr. P. Nevin. There is a R. C. chapel in the village, also a convent of nuns of the Carmelite order, who have a school for the gratuitous instruction of about 100 poor female children, and a select school for 12 young ladies.

DONABATE, or DONAGHBATE, a parish, in the barony of Balrothery, county of Dublin, and province of Leinster, 3 miles (N. by E.)

from Swords containing 386 inhabitants, of which number, 221 are in the village. This parish, which comprises 2366 statute acres, is situated on the eastern coast, near the inlets of Malahide and Rogerstown, and on the proposed line of the Grand Northern Trunk railway from Dublin to Drogheda, for which an act has been obtained. An extensive vein of green and white porphyry runs through it from east to west: the surrounding soil is limestone gravel and conglomerate grit. Contiguous to the village is Newbridge, the extensive demesne of Charles Cobbe, Esq. The house, which is a noble mansion, was erected by Archbishop Cobbe, about 1730, and contains several valuable paintings by the old masters, which were collected on the continent by the Rev. M. Pilkington, author of the Dictionary of Painters, who was vicar of this parish; the drawing-room contains several of the paintings described by him. Near this mansion is Turvey, the property of Lord Trimleston. There is a martello tower near the shore, and a constabulary police force is stationed in the village. The living is a vicarage, in the diocese of Dublin, episcopally united from time immemorial to the vicarage of Portrahan, or Portrane; the rectory is impropriate in the Rev. W. Hamilton and his heirs. The tithes amount to £220, of which £133. 6. 8. is payable to the impropriator, £66. 13. 4. to the vicar, and £20 to the economy estate of St. Patrick's cathedral, Dublin, as the rectorial tithes of the merged parish of Kilereagh. The glebe-house was built in 1810, by aid of a gift of £100 and a loan of £320 from the late Board of First Fruits; and there is a glebe of nine acres, for which a rent of £29 per annum is paid. The church stands in a commanding situation, and contains a handsome marble monument to the memory of Dr. Cobbe, Archbishop of Dublin, who died in 1765: contiguous to the ancient tower is a ruined chapel, in which are several sepulchral monuments of the Barnewall family, the oldest of which is of the 16th century: the Ecclesiastical Commissioners have recently granted £184. 7. 6. for the repairs of the church. In the R. C. divisions this parish is the head of a union or district, comprising also Portrane, where the chapel is situated. On a commanding situation in the demesne of Newbridge are the remains of the ancient castle of Lanistown, and about a mile from the village are the ruins of Kilcreagh church.

DONNYBROOK (St. Mary), a parish, partly in the half-barony of Rathdown, county of Dublin, but chiefly within the county of the city of Dublin, 2 miles (S. by E.) from Dublin; containing 10,394 inhabitants. It includes the villages of Ballsbridge, Clonskea, Donnybrook, Old Merrion, Sandymount, and Ringsend with Irishtown, each of which is described under its own head. The village of Donnybrook is chiefly remarkable for its fair, the patent for which was granted by King John, to continue for 15 days, commencing on the Monday before the 26th of August. On the following day great numbers of horses, cattle, and sheep are sold; but the principal object is amusement and diversion. It is held in a spacious green belonging to Messrs. Maddens, who derive from it annually about £400. A twopenny post has been established here, since the erection of the Anglesey bridge over the Dodder. A hat manufacture was formerly carried on to a great extent, but it has greatly decreased; there are some sawmills in the village, and a branch of the city police is stationed here. The parish is situated on the river Dodder, and comprises 1500 statute acres, as applotted under the tithe act; the lands are fertile and under good cultivation; and near the village is a quarry of excellent building stone, in which organic remains have been found. Exclusively of the gentlemen's seats described under the head of the several villages near which they are respectively situated, are Annfield, the residence of R. Percival, Esq., M. D.; Mount Errol, of Sir R. Baker, Knt.; Montrose, of J. Jameson, Esq., Swanbrook, of Alderman F. Darley; Gayfield, of T. P. Luscombe, Esq., Commissary-General; Priest House, of J. Robinson, Esq.; Stonehouse, of J. Barton, Esq.; Woodview, of E. J. Nolan, Esq.; Nutley, of G. Roe, Esq.; Thornfield, of W. Potts, Esq.; Airfield, of C. Hogan, Esq.; Simmons Court Hall, of G. Howell, Esq.; Belleville, of Alderman Morrison; Flora Ville, of M. Fitzgerald, Esq.; Donnybrook Cottage, of A. Colles, Esq., M. D.; Simmons Court, of P. Madden, Esq.; and Glenville, of J. O'Dwyer, Esq. Within the parish are iron-works, an extensive calico-printing establishment, a distillery, and salt works. The Dublin and Kingstown rail-road, the road from Dublin by Ballsbridge, and the road to Bray through Stillorgan, pass through it. That part of the parish which is in the county of the city is within the jurisdiction of the Dublin court of conscience. It is a chapelry, in the diocese of Dublin, and forms part of the corps of the archdeaconry of Dublin. The tithes amount to £166. 3. 0¾. to which is added about £300 collected as minister's money: there is no glebe-house, and the glebe comprises only about three-quarters of an acre. The church is a spacious and handsome edifice, in the early style of English architecture, with a tower surmounted by a well-proportioned spire; and was erected at Simmons Court (the old church in the village having fallen into decay), by a loan of £4154 from the late Board of First Fruits, in 1829. In the R. C. divisions the parish is united to those of St. Mark, Tawney, and St. Peter; there are chapels at Donnybrook and Irishtown, and a spacious chapel is now in progress near Cottage-terrace, Baggot-street. In the avenue leading to Sandymount is a convent of the Sisters of Charity, a branch from the establishment in Stanhope-street, Dublin; the sisters are employed in visiting the sick and in attending a school for girls; attached to the convent is a small neat chapel. There is a place of worship for Wesleyan Methodists close to the village of Donnybrook. A school for boys and another for girls are supported by subscription; and there is a dispensary at Ballsbridge. The hospital for incurables is in this parish, and is chiefly supported by Grand Jury presentments; and the Bloomfield retreat for lunatics was established by, the Society of Friends. There are cemeteries at Donnybrook and Merrion; and at Simmons Court are the remains of an old castle, consisting of a massive pointed archway. In the grounds of Gayfield is a medicinal spring, the water of which is similar in its properties to that of Golden Bridge. Lord Chief Justice Downes was born in the castle of Donnybrook, now a boarding school.

DOULOUGH'S (ST.), a parish, in the barony of Coolock county of Dublin, and province of Leinster, 5½ miles (N.E.) from Dublin, on the road to Malahide; containing 345 inhabitants. The land in this parish is of good quality and the soil favourable to the growth of corn, of which large crops are raised; the system of agriculture is improved, and there is abundance of limestone, which is quarried for agricultural and other uses, and in some of which varieties of fossils are found. The surrounding scenery is pleasingly and richly diversified, and from its elevation the parish commands extensive and beautiful views of the sea and the mountains in the neighbourhood. The principal seats, all of which command interesting prospects, are St. Doulough's Lodge, the residence of J. Rutherfoord, Esq.; St. Doulough's, of Mrs. Shaw; Lime Hill, of the Rev. P. Ryan, A. M.; and Spring Hill, of H. Parsons, Esq. It is a curacy, in the diocese of Dublin, and in the patronage of the Precentor of the cathedral of Christ-Church, to whom the rectory is appropriate: the tithes amount to £160, payable to the incumbent. The church is a neat modern edifice, adjoining the ancient structure, which is still preserved as a singular and interesting relic of antiquity. In the R. C. divisions it forms part of the union or district of Baldoyle and Howth. About 60 children are taught in the parochial school, which is supported by subscription, aided by the incumbent. The ancient church of St. Doulough, which is still tolerably entire, is one of the oldest and most singular religious edifices in the country: it is situated on an eminence at the extremity of an avenue about 50 yards in length, at the entrance of which is a low granite cross supposed to have been originally placed over the south porch. The church is about 48 feet long and 18 feet wide, with a massive square embattled tower, and is built of the limestone found in the neighbourhood, with the exception of the mullions of the windows, the keystones of the arched roofs, and the more ornamental details, which are of oolite or fine freestone, probably imported in a previously finished state from Normandy or England. The south porch, which rises like a vast buttress at the south-eastern angle of the tower, contains a low and imperfectly pointed doorway leading into a crypt with a stone roof groined, and divided into two small apartments, one of which is almost entirely occupied with the altar-tomb of St. Doulough, the staircase leading to the tower, and the pillars supporting the roof. From this a low doorway leads into the eastern portion of the church, which is 22 feet long and 12 feet wide, lighted at the east end by a trefoiled window, and two smaller windows on the south and one on the north side. This part of the church and also the tower are evidently of much later date than the rest of the building, which is supposed to have been erected in the 10th century; the groining of the roof, the tracery of the windows, and other details contrasting strongly with the ruder portions of the structure. Between the south windows of the church, and projecting into its area, is the staircase leading through the upper portion of the porch to the tower, and opening into a small apartment with two pointed windows, beyond which is an apartment immediately under the roof, 36 feet in length and very narrow, having that portion of it which is under the tower rudely groined. In the south porch a staircase leads from the apartment in which is St. Doulough's tomb, to a very small apartment, called St. Doulough's bed, 5 feet long, 2 feet wide, and 2½ high, and lighted only by a loophole; the entrance is extremely low and narrow; the roof is vaulted, and in the floor is a small hole, through which a bell rope appears to have passed. The roof of the church forms a very acute angle, and the stones of which it is constructed are so firmly cemented that it is impervious to water, though it has been exposed to the weather for eight or nine centuries. This singular edifice comprises within its narrow limits seven different apartments, two staircases, and a great variety of windows of various designs, and door cases all differing in character. Near the church is a well, dedicated to St. Catharine, enclosed within an octagonal building with a groined roof of stone; of this building, with which a subterraneous passage communicated from the crypt in which is St. Doulough's tomb, the faces towards the cardinal points, in which are loopholes, are raised to a second story and crowned with a pediment, in which is a lancet-shaped window; the door is on the south side, and the whole is finished with a pyramidal dome, of which the upper part is wanting. The interior of the building is circular, and has three deep recesses in the walls, in which are stone seats. In the centre of the area is the well, encircled by a ring of stone two feet in depth and 5 inches thick on the edge. In each spandril of the arched ceiling, and over each recess in the walls, is a sunken panel, and the interior was formerly decorated with paintings of scriptural subjects.

DRIMNAGH, or DRIMNA, formerly a parish, in the barony of Uppercross, county of Dublin, and province of Leinster, 2 miles (W.S.W.) from Dublin, on the road to Naas and on the Grand Canal. This ancient parish has merged into that of Clondalkin. There is a paper-mill at Lansdowne Valley; and near the Blue Bell is a woollen factory, at which coarse cloths are manufactured. In the direction of Crumlin stands Drimna Castle, formerly the head of a manor, of which the Barnewall family were lords from the time of John to that of Jas. I., and which was a place of some consequence in the reign of Chas. I. It is the property of the Marquess of Lansdowne, and is an irregular pile, occupied by Mr. E. Cavanagh. The church is in ruins. In the R. C. divisions it is part of the district of Lucan, Palmerstown, and Clondalkin.

DUBLIN (County of), a maritime county of the province of Leinster, bounded on the east by the Irish Sea, on the north and west by the county of Meath, on the west and south-west by that of Kildare, and on the south by that of Wicklow. It extends from 53° 10' to 53° 37' (N. Lat.), and from 6° 4' to 6° 36' (W. Lon.), and comprises an area, according to the Ordnance survey, of 240,204 statute acres, of which 229,292 acres are cultivated land, and the remainder unprofitable bog and mountain. The population, in 1821, exclusively of the metropolis, was 150,011, and in 1831, 183,042.

The earliest inhabitants of this tract of whom we have any authentic notice were a native people designated by Ptolemy *Blanii* or *Eblani,* who occupied also the territory forming the present county of Meath, and whose capital city was Eblana, presumed on good authority to have been on the site of the present city of Dublin. By some writers it is stated that in subsequent remote ages the part of the county lying south and east of the river Liffey formed part of the principality of *Croigh Cuolan;* while that to the north was included in the principality of *Midhe,* or *Meath.* The *Eblani,* whatever may have been their origin, probably enjoyed peaceable possession of the soil until the commencement of the Danish ravages, and the seizure and occupation of Dublin by these fierce invaders. At this era, the tract now described experienced its full share of calamities, until the celebrated battle of Clontarf, which terminated in the overthrow of the military power of the Ostmen in Ireland. But that this people had made extensive settlements within its limits, which they were subsequently allowed to retain as peaceable subjects of the native Irish rulers, is proved by the fact that, at the period of the English invasion, a considerable part of the county to the north of the Liffey was wholly in their possession, and from this circumstance was designated by the Irish *Fingall,* a name signifying either the "white foreigners" or "a progeny of foreigners;" the word "*fine*" importing, in one sense, a tribe or family. The country to the south of Dublin is stated, but only on traditional authority, to have been called, at the same period, *Dubhgall,* denoting the territory of the "black foreigners," from its occupation by another body of Danes. Though all Fingall was granted by Hen. II. to Hugh de Lacy, Lord of Meath, yet the number of other proprietors, together with the circumstance of its being the centre of the English power in Ireland, prevented the county, which was one of those erected by King John in 1210, from being placed under palatine or other peculiar jurisdiction. It originally comprised the territories of

49

the O'Birnes and O'Tooles in the south, which were separated from it and formed into the present county of Wicklow, so lately as the year 1603. At an early period, the jurisdiction of the sheriff of Dublin appears even to have extended in other directions far beyond its present limits; for, by an ordinance of parliament, about the close of the 13th century, preserved in the Black Book of Christ-Church, Dublin, it was restricted from extending, as previously, into the counties of Meath and Kildare, and into some parts even of the province of Ulster.

It is in the diocese and province of Dublin, and, for purposes of civil jurisdiction, is divided into the baronies of Balrothery, Castleknock, Coolock, Nethercross, Newcastle, Half Rathdown, and Uppercross, exclusively of those of St. Sepulchre and Donore, which form parts of the liberties of the county of the city. The irregularities of form in the baronies are very great: that of Newcastle is composed of two portions, that of Nethercross of six, and that of Uppercross of five, of which three constituting the parishes of Ballymore-Eustace, Bally-bought, and Tipperkevin, on the confines of Wicklow and Kildare, are wholly detached from the rest of the county: the irregularities of the two latter baronies are owing to their constituent parts having been formerly dispersed church lands, enjoying separate jurisdictions and privileges, but ultimately formed into baronies for the convenience of the civil authority. The county contains the ancient disfranchised boroughs and corporate towns of Swords and Newcastle; the sea-port, fishing, and post-towns of Howth, Kingstown, Balbriggan, and Malahide; the fishing-towns of Rush, Skerries, and Baldoyle; the inland post-towns of Cabinteely, Lucan, Rathcool, and Tallaght; the market-town of Ballymore-Eustace, and the town of Rathfarnham, each of which has a penny post to Dublin; besides numerous large villages, in some degree suburban to the metropolis, of which, exclusively of those of Sandymount, Booterstown, Blackrock, Donnybrook (each of which has a penny post), Dolphinsbarn, Irishtown, Rathmines, and Ringsend, which are in the county of the city, the principal are those of Finglas, Golden-Ball, Dalkey, Drumcondra, Stillorgan, Raheny, Dundrum, Roundtown, Ranelagh, Artaine, Clontarf, Castleknock, Chapelizod, Glasnevin (each of which has a twopenny post to Dublin), Donabate, Portrane, Garristown, Belgriffin, St. Doulough's, Old Connaught, Killiney, Bullock, Lusk, Newcastle, Saggard, Balrothery, Little Bray, Clondalkin, Coolock, Crumlin, Golden-Bridge, Island-

Bridge, Kilmainham, Milltown, Merrion, Phibsborough, Sandford, and Williamstown. Two knights of the shire are returned to the Imperial parliament, who are elected at the county court-house at Kilmainham: the number of electors registered under the 2d of Wm. IV., c.88, up to Feb.1st, 1837, is 2728, of which 788 were £50, 407 £20, and 622 £10, freeholders; 18 £50, 427 £20, and 423 £10, leaseholders; and 12 £50, 30 £20, and 1 £10, rent-chargers: the number that voted at the last general election was 1480. Prior to the Union, the boroughs of Swords and Newcastle sent each two members to the Irish House of Commons. A court of assize and general gaol delivery is held every six weeks, at the court-house in Green-street, Dublin; and at Kilmainham, where the county gaol and court-house are situated, are held the quarter sessions, at which a chairman, who exercises the same powers as the assistant barrister in other counties, presides with the magistrates. The local government is vested in a lieutenant, 17 deputy-lieutenants, and 88 magistrates, with the usual county officers. The number of constabulary police stations is 30, and the force consists of 6 chief and 29 subordinate constables and 113 men, with 6 horses, the expense of maintaining which is defrayed equally by Grand Jury presentments and by Government. The Meath Hospital, which is also the county of Dublin Infirmary, is situated on the south side of the city, and is supported by Grand Jury presentments, subscriptions, and donations, and by an annual parliamentary grant; there are 25 dispensaries. The amount of Grand Jury presentments for the county, in 1835, was £23,458. 2. 7., of which £2188. 9. 10. was expended on the public roads of the county at large; £6904. 14. 0. on the public roads, being the baronial charge; £8365. 7. 0. for public establishments, officers' salaries, &c.; £3106. 8. 8. for police; and £2895 towards repayment of advances made by Government. In military arrangements, this county is the head of all the districts throughout Ireland, the department of the commander-in-chief and his staff being at Kilmainham; it contains six military stations, besides those within the jurisdiction of the metropolis, viz., the Richmond infantry barrack, near Golden-Bridge on the Grand Canal, Island-bridge artillery station, the Portobello cavalry barrack, the Phoenix-park magazine and infantry barrack, and the recruiting depot on the Grand Canal, all of which are described in the account of the city, affording in the whole accommodation for 161 officers, 3282 men, and 772 horses; there are, besides, 26 martello towers and nine batteries on the coast, capable of containing 684 men; and at Kilmainham stands the Royal Military Hospital, for disabled and superannuated soldiers, similar to that of Chelsea, near London. There are eight coast-guard stations, one of which (Dalkey) is in the district of Kingstown, and the rest in that of Swords, with a force consisting of 8 officers and 64 men.

The county stretches in length from north to south, and presents a sea-coast of about thirty miles, while its breadth in some places does not exceed seven. Except in the picturesque irregularities of its coast, and the grand and beautiful boundary which the mountains on its southern confines form to the rich vale below, it possesses less natural diversity of scenery than many other parts of the island; but it is superior to all in artificial decoration; and the banks of the Liffey to Leixlip present scenery of the most rich and interesting character. The grandeur of the features of the surrounding country, indeed, give the environs of the metropolis a character as striking as those, perhaps, of any city in the west of Europe. The mountains which occupy the southern border of the county are the northern extremities of the great group forming the entire adjacent county of Wicklow: the principal summits within its confines are the Three Rock Mountain and Garrycastle, at the eastern extremity of the chain, of which the former has an elevation of 1586 feet, and the latter of 1869; Montpelier hill; the group formed by Kippure, Seefinane, Seechon, and Seefin mountains, of which the first is 2527 feet high, and Seechon 2150 and the Tallaght and Rathcoole hills, which succeed each other north-westward from Seechon, and beyond the latter of which, in the same direction, is a lower range, composed of the Windmill, Athgoe, Lyons, and Rusty hills. From Rathcoole hill a long range diverges south-westward, and enters the eastern confines of Kildare county, near Blessington. In the mountains adjoining Montpelier and Kilmashogue are bogs, covering three or four square miles; but the grandest features of these elevations are the great natural ravines that open into them southward, of which the most extraordinary is the Scalp, through which the road from Dublin to the romantic scenes of Powerscourt enters the county of Wicklow. From their summits are also obtained very magnificent views of the city and bay, and the fertile and highly improved plains of which nearly all the rest of the county is composed, and which form part of the great level tract that includes also the counties of Kildare and Meath. The coast from the boldly projecting promontory of Bray head, with its serrated summit, to the Killiney hills is indented into the beautiful bay of Killiney. Dalkey Island, separated from the above named hills by a narrow channel, is the southern limit of Dublin bay, the most northern point of which is the Bailey of Howth, on which is a lighthouse. The coast of the bay, with the exception of these two extreme points, is low and shelving, but is backed by a beautiful and highly cultivated country terminating eastward with the city. Much of the interior of the bay consists of banks of sand uncovered at low water. About a mile to the north of Howth is Ireland's Eye, and still farther north, off the peninsula of Portrane, rises Lambay Island, both described under their own heads. Between Howth and Portrane the coast is flat, and partly marshy; but hence northward it presents a varied succession of rock and strand; off Holmpatrick lie the scattered rocky islets of St. Patrick, Count, Shenex, and Rockabill.

The soil is generally shallow, being chiefly indebted to the manures from the metropolis for its high state of improvement. It is commonly argillaceous, though almost every where containing an admixture of gravel, which may generally be found in abundance within a small depth of the surface, and by tillage is frequently turned up, to the great improvement of the land. The substratum is usually a cold retentive clay, which keeps the surface in an unprofitable state, unless draining and other methods of improvement have been adopted. Rather more than one-half of the improvable surface is under tillage, chiefly in the northern and western parts, most remote from the metropolis: in the districts to the south of the Liffey, and within a few miles from its northern bank, the land is chiefly occupied by villas, gardens, nurseries, dairy farms, and for the pasturage of horses. Considerable improvement has taken place in the system of agriculture by the more extensive introduction of green crops and improved drainage, and by the extension of tillage up the mountains. The pasture lands, in consequence of drainage and manure, produce a great variety of good natural grasses, and commonly afford from four to five tons of hay per acre, and sometimes six. The salt marshes which occur along the coast from Howth northward are good, and the pastures near the sea side are of a tolerably fattening quality; but more inland they become poorer. The only dairies are those for the supply of Dublin with milk and butter, which, however, are of great extent and number. The principal manures are lime and limestone gravel, of which the latter is a species of limestone and marl mixed, of a very fertilising quality, and found in inexhaustible quantities. Strong blue and brown marl are found in different parts, and there are likewise beds of white marl; the blue kind is preferred as producing a more durable effect: manures from Dublin, coal ashes, and shelly sand found on the coast, are also used. The implements of husbandry are of the common kind, except on the farms of noblemen and gentlemen of fortune. The breed of cattle has been much improved by the introduction of the most valuable English breeds, which have nearly superseded the native stock. The county is not well wooded with the exception of plantations in the Phoenix Park and the private grounds of the gentry: there are various nurseries for the supply of plants. The waste lands occupy 10,912 statute, acres: the largest tract is that of the mountains on the southern confines, extending about fifteen miles in length and several in breadth. The scarcity of fuel, which would otherwise press severely on the industrious classes, from the want of turf nearer home, which can be had only from the mountains in the south and the distant commons of Balrothery and Garristown on the north, is greatly diminished by the ample supplies brought by both canals and by the importation of English coal.

The county presents several interesting features in its geological relations. Its southern part from Blackrock, Kingstown, and Dalkey forms the northern extremity of the great granitic range which extends through Wicklow and part of Carlow. The granite tract is bordered by a range of incumbent mica slate, which extends eastwards from Shankill and the Scalp to the hills of Killiney, and on the western side commences near Rathfarnham, passes to the south of Montpelier hill, and occupies the upper part of the hollow which separates Seefinane mountain, on the east, from Seechon on the west: in this hollow are displayed some curious intermixtures of the strata of inica slate, granite, and quartz. In the descent from Seechon mountain, both south-westward and north-westward, towards Rathcool, the mica slate passes into clay slate, containing frequent beds of greenstone, greenstone slate, and greenstone porphyry, and occasionally likewise of quartz. The Tallaght hills consist of clay slate, greenstone, and greenstone porphyry, interstratified; the latter rocks more particularly abounding in the eastern quarter. Rathcoole hills, and the range extending from them south-westward, are composed of clay slate, clay slate conglomerate, and grauwacke slate, alternating with each other. The low group west of Rathcoole is composed of clay slate, grauwacke, gratiwacke slate, and granite, of which the last is found remarkably disposed in subordinate beds in the prevailing grauwacke slate of Windmill hill whence some of them may be traced westward to near Rusty hill. This county contains the only strata of transition rocks known to exist in the eastern part of Ireland. They appear in detached portions along the coast from Portrane Head, by Loughshinny, Skerries, and Balbriggan to the Delvan stream, the northern limit of the county. The rest of the county, comprising nearly the whole of its plain surface, is based on floetz limestone, commonly of a blueish grey colour, often tinged with black, which colour in some places entirely prevails, especially where the limestone is inter-stratified with slate clay, calp, or swinestone, or where it abounds in lydian stone. The black limestone in the latter case is a hard compact rock, often of a silicious nature, requiring much fuel for its conversion into lime. Calp, or "black quarry stone," which is generally of a black-ish grey colour and dull fracture, and may be considered as an intimate mixture of limestone and slate clay, forms the common building stone of Dublin; it is quarried to a great extent at Crumlin and Rathgar. Besides carbonate of lime, it includes considerable quantities of silex and alumen, traces of the oxydes of iron and manganese, and a small proportion of carbon, which gives to it its dark colour: by exposure to the air it undergoes a gradual decomposition. The elevated peninsula of Howth consists of irregular alternations of clay slate and quartz rock, both pure and intermixed, on its southern coast the strata present some extraordinary contortions. The only metallic ore at present found in considerable quantity is lead, once abundantly raised near the commons of Kilmainham, and at Killiney; a much more productive vein on Shankill is now being worked by the Mining Company of Ireland. White lead is found in small quantities; the ore is smelted and refined at Ballycorus, in the immediate vicinity of the mine, on Shankill is a tower for the manufacture of shot. At Loughshinny is a copper mine, and at Clontarf a lead mine, both now abandoned. On the south-western side of Howth, grey ore of manganese and brown iron-stone have been obtained in considerable quantities; and a variety of earthy black cobalt ore has been found there. Coal is supposed to exist near the northern side of the county, and unsuccessful trials have been made for it near Lucan. Among the smaller minerals may be enumerated schorl or tourmaline and garnet, frequently found in the granite; beryl, a variety of emerald, which occurs in several places; and spodumene, which is in great request from its containing eight per cent. of a newly discovered alkali, called lithia, is procured at Killiney, as is also a mineral closely resembling spodumene, designated killinite by Dr. Taylor, its discoverer, from its locality. The limestone strata usually abound with petrifactions, specimens of which, remarkable for their perfection and variety, may be obtained at St. Doulough's, and at Feltrim, about seven miles north-east of Dublin. The shores of the county particularly from Loughlinstown to Bray, abound with pebbles of all colours, often beautifully variegated, which bear a polish, and are applied to a variety of ornamental uses.

The manufactures are various, but of inferior importance. The most extensive is that of woollen cloth, carried on chiefly in the liberties and vicinity of Dublin. The manufacture of paper is carried on in different parts, more particularly at Rockbrook and Templeoge. There are also cotton-works, bleach and dye-works, and ironworks, besides minor establishments, all noticed in their respective localities. The banks of the numerous small streams by which the county is watered present divers advantageous sites for the erection of manufactories of every kind within a convenient distance of the metropolis. The great extent of sea-coast affords facilities for obtaining an abundant supply of fish. Nearly 90 wherries, of which the greater number belong to Skerries and Rush, and the others to Howth, Baldoyle, Malahide, Balbriggan, and Ringsend, are employed in this occupation: there are also about twenty smacks and five seine nets occupied in the salmon fishery between Dublin and Kingstown; the former, in the season, are likewise engaged in the herring fishery; and at Kingstown and Bullock are also a number of yawls, employed in catching whiting, pollock, and herring. On the river Liffey, from Island-Bridge to the light-house at Poolbeg, there is a considerable salmon fishery. The harbours are mere fishing ports, except that of Dublin, and its dependencies Howth and Kingstown, upon the improvement of both of which vast sums have been expended, with but partial success.

The chief river is the Anna Liffey ("the water of Liffey"), which has its principal source at Sally gap, in the Wicklow mountains, and taking a circuit westward through Kildare county, enters that of Dublin near Leixlip, where it is joined by the Rye water from Kildare, and pursues a winding eastern course nearly across the middle of it, descending through a deep and rich glen by Lucan and Chapelizod: below the latter it flows through some pleasing scenes on the borders of Phoenix Park: at Island-Bridge it meets the tide, and a little below it enters the city, to the east of which it discharges its waters into the bay of Dublin. The river is navigable for vessels of 300 tons up to Carlisle bridge, the nearest to the sea; for small craft that can pass the arches, up to Island-Bridge, and for small boats beyond Chapelizod: so circuitous is its course, that although the distance from its source to its mouth, in a direct line, is only ten miles, yet, following its banks, it is no less than forty. Numerous streams which supply water to many mills, descend into the Liffey: the principal are the Dodder, the Brittas or Cammock, and the Tolka; a stream called the Delvan forms the northern boundary of the county at Naul. The two great lines of inland navigation commence in Dublin city, but as they run in parallel directions within a few miles of each other during some parts of their course, the benefits anticipated from them have not been realised to the utmost extent. The Grand Canal was originally commenced in the year 1755, by the corporation for promoting inland navigation in Ireland: in 1772, a subscription was opened, and the subscribers were incorporated by the name of the Company of Undertakers of the Grand Canal, who, by the completion of this work, have connected the capital both with the Shannon and the Barrow. Its entire cost was £844,216, besides £122,148 expended on docks. One-third was defrayed by parliament. The Royal Canal, incorporated by a charter of Geo. III., in 1789, and afterwards aided by a grant of additional powers from the legislature, is navigable from Dublin to Longford and Tarmonbarry, near the head of the navigable course of the Shannon, an extent of 92 miles: its construction cost £776,213, which was wholly defrayed at the public expense. The roads and bridges are for the most part in excellent order, being frequently repaired at great expense. The Circular Road is a turnpike, nearly encompassing the metropolis, beyond which the Grand and Royal canals for a considerable distance run nearly parallel: from these limits of the city the great mailcoach roads branch in every direction, and all, excepting the south-east road through Wicklow to Wexford. are turnpikes.

Of the ancient round towers which form so remarkable a feature in the antiquities of Ireland, this county contains three, situated respectively at Lusk, Swords, and Clondalkin. There is a very fine cromlech at Glen Druid, near Cabinteely, and others at Killiney, Howth, Mount Venus (in the parish of Cruagh), Glen Southwell or the Little Dargle, and Larch hill, which last is within a circle of stones; and there are numerous raths or moats in various parts. The number of religious houses existing at various periods prior to the Reformation was 24, of which there are at present remains only of those of Larkfield and Monkstown; but there are several remains of ancient churches. Although always forming the centre of the English power in Ireland, the unsettled state of society caused the surface of the county, at an early period, to be studded with castles, of which the remains are still numerous; these, with the ancient castles yet inhabited, and the principal gentlemen's seats are noticed in their respective parishes. Among the minor natural curiosities are some chalybeate springs, of which the best known are, one at Golden-Bridge, one in the Phoenix Park, and one at Lucan. Southwell's Glen, about four miles south of the metropolis, is worthy of notice as a remarkably deep dale, lined with lofty trees, and adorned by a waterfall. From the district of Fingal, which is the ancient name of a large tract of indefinite extent to the north of Dublin, the distinguished family of Plunkett derives the titles of Earl and Baron.

DUBLIN, the metropolis of Ireland, and a city and county of itself, in the province of Leinster, situated in 53° 21' (N. Lat.) and 6° 17' (W. Lon.), 339 miles (N.W.) from London; containing, in 1831, 265,316 inhabitants, of which number, 204,155 are within the boundary of the civic jurisdiction, and the remainder in the county of Dublin.

The existence of this city, under the name of the city *Eblana*, was first noticed by Ptolemy, the Roman geographer, who lived about the Year 140. Shortly after it is mentioned by the native historians, as being fixed on as the eastern boundary of a line of demarcation drawn westwards across the island to Galway, for the purpose of putting an end to a war between two rival monarchs, Con-Cead-Cathach, King of Ireland, and Mogha Nuagad, King of Munster; the portion of the island to the north of the boundary line being assigned to the former, the southern portion to the latter, of the contending parties. The city originally occupied the summit of the elevated ridge that now forms its central portion, extending from the Castle westwards towards Kilmainham, and was at first called by the native Irish *Drom-Col-Coille*, or the "Hill of Hazel wood," from the number of trees of that species which grew on it. The correctness of this conjecture as to the origin of the name is confirmed by the fact that, on clearing away the foundations of the old chapel royal in the castle, some years since, to prepare for the erection of the beautiful structure that now supplies its place, they were ascertained to have been laid on piles of hazelwood. Another ancient name, still retained by the natives, is *Bally-Ath-Cliath-Duibhlinne*, the "Town of the Ford of Hurdles on the Blackwater," given to it in consequence of the people having access to the river by means of hurdles laid over its marshy borders, before it was embanked. By the Danish settlers in the district of Fingal, to the north of the city, it was called *Divelin*, and by the Welsh it is still called *Dinas Dulin*.

The only circumstance on record connected with the city, during a long interval, is that the inhabitants of Leinster were defeated in a great battle fought at Dublin, by Fiacha Sraotine, monarch of Ireland, in 291. After which its annals present a total blank until the year 448, when, according to Josceline, Alphin Mac Eochaid, King of Bally-Ath-Cliath, was converted to Christianity by the preaching of St. Patrick, and baptised by him at a spring on the southern side of the city, near the tower of the cathedral afterwards dedicated to that saint, and still known by the name of St. Patrick's well. The Black Book of Christ-Church, a manuscript of high antiquity and repute, states that St. Patrick celebrated mass in one of the arches or vaults built by the Danish or Ostman merchants as a depository for their goods, long before the fleets of that nation appeared on the coast with the intention of taking military occupation of the country. It was not till the beginning of the ninth century that these marauders, who afterwards harassed all the northern coasts of Europe by their predatory invasions, divested themselves of the character of merchants, in which they had hitherto maintained an intercourse with the people of Ireland, to assume that of conquerors. In 836, the Ostmen or Easterlings, by which name the Danes were then known, entered the Liffey in a fleet of sixty ships in aid of their countrymen, who had ravaged the land and even fixed themselves in some districts several years before. Dublin now submitted to them for the first time; and they secured themselves in the possession of it by the erection of a strong rath, which enabled them not only to overawe the city but to extend their power through Fingal, to the north, and to Bray and the Wicklow mountains to the south. The district from that time was the principal Danish settlement in Leinster; Fin-Gal, to the north of the river, having acquired its name, as being the territory of the "White Strangers," or Norwegians; and the tract to the south being distinguished by the appellation of Dubh-Gal, or the territory of the "Black Strangers," from the Danes.

But the invaders did not enjoy their newly gained acquisition in tranquillity. On the death of their king Tor-magnus or Turgesius, who, after having reigned despotically over a great part of the island for more than 40 years, was defeated and put to death, in 845, by Malachy, King of Ireland, the Danes were driven out of Dublin, and the city plundered by the Irish of Meath and Leinster. In the year following, however, they regained possession of it and secured themselves by adding new fortifications to those already constructed, and were still further strengthened by the arrival of Amlave, or Aulaffe, who, having landed in 853 with a powerful reinforcement of Danes and Norwegians, assumed the supreme authority over all the Danish settlers; and in the hope of enjoying quiet possession of his newly acquired dignity, he concluded a truce with the neighbouring Irish chieftains, but it continued only for three years. The annals of the remainder of this century are occupied with recitals of reciprocal attacks of the Irish and the foreigners, in which the one party failed to expel the invaders, and the other was equally unsuccessful in enlarging the bounds of their authority, or even of fixing it on a permanent basis in the capital of the district that acknowledged their sway: in one of those conflicts, Clondalkin, the favourite residence of Aulaffe was burnt and upwards of one hundred of his principal followers were slain; in another he retaliated on the enemy, by plundering and burning the city of Armagh. So firmly did the Danish king feel himself fixed in his restored dominion, that he proceeded with his son Ivar in a fleet of 200 vessels to aid his countrymen Hinguar and Hubba, then contending against the Saxons in the West of England, and returned next year laden with booty. On the death of Aulaffe, which took place the year following, his son Ivar succeeded him in the government of

Dublin, where the opinion of his power was such that the Irish annals give him the title of King of the Normans of all Ireland. A few years after, the men of Dublin fitted out an expedition under the command of Ostin Mac Aulaffe against the Picts of North Britain, in which they were successful. Encouraged by these instances of good fortune, they again invaded South Wales, but were driven out with great loss; to wipe off which disgrace they made an incursion into Anglesey, a few years after, and ravaged it with fire and sword. During all this period hostilities were carried on between them and the Irish with little intermission. The annals of the tenth century state that Dublin was four times taken by the Irish, and the Danes expelled from it, but they invariably returned in strength sufficient to re-establish themselves, and often to retaliate severely on their enemies. This century is remarkable for other events connected with Dublin. Aulaffe Mac Godfrid, the king, was defeated in Northumberland by Athelstan, King of England; and about the middle of the century, the Ostmen of Dublin embraced Christianity. The first public proof of their conversion was the foundation of the monastery of the Blessed Virgin, near Ostmanstown, on the northern bank of the Liffey. About the same time, Edgar, King of England, is said to have subdued Wales, the Isle of Man, and part of Ireland, particularly the city of Dublin, of which mention is made in his charter dated at Gloucester, in 964.

Towards the close of the century, the power of the Danes in this part of Ireland began to decline. In 980, they were defeated in a memorable battle at Taragh by Melaghlin, King of Ireland, who, following up his success, ravaged Fingal with fire and sword, and compelled the inhabitants of Dublin to pay a tribute of an ounce of gold for every capital messuage and garden in the city. Reginald, the Danish king, was so much affected by his losses that he undertook a pilgrimage to the Isle of Iona, where he died. The last year of the century was rendered still more memorable by the capture of Dublin by the celebrated Brian Boriomhe, King of Munster, who, after exacting hostages to secure his conquest, permitted the Danes to retain possession of it, a concession of which they immediately took advantage by strengthening it with several additional fortifications. Still, however, their power, though diminished, was not destroyed; for, in the commencement of the ensuing century, Brian Boriomhe, in order effectually to crush them, found it necessary to form a confederacy of most of the subordinate kings of Ireland. The result was the celebrated battle of Clontarf, fought in 1014, in which the Danes were totally defeated, and the shattered remains of their army forced to shut themselves up in Dublin. But the triumph of the conquerors was diminished by the death of their leader, who received a mortal wound at the moment of victory: his son, a number of his nobles, and 11,000 of his soldiers shared his fate. The Danes still kept possession of the city. In 1038, Christ-Church was founded by Sitric the king, and by Donat, the first Danish bishop of Dublin; Aulaffe, Sitric's son, who succeeded him, fitted out a large fleet in order to reinstate Conan, the prince of North Wales, who had fled to Ireland to escape from the cruelties of Grufydd ab Llewelyn, an usurper, and had afterwards married Sitric's daughter. The expedition, though at first so successful as to have gained possession of Grufydd's person by stratagem, ultimately failed; for the Welsh, on hearing of his capture, assembled in great numbers, rescued Grufydd, and drove Conan and his Danish auxiliaries to their ships with great slaughter. A second expedition fitted out the ensuing year was equally unfortunate: the greater part of Conan's fleet was destroyed by a tempest and himself driven back on the Irish shore. He made no further attempt to regain his throne, but spent the remainder of his life with his father-in-law in Dublin.

The city was soon after exposed to the assaults of a new enemy. In 1066, Godred Crovan, King of Man, obtained possession of it and overran a large portion of Leinster, over which he assumed the title of king, which he retained till his death, together with that of Man and of the Hebrides. On his demise the sovereign power again devolved on the Danes, who elected Godfrey Meranagh to succeed him. The Danes, though constantly exposed to the hostilities of the natives, against whom they had great difficulty in maintaining their position in the country, increased their difficulties by their internal dissensions. In 1088, those of Dublin besieged the city of Waterford, which was also inhabited by a colony of the same nation, entered it by storm and burnt it to the ground; and in the following year, the united Danish forces of Dublin, Wicklow, and Waterford proceeded to Cork with a similar intention, but were routed on their march thither and forced to return with considerable loss. For some time after the district appears to have been subject to the kings of Ireland, as no mention is made of any Danish ruler there. At the same time it appears that the kings of England endeavoured to obtain some influence in the affairs of Ireland, for it is stated that Rodolphus, Archbishop of Canterbury, by the orders of Hen. I., consecrated one Gregory Archbishop of Dublin, in 1121, and that this act was done with the concurrence of Turlogh O'Brien, then King of Ireland. Afterwards, however, Dermod Mac Murchad, or Mac Murrough, King of Leinster, exercised paramount authority in the city. He founded the nunnery of St. Mary de Hogges, and the priory of Allhallows, both in its immediate vicinity, and, after overrunning all the surrounding country, forced the Danish residents there to acknowledge his supremacy, which he retained until the commencement of the reign of Roderic O'Conor, King of Ireland, who, on his attainment of the supreme monarchy, was recognised as King of Dublin by the inhabitants, and they in return received from him a present of four thousand oxen.

After the reduction of Wexford by the English forces, who landed at Bannow bay, in 1169, under the command of Robert Fitz-Stephen, to assist Dermod Mac Murrough in the recovery of Leinster, the combined force marched upon Dublin. The garrison, intimidated by the reports of the numbers and ferocity of the assailants, sued for peace, which was granted on the payment of tribute secured by hostages. Asculph Mac Torcall, the Danish king, was suffered to retain the government, and Dermod retired with his English auxiliaries to the southern part of Leinster, where he was joined by Strongbow, Earl of Pembroke, who had landed with a reinforcement of fifteen or sixteen hundred men, and taken Waterford by storm from the Danes. The combined army thus enforced resolved upon another attack on Dublin, either in consequence of a second revolt, or, as the Irish writers assert, to gratify the vindictive feelings of Dermod, who hoped thus to revenge the injury and insult of his former expulsion. Roderic, King of Ireland, hearing of the intended movement, levied an army of 30,000 men, which he posted at Clondalkin to oppose the invaders; but on their nearer approach he disbanded his troops, and retired across the Shannon. The citizens perceiving themselves thus abandoned, again had recourse to treaty; but while they were preparing to select the hostages required of them, Milo de Cogan, one of the English leaders, forced his way into the place. Asculph and most of the Danes took shelter on board their fleet, and the city was, after much slaughter, taken possession of by the English. Roderic now made a second attempt to expel the strangers, for which purpose he invested Dublin with an army of double the number he had formerly collected, and reduced the place to such straits, that Strongbow deputed Laurence O'Toole, the archbishop, to treat with him for a surrender. The terms offered by the Irish king were not only the surrender of all the towns held by the English, but their total evacuation of the country. When these humiliating conditions were reported, Milo de Cogan protested against thus relinquishing the earnings of so many hard-fought battles, and proposed a general sally upon the enemy. His advice was adopted. The English forces, leaving behind them in the city their Irish auxiliaries, on whose fidelity they had less reliance, and led on by Milo, proceeded to Roderic's head-quarters at Finglass, which they assaulted so suddenly that he was obliged to escape half dressed from a bath, and his whole army was dispersed.

Strongbow being soon after called to England, Asculph Mac Torcall, during his absence, arrived in the harbour of Dublin with a fleet of 60 ships and an army of 10,000 men levied in the isle of Man, the Orkneys, and Norway, and proceeded at once to storm the city. His main body was led on by John de Dene, a Norwegian of great military repute, who was repulsed by Milo de Cogan, with the loss of 500 men; and the Danes being unexpectedly attacked in the rear by another body of the garrison, which had made a sally from a different quarter, they were utterly routed, and their king Asculph made prisoner and put to death. The relics of the Danish army which escaped the sword were cut in pieces by the peasantry through the country, in revenge for their former cruelties, so that scarcely 2000 gained their ships, most of whom were destroyed by a tempest during their voyage home. This defeat put an end to the Danish power in these parts. An attempt made, soon after, to seize on the city by Tiernan O'Rourke, the chieftain of Breffny, who thought that the garrison, exhausted by its late struggle, though successful, would be incapable of making a vigorous resistance to the large force he was bringing against it, also failed.

The arrival of Hen. II., who landed at Waterford with a large fleet and a numerous train in 1172 caused a great change in the state of the city. He had compelled Strongbow to surrender to him all his conquests in Ireland: the lands were restored, to be held by feudal tenure, but the fortified places were retained in the king's hands. Henry, after having received the homage of most of the petty chieftains of the south, arrived in Dublin, in the beginning of winter, and celebrated the feast of Christmas there in great splendour; on which occasion a pavilion of hurdles, after the Irish fashion, was erected in the eastern suburb, where the court was held, and where several of the native princes did homage to him. Hugh de Lacy and William Fitz Aldelm were commissioned to receive the homage of Roderic, King of Ireland, who declined crossing the Shannon. Being unexpectedly hurried away to oppose a revolt of his own sons in Normandy, Henry quitted the city for Wexford, whence he embarked for England on Easter-Monday, leaving Hugh de Lacy in charge of the place as governor, with twenty men at arms, and Robert Fitz-Stephen and Maurice Fitz-Gerald with the same number, as wardens and constables. Milo de Cogan, to whose intrepidity the English had been indebted for their conquest, accompanied Henry on his departure. Previously to his leaving the city, the king granted it a charter, entitling it to the same privileges as Bristol then enjoyed: the original is still preserved in the archives of the corporation. By a subsequent charter of the same king, the citizens are freed from payment of toll, passage, and pontage, throughout England, Normandy, Wales, and Ireland. Three years after Henry's departure, Strongbow made an incursion into Munster, in which he was accompanied by the Ostmen of Dublin, but was surprised on his march by Donald, Prince of Ossory, and defeated, with the loss of 400 of the citizens. Elated with this success, Roderic O'Connor ravaged the country even to the walls of Dublin. Shortly after, Strongbow died of a mortification in his foot, and was buried in Christ-Church, where his monument is still preserved. Previously to his death he had founded the extensive and wealthy preceptory of Knights Templars, on the site on which the Royal Hospital now stands. In the same year, Vivian, the pope's legate, held a synod in the city, at which he caused the title of Hen. II. to the lordship of Ireland to be proclaimed; and denounced an excommunication against all who should refuse allegiance to him. In 1185, John, Earl of Morton, the favourite son of Hen. II., having been invested by his father with the lordship of Ireland, arrived in Dublin, attended by a train of young noblemen; but a series of insurrections taking place, he was recalled.

From the period of the arrival of the English and their conquest of Dublin, the city was considered to be the most appropriate position to secure their possessions and to facilitate their intercourse with their native country. To promote this object, instructions were given by John, shortly after the commencement of his reign, to Meyler Fitz-Henry, to erect a castle on the eastern brow of the hill on which the city stood, for which purpose 300 marks were assigned; an order was also issued to compel the inhabitants to repair and strengthen the fortifications. The necessity of a precautionary measure of this nature was confirmed by a calamity which befel the city in 1209, in which year the citizens, while amusing themselves according to custom on Easter-Monday in Cullen's wood, near the southern suburbs, were attacked unawares by the Irish of the neighbouring mountains and driven into the town, after the slaughter of more than 500 of their number. The day was for a long time after distinguished by the name of Black Monday, and commemorated by a parade of the citizens on the field of the conflict, where they appeared in arms and challenged their enemies to renew the encounter. The castle, however, was not completed till 1220, during the government of Henry de Loundres, Archbishop of Dublin and Lord-Justice. King John on his visit to Ireland in 1210, established courts of judicature on the model of those in England, deposited an abstract of the English laws and customs in the Exchequer, and issued a coinage of pence and farthings of the same standard as the English. Hen. III. granted several charters, which were confirmed and extended by Edw. I., who also fixed a standard for coin in England, according to which that of Ireland was to be regulated: during his reign there were four mints in Dublin, besides others at Waterford and Drogheda. About the close of the 13th and beginning of the 14th century a great part of the city was destroyed by fires, one of which consumed many of the public records, which had been lodged in St. Mary's abbey. An attempt to found an university, made in 1311 by Archbishop Leck, who procured a papal bull for this purpose, failed in consequence of the unsettled state of the country, but was revived with more success in 1320 by Alexander de Bicknor, the next archbishop. In 1312, the mountain septs of the O'Byrnes and O'Tooles made an incursion into Rathcool and Saggard, when the chief force of the city had been despatched into Louth, or Orgial, to quell an insurrection of the Verdons, but on its return the southern invaders were forced to retire into their fastnesses. Three years after, when David O'Toole and some others of his sept made a similar attempt, by placing an ambush in Cullen's wood, the citizens issued out against them with their black banner displayed, and did execution on them for several miles.

The year 1315 is remarkable for the invasion of Edward Bruce, brother of Robert Bruce, King of Scotland, who landed at Carrick-fergus at the head of 6000 men, to establish his claim to the crown of Ireland by force of arms. The citizens, on hearing that he was advancing southwards and had taken Greencastle, in Carlingford bay, one of the border fortresses of the English pale, sent out a strong party by sea, recovered the place, and brought the governor to Dublin, where he was starved to death in prison. This success, however, did not put a stop to the advance of Bruce, who marched upon Dublin with the intention of besieging it. The citizens, on his approach, set fire to the suburb of Thomas-street, in consequence of which St. John's Church without Newgate, and the Magdalene chapel were burnt. The church of the Dominicans was also pulled down, in order to use the stones for repairing and extending the city walls on the north side towards the river. The gallant determination of the citizens had its effect. Bruce, after destroying St. Mary's abbey and plundering the cathedral of St. Patrick, drew off his army and marched westward into Kildare. In consideration of the sufferings and losses of the citizens, Edw. II. remitted half of their fee-farm rent. At the close of the century the city was twice visited by Rich. II.; at first, in 1394, when he marched hither from Waterford, about Michaelmas, at the head of an army of 30,000 foot and 4000 horse, and remained till the beginning of the ensuing summer. His second visit, which took place in 1399, was cut short by the unwelcome news of the insurrection of the Duke of Lancaster, afterwards Hen. IV., which hurried him back to England.

During the reign of Henry IV. the citizens adhered firmly to him throughout the civil war excited by the Earl of Northumberland and Owain Glyndwr, and caused a diversion in his favour by fitting out a fleet with which they invaded Scotland, and, after several landings on the coast, proceeded in like manner along that of Wales, whence they carried away the shrine of St. Cubie and on their return placed it in the cathedral of Christ-Church. In consequence of these services they obtained from the king a confirmation of all their former charters, and the present of a gilded sword to be borne before the mayor in public, in the same manner as before the lord mayor of London. The border war between the citizens and the Irish of the neighbouring mountains was carried on with great fury during this and the succeeding reigns. In 1402, John Drake, the provost, led out a strong party against the O'Byrnes, whom he defeated with a slaughter, as some writers say, of 4000 men, but according to others of 400, and compelled them to surrender the castle of Newcastle-MacKynegan. In 1410, the lord-deputy made another incursion into the territory of the O'Byrnes, but was forced to retreat in consequence of the desertion of a large body of his kernes; and in 1413 the O'Byrnes gave the citizens a signal defeat and carried off many prisoners. In 1431, Mac Murrough, King of Leinster, made an incursion into the vicinity of Dublin, defeated the troops sent out to oppose him, and carried off much booty; but the citizens having collected a fresh body of troops, pursued the enemy the same evening, attacked them unawares, and routed them with great loss. The city was much disturbed, about this time, by the contentions between the Kildare and Ormonde families. To decide one of their disputes, in which Thomas Fitzgerald, prior of Kilmainham, had accused the Earl of Ormonde of treason, a trial by combat was appointed at Smithfield, in Oxmantown; but the quarrel being taken up by the king was terminated without bloodshed. The mayor and citizens, having taken part with the Fitzgeralds in these broils, and grossly insulted the Earl of Ormonde, and violated the sanctity of St. Mary's abbey, were compelled to do penance, in 1434, by going barefoot to that monastery and to Christ-Church and St. Patrick's cathedrals, and craving pardon at the doors. In 1479, the fraternity of arms of St. George, consisting of thirteen of the most honourable and loyal inhabitants in the counties of Dublin, Meath, Kildare, and Louth, was formed by act of parliament, for the defence of the English pale: the mayor of Dublin was appointed one of the commanders of the force raised in the city; the fraternity was discontinued in 1492. A bull for the foundation of an university in the city was published by Pope Sextus in 1475, but was never carried into effect.

When Lambert Simnel claimed the crown of England, in the beginning of the reign of Hen.VII., his title was recognised in Dublin, where he was crowned in Christ-Church, in the presence of the lord-deputy, the lords of the council, the mayor, and all the citizens; after the ceremony was concluded, he was carried in state to the castle, according to the Irish custom, on the shoulders of Darcy of Platten, a man of extraordinary stature. On Simnel's defeat at Stoke, the mayor and citizens made a humble apology to the king for the part they had taken in the affair, pleading the authority and influence of the lord-deputy, the archbishop, and most of the clergy. Their pardon was granted through Sir Richard Edgecumbe, who was specially deputed by Henry to administer the oaths of fealty and allegiance to the Irish after the insurrection: this officer entered Dublin on the 5th of July, 1488, for the fulfilment of his mission, and embarked for England at Dalkey, on the 30th of the same month, after having successfully accomplished the objects for which he had been deputed. In 1504, the mayor and citizens contributed their share to the victory gained by the Earl of Kildare, lord-deputy, over the Irish and degenerate English of Connaught, at Knocktow, near Galway. A few years after, the revival of the controversy between the Earls of Kildare and Ormonde again subjected the citizens to ecclesiastical censures. The two Earls had a meeting in St. Patrick's cathedral, for the ostensible purpose of com-promising their feud; the citizens attended the former as his guard, and on some cause of complaint between them and the Earl of Ormonde's soldiers, they let fly a volley of arrows, some of which struck the images in the roodloft. In atonement for this sacrilegious violation of the building, the mayor was sentenced to walk barefoot before the host on Corpus Christi day yearly, a ceremony which was kept up till the Reformation.

During the early period of the reign of Hen. VIII., the people of Dublin gave several instances of loyalty and courage. In 1513 they attended the lord-deputy in a hosting against O'Carrol, which termi-nated without any remarkable action, in consequence of the death of their leader. In 1516 they routed the O'Tooles of the mountains, slew their chief, and sent his head a present to the mayor: a second expedi-tion, however, was less successful; the O'Tooles drove them back with loss. Afterwards, in 1521, they performed good service under the Earl of Surrey against O'More, in Leix, and O'Conor in Meath. But the most remarkable event connected with the city, during the reign of Hen. VIII., arose out of the rebellion of Lord Thomas Fitzgerald, com-monly called the Silken Knight, from the fantastical fringes with which the helmets of his followers were decorated. This young noble-man had been appointed lord-deputy in the absence of his father, the Earl of Kildare, who was summoned to appear before Henry, to answer some charges brought against him, as chief governor of Ireland and on a false report that his father had been imprisoned and put to death in London, he proceeded, without making further inquiry into the truth of the allegation, at the head of his armed followers, to St. Mary's abbey, where the council was sitting, threw down the sword of state, and notwithstanding the paternal remonstrances of the primate, Archbishop Cromer, bade defiance to the king and declared himself his open enemy. After ravaging Fingal, where he seized and put to death Alan, then archbishop of Dublin, the enemy of his family, he laid siege to the castle, but after several ineffectual attempts to carry it by storm he surrendered to Lord Leonard Grey, and was ultimately sent to England, where he was executed with five of his uncles, who not only had taken no part in the insurrection, but had been active in dissuading him from engaging in it. In recompense for the citizens' gallant defence, the king granted them the dissolved monastery of All Hallows, without Dames Gate, confirmed a grant of £49. 6. 8. made by Rich. II., and released them from an annual rent of £20.

In 1547, the Byrnes and O'Tooles, presuming on the weakness of the government during the minority of Edw. VI., made frequent inroads into the neighbourhood of Dublin, to the great annoyance of the inhabitants. The close vicinity of the mountains and the difficulties of the passes through which they were accessible, rendered the defence of the suburbs difficult, and retaliation hazardous; but at length Sir Anthony St. Leger, lord-deputy, with a body of the standing army, and a considerable number of the city militia, made a successful inroad into their fastnesses, defeated them in a great battle, killed their chief, and brought sixteen of the Fitzgeralds prisoners to Dublin, where they were all executed as traitors. In 1552, the mayor, at the head of the armed citizens, being joined with the townsmen of Drogheda, marched against the O'Reillys of Cavan, whom they put down: but, on their return, the victory was likely to be sullied by a dispute between the two commanders, as to the honour of leading the vanguard; which was at last terminated in favour of the mayor of Dublin, by an order confirming his right of leading the van when going out, and the rear when returning home.

In the first year of Queen Mary's reign, the citizens marched out against the Cavanaghs, who with a large army were devastating the southern part of the county of Dublin, and whom they routed, killing many and compelling the remainder to shut themselves up in Powerscourt castle, whence, having been at length forced to surrender at discretion, after an obstinate resistance, they were taken to Dublin, and 74 of them executed: the rest were pardoned.

Queen Elizabeth, in the beginning of her reign, caused the castle to be fitted up as a residence for the lord-lieutenant, who, previously to this arrangement, had resided at Thomas Court. In 1579, the public records were arranged in Birmingham tower, Dublin Castle; and three years afterwards the courts of law were transferred from the castle to St. Mary's abbey, which occupied nearly the site of the buildings in which they are now held on the north side of the river. In 1586, the king's exchequer, then held without the eastern gate on the ground now called Exchequer-street, was plundered by a party of Irish from the mountains. The year 1591 is memorable for the foundation of Trinity College. In 1599, the Earl of Essex arrived in Dublin at the head of a large army, and after his removal Sir Charles Blount, afterwards Lord Mountjoy, who had been appointed to succeed him in the command of the army raised against the Earl of Tyrone, landed there with 6000 men: but his operations gave rise to no circumstances peculiarly affecting the city.

In 1607, the Government was thrown into the greatest alarm by a letter found on the floor of the council-chamber in the castle, containing intimations of a conspiracy entered into by the Earls of Tyrone and Tyreconnell, and other northern chieftains, to seize the city and excite a general insurrection against the English government. Instant measures were employed to arrest the imputed leaders, several of whom were taken and executed, but the two Earls had sufficient notice of the designs against them to save themselves by flight; their immense estates were confiscated. In 1613, a parliament was held in Dublin, after a lapse of 27 years: it was the first in which representatives were sent from all the counties, and is still more remarkable for a dispute respecting the election of a speaker between the Protestant and Roman Catholic parties, which terminated in the triumph of the former, and the succession of the latter from the House of Commons. In 1614, a convocation was held here, which established the thirty-nine articles of religion; and a subsequent convocation, in 1634, adopted a body of canons for the regulation of the Established Church.

After a period of 40 years of uninterrupted tranquillity, both to the city and the nation, the prospect of its further continuance was destroyed by the discovery of a plot to seize the castle, on the 23rd of October, 1641, as the first movement of a general insurrection against the English Government. The plan was disclosed by an accomplice, on the evening before the day it was to have been put into execution, and thus frustrated as far as the city was concerned. So little had the occurrence of such an event been apprehended that, in the year before, a large portion of the city walls was allowed to fall to ruin. To aid in their repairs, and to meet the other urgent necessities of the state, the citizens were called upon by proclamation to send in their plate, on promise of repayment, an expedient which produced only £1200 towards the relief of the public exigencies. Next year the mayor was invited to the council, to confer on a project for raising £10,000, half in money and the remainder in provisions, to enable the king's army to take the field; but such was the poverty of the place, that the project was relinquished as impracticable. On an alarm of an intended attack on Dublin by the Irish forces of Owen Roe O'Nial and General Preston, in 1646, the Marquess of Ormonde, then lord-lieutenant, determined to strengthen the city by a line of outworks thrown up on its eastern side, between the castle and the college. On this occasion the women set a remarkable example of public spirit, the Marchioness of Ormonde and other ladies placing themselves at their head, and the whole assisting in carrying baskets of earth to the lines. Famine, however, proved the city's best safeguard. The Marquess had caused the country to be laid waste, and the mills and bridges to be destroyed for several miles round, so that the besieging army, amounting to 10,000 foot and 1000 horse, was forced to retire without any attempt of importance. So confident was Ormonde now of his own strength, that he refused admission to commissioners sent by the English parliament with 1400 men, but the very next year he was compelled, by extreme necessity, to surrender the place to them, rather than suffer it to fall into the hands of the Irish; after which, Owen Roe O'Nial, being baffled in another attempt upon the city, revenged himself by ravaging the surrounding country with such fury that from one of the town steeples 200 fires were seen blazing at once. The Marquess of Ormonde returned in 1649, with a determination to regain possession of the city. He first fixed his head-quarters at Finglas, but afterwards removed to Rathmines, on the south side. An unexpected sally of the garrison, to destroy some works he was throwing up at Bagotsrath, led to a general engagement, in which his troops, struck with an unaccountable panic, gave way, with such precipitation, that he had scarcely time to make his escape. The city remained in the hands of the parliament during the remainder of the war. At the close of the same year, Oliver Cromwell landed here with a well-appointed army of 13,000 men: after remaining a short time to refresh his troops, and to arrange his affairs, he left it for Drogheda, which he took, and treated those by whom he was opposed with a degree of cruelty seldom paralleled in the annals of modern warfare. In 1652, the war having been declared at an end, a high court of justice was erected in Dublin, for the trial of persons charged with murder and other atrocities not tolerated by the rules of war, by which, among many others of less note, Sir Phelim O'Nial, the first and principal leader of the insurrection in Ulster, was condemned and executed. In 1659, a party of general officers, well inclined to the Restoration, surprised the castle, and having secured the parliamentary commissioners of Government, who resided there, declared for a free parliament; they then, upon the petition of the mayor and aldermen, summoned a convention, and though the castle was again surprised by Sir Hardress Waller, for the parliament, he was forced to surrender it, after a siege of five days, and Chas. II. was formally proclaimed. Charles, immediately after his restoration, rewarded the services of the citizens by the donation of a cap of maintenance, a golden collar of office, and a foot company to the mayor, and some years after, a pension of £500 was allowed him in lieu of the company. In 1663, several discontented officers, among whom was the notorious Col. Blood, formed a plan to seize the castle, which was discovered by one of the accomplices.

About this period the city began to increase rapidly in extent, and in the number and elegance of its public buildings. The ground to the north of the river, formerly considered as a separate jurisdiction, under the name of Oxmantown, was connected with the city by four new bridges, and has since formed an integral part of it: it had hitherto been but a single parish, but was, some years after, in consequence of the increase of houses and inhabitants, subdivided into three. Numerous improvements were successively carried into effect, and the increase of population kept pace with them. In 1688, King James visited Dublin, where he held a parliament, which passed acts to repeal the act of settlement, to attaint a number of Protestants, and to establish an enlarged system of national education. He also established a mint, in which a quantity of base metal was coined. The year 1690 is marked by the decisive battle of the Boyne, after which James passed one night in Dublin Castle, during his precipitate retreat from the kingdom; in 1701, an equestrian statue of Wm. III. was erected on College Green, to commemorate that victory. On King William's arrival, his first act was to repair in state to St. Patrick's cathedral, to return public thanks for the success which had crowned his arms. Previously to the battle of the Boyne, Sir Cloudesly Shovel, who commanded at sea for the latter monarch, took a frigate out of Dublin harbour, in which much of the plate and valuables of the Roman Catholic nobility and gentry had been embarked, under an apprehension of the event which so soon after decided the fate of their cause in Ireland.

During the period between the revolution and the legislative union, the city increased in an unprecedented manner in extent, wealth, and splendour. The effects are attributable partly to the long period of peace from the former of these eras to the commencement of the American war, but more so to the parliamentary grants which were expended on objects of utility. Afterwards, the regulation which made the lord-lieutenant a fixed resident in Dublin, instead of being a periodical visitor for a few months every second year, when he came over from England to hold a parliament; the shortening of the duration of these assemblies, the removal of the restrictions by which the national industry and the spirit of commercial speculation had been shackled, combined with the general extension of literature and science throughout the western kingdoms of Europe, tended to promote this effect. In 1798, the Leinster provisional committee of the United Irishmen were seized with all their papers, and Lord Edward Fitzgerald, the chief leader of the insurgents, was arrested, after a desperate conflict with his captors, and lodged in prison, where he shortly after died of his wounds. The following statement will show the increase of population from about the middle of the 17th century till the legislative union: in 1682 the number of inhabitants was 64,483; in 1728, 146,075; in 1753, 128,570; in 1777, 138,208; and in 1798, 182,370.

The local events of the period which has elapsed since the Union are too numerous to particularise in a condensed narrative. The principal occurrences are the public meetings and associations for the attainment of political objects, organised insurrections, tumults resulting from those causes and embittered by the acrimony of party spirit, and visitations of famine, during which the working classes suffered great distress. Two events, however, deserve more particular notice. In 1803, a sudden and alarming insurrection broke out in the city: it was planned and carried into effect by Robert Emmet, a young gentleman of respectable family, who, at his own sole expense and with the aid of a few associates of desperate fortune, secretly formed a depot of arms and ammunition in a retired lane off Thomas-street, whence he issued early in the night of the 23rd of July, at the head of a band chiefly brought in from the neighbouring counties of Kildare and Wicklow, and was proceeding to the castle, when the progress of his followers was checked by the coming up of Lord Kilwarden, chief justice of the king's bench, who, on hearing a rumour of insurrection at his country seat, had hurried to town in his carriage with his daughter and nephew. Both the males were killed; the lady, being allowed to pass in safety, gave the alarm at the castle, and detachments being immediately sent out, the undisciplined multitude was at once dispersed with some loss of life, and the leaders, who had escaped to the mountains, were soon after taken and executed. On the accession of Geo. IV., in 1820, his majesty received a deputation from Dublin, consisting of the lord mayor and city officers, on his throne: this was the first address from the city thus honoured. The next year, on the 12th of August, the king's birth-day, he landed in Ireland, and after remaining till Sept. 3rd, partly at the Phoenix Lodge, and partly at Slane Castle in Meath, during which time he visited most of the public institutions of Dublin, and held a chapter of the order of St. Patrick, at which nine knights were installed, he sailed from Dunleary (since called Kingstown) amidst the enthusiastic acclamations of an unprecedented multitude.

EXTENT AND GENERAL DESCRIPTION OF THE CITY.

The city, which was originally confined to the summit of the hill, on the eastern brow of which the castle now stands, and whose circuit within the walls was little more than a mile round, and its suburbs confined to the few adjacent streets, now occupies a space covering 1264 acres, and is about nine miles in circumference. It is situated at the western extremity of Dublin bay, and at the mouth of the Liffey, which passes nearly through the middle of it. The hill, which now forms the central part of the city, stands in the lowest part of the basin of the Liffey, which rises gradually on the southern side into the beautiful line of the Wicklow mountains, that skirt the boundary of the county, and still more gradually on the north and west till it loses itself in the extended plains of Fingal and Kildare. It is somewhat more than three miles long in a direct line from east to west, and of nearly equal breadth from north to south, and contains upwards of 800 streets and 22,000 houses: the foot-paths are well flagged, and the carriage ways partly paved and partly Macadamised. The paving, lighting, and cleansing of the public avenues is regulated by an act passed in the 47th, and amended by one of the 54th, of Geo. III., authorising the lord-lieutenant to appoint three cornrnissioners, who are a corporation under the title of the "Commissioners for Paving, Cleansing, and Lighting the City of Dublin:" the total annual expenditure averages about £30,000. Several local acts have been passed for the supply of gaslight, and there are four companies, the Dublin Gas Company, the Hibernian Gas-light Company, the Oil Gas Company, and the Alliance Company. An ample supply of water is obtained by pipes laid down from reservoirs on both sides of the river to the houses and the public fountains, under a committee appointed in pursuance of acts passed in the 42nd and 49th of Geo. III., the expense of which is defrayed by a rate called the pipe-water tax, producing about £14,000 annually. Three basins have been formed; one at the extremity of Basin-lane, in James-street, half a mile in circumference and surrounded by a broad gravel walk, formerly a favourite promenade; another at the upper end of Blessington-street, encompassed by a terrace, for the supply of the northern side of the city; and the third on the bank of the canal, near Portobello harbour, for the supply of the south-eastern part. Considerable improvements have been made by the Commissioners "for opening wide and convenient streets," appointed under an act of the 31st of Geo. II., whose powers were subsequently extended by various successive acts till the 51st of Geo. III. Their funds, till recently, were derived from a tonnage upon coal and a local rate, called "the wide street tax," the former of which ceased in 1832, and the funds arising from the latter amount to about £5500 per ann. Among the chief improvements are the opening of a passage from the Castle to Essex bridge, an enlargement of the avenue from the same place to the Parliament House (now the Bank of Ireland), the opening of

Westmoreland-street and Sackville-street, the clearing away the buildings that interfered with the free thoroughfare along the quays on both sides of the river, the entrance into the city by Great Brunswick-street, besides various improvements in the vicinity of the cathedrals of Christ-Church and St. Patrick. In short, the city may be said to have been new-moulded since the year 1760, through the instrumentality of this Board, as there is no portion of it which does not exhibit in a greater or smaller degree the results of its labours in improvements tending to augment its beauty or to add to its salubrity. A circular road nearly nine miles in circuit, carried round the city, affords great facilities of communication throughout all the outlets, and also walks and drives of much beauty. Some portions of this road, however, particularly on the southern side, are already absorbed into the city by the continued extension of the streets; and most of the other parts, particularly on the eastern side, are likely, from the same cause, shortly to lose their distinguishing characteristic of an encircling avenue. On the north side of this road is the Royal Canal, and on the south, the Grand Canal; both terminating in docks near the mouth of the Liffey: and beyond these are, on the north, a small river called the Tolka, formerly called Tulkan and Tolekan, which empties itself into the sea at Ballybough bridge; and on the south, the river Dodder, which, curving northward, terminates with the Liffey at the harbour, forming two striking natural boundaries towards which the city is gradually extending itself. The city is now closely connected with the harbour of Kingstown by a railway formed under an act of parliament of the 1st and 2nd of Wm. IV., which was opened in Dec. 1834. The number of passengers conveyed upon it during the months of May, June, July, and August, 1836, was 523,080: the greatest number conveyed in one day was 13,000.

In addition to the splendid line of communication afforded by the quays on both sides of the river, there are several noble avenues of fine streets, among which, that from the northern road is peculiarly striking, especially on entering Sackville-street, which is conspicuous for its great width, the magnificence and beauty of the public buildings which embellish it, and the lofty monument to Admiral Viscount Nelson which stands in its centre. It consists of a fluted Doric column on a massive pedestal, inscribed on each side with the name and date of his lordship's principal victories, and over that which terminated his career is a sarcophagus: the whole is surmounted with a colossal: statue of the Admiral, surrounded by a balustrade, to which there is an ascent by a spiral staircase in the interior. The structure was completed at an expense of nearly £7000. On the southern side of the city, the avenue from Kingstown is equally imposing. Both meet in College-green, a spacious area surrounded with noble buildings, and having in its centre an equestrian statue of Wm. III., of cast metal, upon a pedestal of marble. Of the public squares, *St. Stephen's-green,* situated in the south-eastern quarter, is the most spacious, being nearly a mile in circuit: in the centre is an equestrian statue of Geo. II., finely executed in brass by Van Nost; *Merrion-square,* to the east of the former, is about three-quarters of a mile in circuit; on the west the lawn of the Royal Dublin Society. *Fitzwilliam-square* has been recently built and is much smaller than either of the others; the houses are built with much uniformity in a neat but unornamented style; some of them have basements of granite and the upper stories of brick. *Mountjoy-square,* in an elevated and healthy situation in the north-eastern part of the city, is more than half a mile in circuit; the houses are uniformly built and present an appearance very similar to those in Fitzwilliam-square. *Rutland-square* is on the north side of the river, at the upper end of Sackville-street: three sides of it are formed by Granby-row, Palace-row, and Cavendish-row, the fourth by the Lying-in Hospital and the Rotundo. The areas of the several squares are neatly laid out in gravel walks and planted with flowering shrubs and evergreens. A line drawn from the King's Inns, in the north of Dublin, through Capel-street, the Castle and Aungier-street, thus intersecting the Liffey at right angles, would, together with the line of that river, divide the city into four districts, strongly opposed to each other in character and appearance. The south-eastern district, including St. Stephen's-green, Merrion-square, and Fitzwilliam-square, is chiefly inhabited by the nobility, the gentry, and the members of the liberal professions. The north-eastern district, including Mountjoy and Rutland-squares, is principally inhabited by the mercantile and official classes. The south-western district, including the liberties of St. Sepulchre and Thomas-court, and formerly the seat of the woollen and silk manufactures, is in a state of lamentable dilapidation, bordering on ruin: and the north-western district, in which are the Royal barracks and Smithfield (the great market for hay and cattle), presents striking indications of poverty.

The Liffey is embanked on both sides by a range of masonry of granite, forming a continuation of spacious quays through the whole of
the city, and its opposite sides are connected with nine bridges, eight
of which are of elegant design and highly ornamental. *Carlisle bridge,*
the nearest to the sea, and connecting Westmoreland street on the
south with Sackville-street on the north, is a very elegant structure of
three arches: it is 210 feet in length and 48 feet in breadth, and was
completed in 1794. *Wellington bridge,* at the end of Liffey-street, 140
feet long, consists of a single elliptic arch of cast iron, and was erected
in 1816, for the accommodation of foot passengers only, at an expense
of £3000, which is defrayed by a halfpenny toll. *Essex bridge*, connecting Capel-street with Parliament-street, and fronting the Royal
Exchange, was built in 1755, on the site of a former structure of the
same name, at an expense of £20,661; it is a handsome stone structure
of five arches, 250 feet in length and 51 in width, after the model of
Westminster bridge, London. *Richmond bridge,* built on the site of
Ormond bridge, which had been swept away by a flood, was commenced in 1813; it connects Winetavern-street with Montrath-street,
and was completed at an expense of £25,800, raised by presentments
on the city and county, and opened to the public on St. Patrick's day,
1816; it is built of Portland stone, with a balustrade of cast iron, and is
220 feet long and 52 feet wide, consisting of three fine arches, the keystones of which are ornamented with colossal heads, on the one side
representing Peace, Hibernia, and Commerce; and on the other, Plenty,
the river Liffey, and Industry. *Whitworth bridge* supplies the place of the
old bridge built by the Dominican friars, which had been for a long
time the only communication between the city and its northern suburbs: the first stone was laid in 1816, by the Earl of Whitworth, then
lord-lieutenant; it is an elegant structure of three arches, connecting
Bridge-street with Church-street. *Queen's bridge,* a smaller structure of
three arches of hewn stone, connecting Bridgefoot-street with Queen-
street, is only 140 feet in length: it was built in 1768, on the site of
Arran bridge, which was destroyed by a flood in 1763. *Barrack bridge,*
formerly Bloody bridge, connecting Watling-street with the quay leading to the royal barracks, was originally constructed of wood, in 1671,
and subsequently rebuilt of stone. *King's bridge,* of which the first stone

was laid by the Marquess Wellesley in 1827, connects the military road with the south-eastern entrance to the Phoenix Park, affording to the lord-lieutenant a retired and pleasant avenue from the Castle to his country residence; it consists of a single arch of cast iron, 100 feet in span, resting on abutments of granite richly ornamented, and was completed at an expense of £13,000, raised for the purpose of erecting a national testimonial in commemoration of the visit of Geo. IV. to Ireland, in 1821. *Sarah bridge,* formerly Island bridge, but when rebuilt in its present form named after the Countess of Westmoreland, who laid the foundation stone in 1791, is a noble structure of a single arch, 104 feet in span, the keystone of which is 30 feet above low water mark: this bridge connects the suburban village of Island-Bridge with the north-western road and with one of the entrances to the Phoenix Park; from the peculiar elegance of its proportions, it has been distinguished by the name of the "Irish Rialto".

MANUFACTURE TRADE AND COMMERCE.

The woollen manufacture was carried on in Ireland at a very early period, and attained considerable celebrity both in the English and continental markets; but its first establishment in connection with Dublin did not take place till after the Revolution, when a number of English manufacturers, attracted by the excellent quality of the Irish wool, the cheapness of provisions, and the low price of labour, established regular and extensive factories in the liberties of the city. Soon afterwards the Coombe, Pimlico, Spitalfields, Weavers'-square, and the neighbouring streets, chiefly in the Liberties of the city, were built; and this portion of the metropolis was then inhabited by persons of opulence and respectability: but the English legislature, considering the rapid growth of the woollen manufacture of Ireland prejudicial to that of England, prevailed on King William to discourage it, in consequence of which the Liberties, by the removal of the more opulent manufacturers, soon fell into decay. The trade, however, continued to linger in that neighbourhood and even to revive in some degree by being taken, in 1773, under the protection of the Dublin Society; in so much that, in 1792, there were 60 master clothiers, 400 broad cloth looms, and 100 narrow looms in the Liberties, giving employment to upwards of 5000 persons; but the effect was transitory: ever since, the trade has progressively declined, being at present confined to the manufacture of a few articles for home consumption. The working weavers suffered still further from the loss of time and suspension of their labours, caused by the necessity of teetering their cloths in the open air, which could only be performed during fine weather. To remedy this inconvenience, Mr. Pleasants, a philanthropic gentleman of large fortune, erected at his own cost a tenter-house near the Weavers'-square, in which that process might be performed in all states of the weather: the expense of its erection was nearly £13,000; a charge of 2s. 6d. is made on every piece of cloth, and 5d. on every chain of warp, brought in. The linen manufacture was carried on at a very early period for domestic consumption, long before it became the great staple of the country; in the latter point of view it owes its extension chiefly to the Earl of Strafford, who during his lieutenancy embarked £30,000 of his private property in its establishment. After the depression of the woollen trade, great encouragement was given by parliament to the linen manufacture as a substitute; and in the 8th of Queen Anne an act was passed appointing trustees, selected from among the most influential noblemen and gentlemen of large landed property in each of the four provinces, for the management and disposal of the duties granted by that statute for its promotion; and in 1728 a spacious linen hall was erected by a grant of public money under the direction of the Government, from whom the offices and warehouses are rented by the occupants: the sales commence every morning at 9 o'clock and close at 4 in the afternoon, but though the linen manufacture is still extensively carried on in some parts of Ireland, very little is made in the immediate vicinity of the city, and the sales at the hall are consequently much diminished. The cotton manufacture was first introduced about the year 1760, and was greatly promoted by Mr. R. Brook, who in 1779 embarked a large capital in the enterprise; it was further encouraged by grants from parliament and carried on with varying success in the neighbourhood of the city. Since the withdrawing of the protecting duties the trade has progressively declined in Dublin, and may now be considered as nearly extinct there.

The silk manufacture was introduced by the French refugees who settled here after the revocation of the Edict of Nantz; and an act of parliament was soon after passed by which the infant manufacture was placed under the direction of the Dublin Society. This body estab-

lished an Irish silk-warehouse in Parliarnent-street, the management of
which was vested in a board of 12 noblemen (who were directors), and
a committee of 12 persons annually chosen by the guild of Weavers,
to examine the quality of the goods sent in by the manufacturers, and
to whom the Dublin Society allowed a premium of 5 per cent. on all
goods sold in the warehouse. While the trade was thus managed, the
sales on an average amounted to £70,000 per annum, and the manufacture attained a high degree of perfection; but by a subsequent act
of parliament, passed in the 26th of Geo. III., the society was prohibited from disposing of any portion of its funds for the support of an
establishment in which Irish silks were sold, and from that period the
silk-warehouse department was discontinued and the manufacture
rapidly declined. However, the tabinets and poplins, for which Dublin
had been so peculiarly celebrated, are still in request, not only in Great
Britain, but in the American and other foreign markets; but the
demand is limited, and the number engaged in the manufacture pro-
portionably small. The tanning and currying of leather is carried on to
a considerable extent; the number of master manufacturers in both
branches exceeding 100. There are l6 iron foundries, in some of which
are manufactured steam engines and agricultural implements on an
extensive scale: the number of brass foundries is 25. Cabinet making
is also carried on to a considerable extent. The same may be said of the
coach-making trade; the demand for jaunting cars, a vehicle peculiar
to the country, is very great. There are not less than 20 porter and ale
breweries, several of which are on a very large scale, particularly the
former, upwards of 120,000 barrels being brewed annually, a considerable portion of which is exported. There are 14 distilleries and rec-
tifying establishments; some of these are likewise very extensive. There
are also numerous establishments in the city and its vicinity for the
manufacture and production of a variety of articles both for home
consumption and exportation, amongst which may be noticed, flint
glass, sail-cloth, canvas, turpentine, vitriol, vinegar, soap, starch, size,
glue, paper, parchment, vellum, hats, also silk and calico-printing, and
in Dublin is made the celebrated Lundyfoot snuff by Messrs. Lundy
Foot & Co.

Several acts of parliament have at different periods been passed for
improving the port of Dublin, the last of which, 26th of Geo. III., constituted the present corporation for "preserving and improving the

port of Dublin," commonly known by the name of the Ballast Board, in which was vested the care, management, and superintendence of the whole of the river and the walls bounding it. Its jurisdiction was subsequently extended by several successive acts; and the management of the port and harbour of Kingstown was also vested in this corporation; but in 1836, an act was passed by which the port was placed under the control of the Board of Works. The receipts on account of the port average about £30,000 per annum. The Ballast Board has the charge of all the lighthouses in Ireland, of which there are six connected with the port of Dublin.

The commerce of the port consists of various branches, of which the most important is the cross-channel trade, which has increased considerably, owing to the facilities afforded by steam navigation; the agricultural produce of the midland counties being brought hither for exportation, in return for which, groceries, and other commodities for domestic consumption are sent back. The first steam-boat that crossed the channel to this port was from Holyhead in 1816, but it was not till 1824 that steam-boats were employed in the transmission of merchandise: the passage by steam to Liverpool is performed on the average in 14, to London in 80, to Bristol in 24, to Cork in 20, to Belfast in 14, and to Glasgow in 24 hours. The City of Dublin Steam-packet Company, in 1824, was the first that introduced a line of packets between this port and Liverpool, also in 1825 between this port and Belfast, for the conveyance of passengers and merchandise: the capital of this company amounts to £450,000, subscribed in £50 and £100 shares, of which £350,000 is held by Dublin shareholders. It employs 18 vessels between this port and Liverpool and Belfast; nine on the river Shannon, and in the summer a vessel to Bordeaux; also 52 trade boats on the Grand and Royal Canals. Besides the above company, there are the Dublin and London Steam Marine Company, which has six vessels plying between this port and Falmouth, Plymouth, London, and Belfast; the St. George's Company, which has a vessel each to Cork, Bristol, and Greenock; also in the summer one to Whitehaven, calling at Douglas (Isle of Man); the British and Irish Steam-packet Company, which has two vessels plying between this port and Plymouth, London, and Belfast; and the Dublin and Glasgow Steam-packet Company, which has two vessels plying between this port and Glasgow and Cork: thus making 33 steam-packets trading from and to this port, from 250 to

800 tons' burden, and from 100 to 280-horse power each. The number of vessels that entered inwards at the port in the year ending Jan. 5th, 1792, was 2807, of the aggregate burden of 288,592 tons; in 1800, 2779, of 280,539 tons; in 1815, 3046, of 304,813 tons; and in 1813, 3412, of 363,685 tons. In the year ending Jan. 5th, 1836, the number of vessels that entered inwards was 34 foreign and 209 British, and that cleared outwards, 25 foreign and 107 British, exclusively of those that cleared out in ballast: during the same period, 3978 coasting vessels entered inwards and 1937 cleared outwards, exclusively of those which go out in ballast, chiefly to and from various parts if Great Britain; and 2087 colliers entered inwards, nearly the whole of which leave in ballast. The number of vessels belonging to the port in 1836 was 327. After the year 1824, no correct statement can be furnished of the imports and exports of Ireland, as the trade between that country and Great Britain was then placed on the footing of a coasting trade, and no entry was made at any custom-house except of goods on which duty was to be paid. Any statement of the quantities of corn, cattle, &c., now exported is, there-fore, merely one of probable quantities. The principal articles of Irish produce and manufacture exported from Dublin for Great Britain, for the year ending Jan. 5th, 1831, were bacon, 7461 bales; barley, 10,093 barrels; wheat, 40,000 barrels; beef, 18,084 tierces; bere, 10,651 barrels; butter, 41,105 firkins; candles, 1701 boxes; eggs, 3300 crates; feathers, 1570 packs; flour, 10,356 sacks; hams, 88 casks; herrings, 259 casks; hides, 6781 bundles; lard, 365 casks; leather, 693 bales; linen, 3648 boxes; malt 103 barrels; oats, 153,191 barrels; oatmeal, 16,482 bags; porter, 29,800 hogsheads; printed cottons, 2100 packages; whiskey, 800 pun-cheons; wool, 3500 packs; oxen, 69,500; pigs, 58,000; and sheep, 80,000. For some years previous to 1830, the quantity of tobacco imported had been diminished by the increased cultivation of that plant in Ireland, but the legislature prohibited the cultivation in 1833, and the importa-tion of foreign tobacco has since greatly increased. The large quantity of soap imported in 1835 is attributable to a drawback allowed on exportation from Great Britain, which was found to exceed the excise duty previously paid. The duty has since been altered, and the impor-tation of soap has been thereby diminished. In 1830, the quantity imported into all Ireland was 6,559,461 lb. of hard and 120,992 lb. of soft soap, the drawback allowed being £82,875. 9. 11. The quantities of the principal articles imported in the year ending Jan. 5th, 1836,

were–coal, 340,000 tons, chiefly from Whitehaven and Scotland; soap, 3,350,000 lb.; coffee, 2,200 packages; sugar, 15,000 hogsheads; tea, 52,500 chests; pepper, 2000 packages; spirits, 700 casks,–spirits (in bottle), 1200 cases; wine, 7100 casks,–wine (in bottle), 1500 cases; tobacco, 1150 hogsheads; deals, 2000 great hundreds; staves, 3500 great hundreds; and timber, 11,600 logs. There is no sugar-refinery in Dublin, although at one period the number was very considerable; all the refined sugar now used is imported from Great Britain. It will be perceived by the above statement that the direct foreign import trade is not so great as might be expected from the consumption of a large population; but the articles required can, by steam-vessels, be expeditiously brought from Liverpool, into which port they are imported, in many instances, on much lower terms than they could be imported into Dublin direct.

There is very little foreign export from Dublin. The trade with the Baltic in timber, staves, &c., is greatly diminished by the high rate of duty imposed and the low rate at which Canada timber is admitted. From St. Petersburgh, Riga, Archangel, &c., there is a considerable import of tallow, hemp, and tar, with some linseed, bristles, &c.; from Spain and Portugal the chief import is wine, with some corkwood, raisins, barilla, and bark; from France the imports are wine in wood and bottle, claret, champagne, &c., also corkwood, prunes, dried fruits, and some brandy; from the Netherlands the imports are bark and flax; from Holland, tobacco pipes, bark, cloves, and flax-seed, and small quantities of gin, Burgundy pitch, Rhenish wines, madder, &c. With the West Indies the trade is chiefly in sugar from Jamaica, Demerara, and Trinidad, estates in the last-named island being owned in Dublin. Coffee is imported in small quantities and also rum, but very little foreign spirits are consumed in Ireland, in consequence of the low price and encouragement given to the use of whiskey. Beef and pork in casks, and soap and candles in boxes, were formerly exported to the West Indies in large quantities, but the trade is now nearly lost in consequence of permission being given to the colonists to import these articles from Hamburgh, Bremen, &c., where they can be purchased at lower prices than in Ireland. To the United States of America formerly there was a very large export of linen, principally to New York, and flax-seed, staves, turpentine, clover seed, &c., were brought back; but the bounty on the export of linen having been withdrawn, the trade between the United States and Dublin has greatly diminished. The export of linen and import of flax-seed is now chiefly confined to Belfast and other northern ports. The American tobacco which is either sold or consumed in Dublin is brought from Liverpool. With British America the trade is very great in timber, as a return cargo of vessels sailing thither from Dublin with emigrants. With Newfoundland there is no direct trade; the cod and seal oil consumed are imported from Liverpool or brought by canal from Waterford, which has a direct trade with Newfoundland; dried codfish and ling being much used in the southern counties, but not in the northern or midland. With China there are three vessels owned in Dublin, besides others engaged in the tea trade; the number of chests directly imported is, therefore, considerable. With South America there is no direct trade, the Dublin tanners being abundantly supplied with native hides, and any foreign hides required being brought from Liverpool, whence also is imported the cotton wool consumed in the Dublin factories. With Turkey the trade is confined to the importation from Smyrna of valonia, figs, raisins, and small quantities of other articles; madder-roots and emerystone being always transhipped for Liverpool. With Leghorn there is a considerable trade for cork-tree bark, and small quantities of hemp in bales, oil, marble, &c., are also imported, but very little communication is kept up with Trieste or other Italian ports. With Sicily the trade is in shumac and brimstone; the latter article in considerable quantities for the consumption of vitriol and other chymical works.

The markets are under the superintendence of a jury; the sheriffs being required, under the 73rd sec. of the 13th and 14th of Geo. III, cap. 22, to summon 48 of the most respectable citizens, of whom 24 are sworn in at the general quarter sessions, and any three are empowered to visit and examine the commodities, and report to the lord mayor, who is authorised to condemn the provisions, and impose a fine to the extent of £10. The principal wholesale market is in Smithfield, a narrow oblong area in the north-eastern part of the city, the site of which is the property of the corporation, as part of their manor of Oxmantown: the market days for the sale of black cattle and sheep are Monday and Thursday, and for hay and straw, Tuesday and Saturday. There is also a considerable market for hay, straw, potatoes, butter, fowls, and eggs, in Kevin-street, over which, though it is within the liberty of St. Sepulchre, and is alleged to be exempt from the corporate jurisdiction, the officers being appointed by the archbishop, the lord mayor claims a right of superintendence, and the weights and measures used there are sanctioned by his authority. The great market for the sale of potatoes is on the north side of the river, in Petticoat-lane; a small portion of the present site is corporate property, and was the ancient potatoe market of the city; it is now rented from the corporation by two persons, who are joint weighmasters and clerks of the market, under the lord mayor; the market is commodious, and the avenues to it convenient. The wholesale fish market is held in an enclosed yard in Bootlane: there is also a wholesale fruit market in the Little Green, and one for eggs and fowls contiguous thereto in Halton-street. There are ten retail markets for butchers' meat, poultry, vegetables, and fish; namely, Northumberland market on Eden Quay, which is kept with peculiar neatness; Meath market, in the Earl of Meath's liberty; Ormond market, on Ormond quay; Castle market, between South Great-George's-street and William-street; Patrick's market, in Patrick-street; City market, in Blackhall-row; Clarendon market, in William-street; Fleet-market, in Townsend-street; Rotundo, or Norfolk-market, in Great-Britain-street; and Leinster-market, in D'Olier-street. The want of well regulated slaughterhouses, in situations which would prevent offensive exposure, is severely felt.

Fairs. – A fair is annually held at Donnybrook, about two miles from the city, but within the limits of the jurisdiction of the corporation, under several charters: the first, granted in the 16th of John, authorises its continuance for sixteen days, though of late years it has been limited to a week or eight days: it commences on Aug. 26th. The number of cattle sold is inconsiderable, as it is frequented more for purposes of amusement and conviviality than of business. The corporation have little interest in it, excepting the preservation of order; it yields the proprietor of the ground about £400 per annum. A fair is held in James'-street on St. James's day (July 25th), chiefly for pedlery. The fairs of Rathfarnham and Palmerstown, though beyond the limits of the corporate jurisdiction, are within that of the city police.

PUBLIC BUILDINGS CONNECTED WITH COMMERCE.

The Royal Exchange is situated on the ascent of Cork hill, near the principal entrance to the Castle, and also nearly opposite to

Parliament-street. The building was completed in 1779, at the expense of £40,000, raised partly by parliamentary grants, partly by subscriptions, and partly by lotteries. It forms a square of 100 feet, presenting three fronts, the fourth side being concealed by the adjoining buildings of the castle. The ground plan of the interior represents a circle within a square. The circle is formed by twelve fluted columns of the composite order, forming a rotundo in the centre of the building; above their entablature is an attic, ten feet high, having a circular window corresponding with each of the subjacent intercolumniations, and above the attic rises a hemispherical dome of very chaste proportions, crowned by a large circular light, which, together with the zone of windows immediately underneath, throws an ample volume of light into the body of the building. At the eastern and western ends of the north front are geometrical staircases leading to the coffee-room and other apartments now employed as courts for the Bankrupt Commission, meeting-rooms for the trustees, and accommodations for inferior officers. In the lower hall is a fine marble statue of the late Henry Grattan, and on the staircase leading to the coffee-room another of Dr. Lucas, who preceded Grattan in the career of patriotism. The increase of commercial business since the erection of this building having required additional accommodation in a situation more convenient for mercantile transactions, the Exchange has been gradually deserted and the meetings held there transferred to the Commercial Buildings in College-green. *The Commercial Buildings* form a plain but substantial square of three stories, constituting the sides of a small quadrangle and wholly unornamented except in the principal front to College-green, which is of hewn stone and has a central entrance supported by Ionic columns. On the left of the grand entrancehall and staircase is a news-room, 60 feet long and 28 feet wide, occupied by the members of the Chamber of Commerce (established in 1820 to protect and improve the commerce of the city); and on the right is a handsome coffee-room, connected with that part of the building which is used as an hotel. The north side of the quadrangle is occupied by the Stock Exchange and merchants' offices, and on the east and west are offices for the brokers. It was built by a proprietary of 400 £50 shareholders, and was completed in 1799, under the superintendence of Mr. Parkes. *The Corn Exchange* was built by merchants who were incorporated in 1815, under the designation of the "Corn Exchange Buildings' Company," with leave to augment their capital to £15,000; the business is managed by a committee of 15 directors. The building, which is two stories high, has a neat front of mountain granite towards Burgh Quay; the interior contains a hall, 130 feet long, separated longitudinally from walks on each side by a range of cast iron pillars supporting a cornice, which is continued round the inner hall and surmounted by an attic perforated with circular windows; the hall is furnished with tables for displaying samples of grain, and in the front of the building is a large room on the upper story for public dinners or meetings of societies, by the rent of which and of the tables the interest of the capital, estimated at £25,000, is paid. The Ouzel Galley Society was established in 1705 for the arbitration of differences respecting trade and commerce. The arbitrators must be members of the society, who are among the principal merchants in the city: the surplus of expenses incurred in this court are appropriated to the benefit of decayed merchants.

The *Bank of Ireland* was established in 1783, under an act of parliament, with a capital of £600,000, which, on a renewal of the charter in 1791, was increased to £1,000,000, and by subsequent renewals, the last in 1821, the bank was authorised to enlarge its capital to £3,000,000. The proprietors are incorporated by the name of "The Governor and Company of the Bank of Ireland," and the establishment is under the management of a governor, who must be a proprietor of £4000 stock, a deputy-governor, holding £3000, and 15 directors holding £2000 each; all these are elected by the court of proprietors, and five directors must vacate annually, but not in rotation. Agencies have been established in most of the principal cities and towns in Ireland, and connections have been formed with the Bank of England and the Royal Bank of Scotland, for facilitating the transmission of money. The building is nearly of a semicircular form, and stands on an acre and a half of ground, and previously to the Union was occupied as the Parliament House. The principal front consists of a colonnade of the Ionic order extending round three sides of a quadrangular recess, and supporting an entablature and cornice surmounted by an attic, which is broken only in the central range by a projecting portico of four columns of the same order, sustaining a triangular pediment, in the tympanum of which are the royal arms, and on the apex a statue of Hibernia, with one of Fidelity on the right, and of

Commerce on the left extremity of the attic. The east front, in College-street, has a noble portico of six Corinthian columns projecting far into the surrounding area, and supporting an enriched cornice surmounted by a triangular pediment, on the apex of which is a statue of Fortitude, with Justice at one end and a figure of Liberty at the other: this portico, which differs from the style of architecture of the rest of the structure, was formerly the entrance to the House of Lords. The west front, which faces Foster-place, has in the centre an Ionic portico of four columns, supporting an entablature and cornice crowned with a triangular pediment, corresponding in style with the principal front. Within the central portico are two entrances leading to the Cash office, communicating at each end with corridors leading to the various offices in the establishment. This part of the building stands on the site of the former House of Commons. The former House of Lords, which remains unaltered, is now appropriated to the use of the court of proprietors; it is of rectangular form, with a semicircular recess at one extremity, in which the throne was placed, and in which has since been set a statue of white marble of Geo. III. In the rear of the interior is a department for printing bank notes, the machinery of which is wholly worked by steam, and arranged with such ingenuity as in a great measure to baffle any attempt at forgery, and at the same time to add greatly to the expedition with which the process of printing is carried on, while it affords a check upon the workmen employed, by means of a self-acting register, which indicates the quantity of work done and the actual state of that in progress at any moment required. The *Hibernian Joint Stock Banking Company* is managed by a governor, deputy-governor, and 7 directors; it transacts business at a house in Castle-street, built for the late private banking establishment of Lord Newcomen. The *Provincial Bank of Ireland* is managed by a court of directors in London, and has an office in William-street and agencies throughout the country parts. The *National Bank of Ireland* was formed under the provisions of the same act, with a capital of two millions subscribed in London and Ireland, to be applied to the support of banking establishments connected with it in Ireland, by contributing to each a sum equal to that locally subscribed; it has also branches in the principal towns. The private banking establishments are those of La Touche and Co., Castle-street; Ball and Co, Henry-street; Boyle and Co., College-green; and the Royal

Bank, Foster-place. There are two Savings' Banks, both formed in 1818, one in Meath-street, the other in Cuffe-street, in St. Peter's parish. The former has two branches in Marlborough-street and at the Linen-hall, by which the benefits of the system have been extended to the northern division of the city. The Money Order office, held in the general Post-Office, furnishes means for the secure transmission of small sums.

The *Custom-house* is a stately structure of the Doric order, situated on the north bank of the Liffey, below Carlisle bridge. It was erected under the superintendence of Mr. Gandon in 1794, at an expense of £397,232. 4. 11, which the requisite furniture and subsequent enlargements have increased to upwards of half a million sterling. The building is 375 feet in length and 205 feet in depth, and has four fronts, of which the south is entirely of Portland stone, and the others of mountain granite. On the cast of the custom-house is a wet dock capable of receiving 40 vessels, and along the quay is a range of spacious warehouses. Beyond these an extensive area, enclosed with lofty walls, contains a second wet dock, consisting of two basins, the outer 300 feet by 250 and the inner 650 by 300; still further eastward, and on the same line with the principal building, are the tobacco and general warehouses, the latter of which were burnt down in 1839, but have been rebuilt. The business of the customs and excise for all Ireland was transacted in the custom house, until the consolidation of the boards of Customs and Excise into one general board in London, since which period it has been confined to that of the Dublin district, and a great part of the building is applied to the accommodation of the following departments:– the Stamp Office; the Commissariat; the Board of Works; the Record Office for documents connected with the vice-Treasurer's Office; the Quit-Rent Office; and the Stationery Office. The amount of duties paid in 1836, for goods imported and exported, was £898,630. 5. 1.; and the excise duties of the Dublin district during the same period amounted to £419,935. 14. 4½.

The General Post-Office situated in Sackville street, is a very fine building of granite, 223 feet in length, 150 feet in depth, and three stories high. In the centre of the front is a boldly projecting portico of six fluted Ionic columns supporting an entablature and cornice, which are continued round the building and surmounted by a triangular pediment, in the tympanum of which are the Royal arms, and on the apex a figure of Hibernia, with one of Mercury on the right, and of Fidelity on the left; the whole of the building is crowned with a fine balustrade rising above the cornice. This structure was raised under the direction of Mr. Francis Johnston, architect, at an expense of £50,000. Over the mantel-piece in the Board-room is a marble bust of Earl Whitworth, by whom the first stone was laid in 1815. The establishment, which had been under the direction of two postmasters-general, was, in 1831, consolidated with the English Post-Office, and placed under the control of the postmaster-general of the united kingdom. Letters are delivered throughout the city three times a day by the penny post department, and once a day to 17 stations within 12 miles of it on payment of two pence.

LITERATURE AND SERVICE.

The Royal Dublin Society originated, in 1731, in the private meetings of a few scientific gentlemen, among whom were Dr. Price and Dr. Madden, and was supported entirely by their own contributions until the year 1749, when they were incorporated by royal charter, under the name of "the Dublin Society for promoting husbandry and other useful arts in Ireland," and received an annual grant of £500, which was gradually augmented to £10,000, until lately, when it has been reduced to £5000. It is under the patronage of the king and the lord-lieutenant (the latter being president), and there are seven vice-presidents, two honorary secretaries, and an assistant secretary. The literary and scientific department consist of a professor of botany and agriculture, a professor of chymistry, a professor of mineralogy and geology, a librarian, teachers of landscape, figure, and ornamental drawing and of sculpture, and a curator of the botanic garden. The society, which in 1821 was honoured with the designation of "Royal," held its meetings in Shaws-court till 1767, when the members removed to a building which they had erected in Grafton-street, whence, in 1796, they removed to Hawkins-street, where they erected an edifice for their repository, laboratory, library, and galleries; and in 1815 they purchased, for £20,000, the spacious and splendid mansion of the Duke of Leinster, in Kildare-street. This building is 140 feet in length and 70 in depth, and is approached from the street by a massive gateway of rusticated masonry: the principal front is of the Corinthian order, richly embellished; before it is a spacious court, and in the rear an extensive lawn fronting Merrion-square. The entrance-hall is enriched with casts taken from figures by the first masters, and there are also several busts executed by artists who had been pupils of the society. The library, in the east wing, is 64 feet long and 24 feet wide, and is surrounded by a light gallery; it contains 12,000 volumes, and is rich in botanical works. The museum occupies six rooms, containing miscellaneous curiosities, specimens of animals, mineralogy, geology, &c.; the specimens of the mineralogical department are classified on the Wernerian system. The lecture-room is capable of accommodating 400 auditors. The apartments for the use of members are all on the ground-floor. The drawing schools occupy a range of detached buildings; they are appropriately fitted up, and are attended by 200 pupils. The botanical studies are under the direction of a professor, who delivers lectures both at the Society house and in the botanic gardens at Glasnevin. These are about a mile from the city, occupying a space of more than 27 acres, watered by the Tolka, and containing every requisite variety of soil for botanical purposes. The garden is formed into subdivisions for agricultural and horticultural specimens: it has the house of the professor and the lecture-rooms near the entrance, and is open to the public on Tuesdays and Fridays; the admission is free, as also to the lectures, schools, and museum. *The Royal Irish Academy* was instituted, in 1782, by a number of gentlemen, members of the University, chiefly to promote the study of polite literature, science, and antiquities, and was incorporated in 1786: it is assisted in its objects by a parliamentary grant of £300 per annum, and honoured with the patronage of the King; and is under the superintendence of a visitor (who is the lord-lieutenant for the time being), a president, four vice-presidents and a council of 21, a treasurer, librarian, and two secretaries. Its literary management is entrusted to three committees, respectively superintending the departments of science, polite literature, and antiquities. At the annual meetings premiums, accruing from the interest of £1500 bequeathed by Col. Burton Conyngham, are awarded for the best essays on given subjects, for which persons not members of the academy may become competitors; the successful essays are sometimes published in the transactions of the academy, of which 17 volumes in quarto have already appeared. The library contains some very valuable manuscripts relating to Ireland: the large room for meetings of the academy is embellished with portraits of their presidents.

The Library of Trinity College, by much the largest not only in Dublin but in Ireland, is described under the head of the institution of which it forms a portion: the King's Inns library is also noticed in like manner. *St. Patrick's or Marsh's library* was founded by Dr. Narcissus Marsh, archbishop of Dublin, in the vicinity of St. Patrick's cathedral; it contains the celebrated Dr. Stillingfleet's collection and some manuscripts. The apartment for the books consists of two Galleries meeting at a right angle, in which is the librarian's room. The library is open on liberal terms, a certificate or letter of introduction from some respectable and well-known character being all that is required: it is under the government of trustees appointed by act of parliament. *The Dublin Library Society* originated in the meeting of a few individuals at a bookseller's in Dame-street to read newspapers and periodicals. Having formed a regular society, a library was opened, in 1791, in Eustace-street, which was removed in 1809 to Burgh-quay, and finally, in 1820, to a building in D'Olier-street, erected for the special purpose, by shares. The building is plain but elegant, and contains a spacious apartment for the library, another for newspapers and periodicals, and a few smaller rooms for committees and house officers. The public rooms are ornamented with busts of John Philpot Curran, Daniel O'Connell, Henry Grattan, Archibald Hamilton Rowan, and Dean Kirwan, and with portraits of the first Earl of Charlemont and of Curran. The medical libraries of the College of Surgeons and Sir Patrick Dun's hospital are well selected and rapidly increasing. Steevens's Hospital, the Royal Hospital, Christ-Church, and Strand-street Meeting-house have each a collection of books, none of any great extent. The private library of the Earl of Charlemont is highly worthy of notice. It is contained in a building attached to the town residence in Palace-row: the entrance to it is by a long gallery, ornamented with antique busts, vases, and altars, which opens into a large vestibule lighted by a lantern, which contains the works on antiquities and numismatics, and has in a recess the statue of Venus and eight busts of ancient and modern characters of celebrity. The principal library contains a fine and well-selected collection of ancient and modern writers on most departments of literature and some of science, very judiciously and happily arranged; also some manuscripts, and an unique collection of

Hogarth's engravings, mostly proofs. Over the chimney-piece is a fine bust of Homer. Attached to the library is a small museum, a medal room, and a smaller library of very elegant proportions, containing busts of the Earl of Rockingham and General Wolfe.

SURGICAL AND MEDICAL INSTITUTIONS.

The Royal College of Surgeons was incorporated in 1784, for the purpose of establishing a "liberal and extensive system of surgical education:" a parliamentary grant was afterwards conferred on it for providing the necessary accommodations. Sums amounting in the whole to £35,000 were granted for erecting and furnishing the requisite buildings; besides which, £6000, the accumulated excess of the receipts over the disbursements of the college, were expended in 1825 in the addition of a museum. The front of the building, which is situated on the west side of St. Stephen's-green, has a rusticated basement story, from which rises a range of Doric columns supporting a tier of seven large windows, the four central columns being surmounted by a triangular pediment, on which are statues of Minerva, Esculapius and Hygeia. The interior contains a large board-room, a library, an apartment for general meetings, an examination hall, with several committee-rooms and offices, four theatres for lectures, a spacious dissecting-room with several smaller apartments, and three museums, the largest of which, 84 feet by 30, with a gallery, contains a fine collection of preparations of human and comparative anatomy; the second, with two galleries, contains preparations illustrative of pathology and a collection of models in wax, presented by the Duke of Northumberland when lord-lieutenant; and the third, attached to the anatomical theatre, contains a collection for the illustration of the daily courses of lectures. The College consists of a president, vice-president, six censors, twelve assistants, secretaries, members, and licentiates. Candidates for a diploma must produce certificates of attendance on some school of medicine and surgery for five years, and of attendance at a surgical hospital for three years, and must pass four half-yearly examinations, and a final examination for letters testimonial in the presence of the members and licentiates on two days: rejected candidates have a right of appeal to a court constituted for the purpose, which is frequently resorted to. Attached to the school are two professors of anatomy and physiology, two of surgery, a professor of chymistry, one of the practice of medicine, one of materia medica, one of midwifery, and one of medical jurisprudence, with four anatomical demonstrators; the lectures commence on the last Monday in October, and close on the last day of April.

The College of Physicians was first incorporated in the reign of Chas II., but the charter being found insufficient, was surrendered in 1692, and a more ample charter was granted by William and Mary, under the designation of the King and Queen's College of Physicians in Ireland. This charter, which conferred considerable privileges, was partly confirmed by successive acts of parliament, which gave the society authority to summon all medical practitioners for examination, to inspect the shops and warehouses of apothecaries, druggists, and chymists, and to destroy all articles for medical use which are of bad quality: it has also a principal share in the superintendence of the School of Physic. No person can be a member of the College who has not graduated in one of the universities of Oxford, Cambridge, or Dublin. The officers of the college consist of a president, vice-president, four censors, a registrar, and a treasurer; the members hold their meetings at Sir Patrick Dun's hospital, of whose bequests for the promotion of medical science they are trustees. *The School of Physic* is partly under the control of the Board of the University, and partly under that of the College of Physicians; the professorships of anatomy, chymistry, and botany being in the appointment of the University, who elect the professors, thence called University professors; those of the practice of medicine, the institutes of medicine, and of the materia medica, called King's professors, derive their appointment and their salaries from the College of Physicians, being chosen by ballot from among the members of that body. The University professors deliver their lectures in Trinity College, and the King's professors in Sir Patrick Dun's hospital. No candidate is qualified for a degree in medicine until he has attended the six courses, and six months at Sir Patrick Dun's clinical hospital.

The School of Pharmacy. Previously to the company of the Apothecaries' Hall having been incorporated, the shops were supplied by the druggists, without any check on the quality of the medical articles supplied. To remedy this defect an act was passed, in 1791, incorporating a body under the title of the "Governor and Company of the Apothecaries' Hall," by whom a building was erected in Mary-street (a respectable edifice of brick, with a basement of hewn stone) for the preparation and sale of drugs, unadulterated and of the best quality, and for the delivery of courses of lectures on chemistry, the materia medica, pharmacy, botany, and the practice of physic, and for the examination of candidates for a diploma to practise as apothecaries. The establishment consists of a governor, deputy-governor, treasurer, secretary, and thirteen directors. Candidates for apprenticeship must undergo an examination in Greek and Latin, and those for the rank of master apothecary must produce certificates of attendance on a course of each of the following departments of medicine; chymistry, materia medica and pharmacy, medical botany, anatomy, and physiology, and the theory and practice of medicine. The diploma of the society of Apothecaries of London also, by the rules of the Dublin company, qualifies the holder to practise in Ireland. *The School of Anatomy, Medicine, and Surgery*, in Park-street, Merrion-square, established in 1824 by a society of surgeons and physicians, contains a museum, a chymical laboratory, an office and reading-room, a lecture-room capable of accommodating 200 persons, a dissecting-room, and rooms for preparations. Private medical schools are numerous, and, combined with the public institutions, and with the extensive practice afforded by the city hospitals, have rendered Dublin a celebrated school of medicine, resorted to by students from every part of the British empire. *The Phrenological Society*, under the direction of a president, vice president, and two committees, was established in 1829. Its meetings are held in Upper Sackville-street, where the society has a large collection of casts illustrative of the theory of the science, and a library of phrenological treatises, which are lent out to the members: the annual subscription is one guinea. *The Association of Members of the College of Physicians* was instituted in 1816; they hold their meetings at their rooms in College-green, for receiving communications on medical subjects and on scientific matters; their object is the promotion of medical science, and among their corresponding members are some of the most eminent medical men in England and on the Continent: the society has published several volumes of transactions.

INSTITUTIONS FOR THE PROMOTION OF THE FINE ARTS AND OTHER
USEFUL AND SCIENTIFIC PURPOSES.

The Royal Hibernian Academy of painting, sculpture, and architecture, founded by royal charter in 1823, consists of fourteen academicians and ten associates, all of whom must be professional painters, sculptors, or architects: the king is patron, the lord-lieutenant vice-patron, and its affairs are under the superintendence of a council. The academy has for the last few years been encouraged by a grant from parliament of £300 per ann.; its first president, the late Francis Johnston, Esq., architect, erected an elegant and appropriate building in Abbey-street, at an expense of £10,000, which he presented to the academy for ever, at a nominal rent of 5s. per ann., and to which his widow subsequently added a gallery for statuary. The building, which is three stories high and of elegant design, has, on the basement story, a recess ornamented with fluted columns of the Doric order: over the entrance is a head of Palladio, emblematical of architecture; over the window on the right, a head of Michael Angelo, illustrative of sculpture; and over the window on the left, a head of Raphael, allusive to painting. The academy has a good collection of casts from the antique, some paintings by the old masters, and a library of works chiefly connected with the fine arts, and of which the greater number were presented by the late Edward Houghton, Esq. *The Royal Irish Institution for promoting the fine arts* was founded, under royal patronage, in 1815: its vice-patron is the Marquess of Anglesey, its guardian, the lord-lieutenant, and its president, the Duke of Leinster: its affairs are superintended by eight vice-presidents (all noblemen), and a committee of directors. The Artists have also formed a society, called the *Artists' and Amateurs' Conversazione,* for cultivating and maintaining a social intercourse with admirers of the fine arts, and thereby promoting their mutual interests. *The Horticultural Society,* patronised by the Lord-Lieutenant and the Duchess of Leinster, and under the direction of the Earl of Leitrim as president, several noblemen as vice-presidents, and a council, was instituted in 1813, and has rapidly increased in prosperity. Prizes are awarded at its annual exhibitions, which are numerously and most fashionably attended. *The Geological Society* was instituted in 1835, and is under the directions of a president, vice-presidents, and a council. Its attention is peculiarly directed to Ireland: it consists of honorary and ordinary members; £30 on admission, or £5 if not resident within 20 miles of Dublin for more than one month in the year, constitutes a member for life; and £1 on admission, and £1 per ann., constitutes an ordinary member. The rooms of the society are in Upper Sackville-street; two parts of a volume of its transactions have been already published. *The Zoological Society*, instituted in 1831, is under the direction of a president, vice-president, and council: £10 paid on admission constitutes a member for life, and £1 on admission and a subscription of £1 per ann., an annual member. The gardens are situated in the Phoenix Park, and occupy a piece of ground near the vice-regal lodge, given for that purpose by the Duke of Northumberland, when lord-lieutenant: they have been laid out with much taste, and are in excellent order, affording a most interesting place of resort; the council have already purchased many fine specimens of the higher classes of animals. They are open to the public daily, on payment of sixpence admission. *The Agricultural Society* was instituted in 1833, and is under the direction of a president (the Marquess of Downshire), several vice-presidents, a committee and subcommittee: it consists of 330 members, who pay an annual subscription of £1, and among whom are most of the principal landed proprietors; its object is the establishment of a central institution for concentrating the efforts made by other societies and by individuals for improving the condition of the people and the cultivation of the soil of Ireland: two annual meetings are held, one in Dublin during the April show of cattle, and the other at Ballinasloe in October. *The Civil Engineers' Society* was established in 1835, for the cultivation of science in general, and more especially of those branches of it which are connected with the engineering department; it is under the direction of a president, vice-presidents, and a committee, and consists of members who must be either civil or military engineers, or architects, who pay one guinea on admission by ballot and an annual subscription of equal amount.

Theatres, clubs, and Musical Societies.

The places of public amusement are few. The Drama is little encouraged by the fashionable and wealthy; the theatre is thinly attended, except on the appearance of some first-rate performer from London, or at the special desire of the lord-lieutenant, the social character of the inhabitants inducing an almost exclusive preference to convivial inter-course within the domestic circle. The first public theatre was built in Werburgh street, by Lord Strafford, in 1635, and was closed in 1641. After the Restoration, a theatre under the same patent was opened in Orange-street, now Smock-alley; and in 1733, a second was opened in Rainsford-street, in the liberty of Thomas-court, and a third in George's-lane. Sheridan had a theatre in Aungier-street, in 1745, which was destroyed in 1754 by a tumult of the audience; and in 1758 another was built in Crow-street, which, with that in Smock-alley, continued open for 25 years, when, after much rivalry, the latter was closed, and a patent granted to the former for the exclusive enjoyment of the privilege of performing the legitimate drama. On the expira-tion of this patent, Mr. Harris, of London, procured a renewal of it from Government and erected the *"New Theatre Royal"* in Hawkins-street, a pile of unsightly exterior but internally of elegant proportions, being constructed in the form of a lyre, handsomely decorated and admirably adapted to the free transmission of the actor's voice to every part of the house: attached to it is a spacious saloon, supported by pil-lars of the Ionic order. A smaller *theatre* has been lately opened in *Abbey-street* for dramatic performances: it is a plain building, neatly fit-ted up. Another small *theatre in Fishamble-street,* originally a music-hall, is occasionally opened for dramatic and other entertainments; and a third, in Great Brunswick-street, called *the Adelphi,* originally intended for a diorama, is used for amateur theatricals. In Abbey-street is a *cir-cus,* in which equestrian performances occasionally take place. During the summer season, *the Rotundo gardens* are open on stated evenings every week, and being illuminated in a fanciful manner and enlivened by the attendance of a military band, and by occasional exhibitions of rope-dancing and fireworks, they afford an agreeable promenade in the open air, and are well attended. In *the Royal Arcade,* in College-green, are some handsome rooms for public amusements. Clubs and societies for convivial purposes are numerous: several club-houses have been opened on the principle of those in London. *The Kildare-street Club,* consisting of about 650 members, was instituted upwards of fifty years since, and takes its name from the street in which its house stands: the accommodations contain a large and elegant card-room, coffee, read-ing, and billiard-rooms; the terms of admission, which is by ballot, are £26. 10., and the annual subscription, £5: it is managed by a committee of 15 members chosen annually. *The Sackville-street Club,* instituted in 1795, consists of 400 members chosen by ballot, who previously pay 20 guineas, and an annual subscription of 5 guineas; the house, which contains a suite of apartments similar in character to those of the Kildare-street Club, has been recently fitted up in a very splendid style. *The Friendly Brothers' Club,* also in Upper Sackville-street, consists of many members who are in connection with similar societies in various countries; the house affords excellent accommodation. *The Hibernian United Service Club,* instituted in 1832, is limited to 500 permanent and 200 temporary members, consisting of officers of the army and navy of every rank, and of field officers and captains of militia of the United Kingdom; the terms of admission by ballot are £10. 10., and the annual subscription £4 for permanent members; honorary members are admitted on payment of the annual subscription only; the club-house is in Foster-street, near the Bank. The *Freemasons* for some years had a hall in Dawson-street: they now hold their meetings in temporary apartments in the Commercial Buildings. The leading *musical societies* are the Beefsteak Club, the Hibernian Catch Club, the Anacreontic, for the performance of instrumental music; the Dublin Philharmonic Society, for the practice of vocal and instrumental music; and the Festival Choral Society, for the cultivation of choral music. Other societies, of a more miscellaneous character, whose names indicate their objects, are the Chess, Philidorean, Shakspeare, Royal Yacht, and Rowing clubs.

MUNICIPAL GOVERNMENT.

The charters granted at various times to the city are carefully preserved from the earliest period in the archives of the corporation. The first was granted in the reign of Hen. II., from which period to the reign of Geo. III. a numerous series of them has been successively issued, either confirming previous grants, or conferring additional privileges. The present constitution of the corporate government is founded partly on the provisions of several of the earlier charters, partly on usage and ancient customs, partly on the new rules laid down in the 25th of Chas. II. and partly on the statutes of the 33rd of Geo. II., and the 11th and 12th of Geo. III. The corporation consists of a lord mayor, 24 aldermen, and a common council. The lord mayor is annually elected from among the aldermen, by a majority of that body, with the approbation of the common council; the alderman next in rotation is generally chosen. Within ten days after his election, he must be presented to the lord-lieutenant and privy council for their approbation, and is sworn into office before the lord-lieutenant on Sept. 30th; he is a justice of the peace for the county of the city, admiral of the port of Dublin, and chief Judge of the Lord Mayor's and Sheriffs' courts; he has the regulation of the assize of bread, and is clerk of the market, and, *ex officio*, a member of certain local boards and trusts. The aldermen, who are also justices of the peace for the city, are elected for life, as vacancies occur, from among such common-councilmen as have served the office of sheriff, and are therefore called sheriffs' peers; each on his election pays £400 late currency, of which £105 is for the Blue-coat hospital, and the remainder for the repair and embellishment of the Mansion-house. The sheriffs are annually elected at Easter by the lord mayor and aldermen out of eight freemen nominated by the common council, and each of them must be in possession of real or personal property to the clear amount of £2000; they must be approved by the lord-lieutenant and privy council; but on payment of a fine of £500, of which £105 is given to the Blue-coat hospital, a freeman so nominated may become a sheriffs' peer without serving the office of sheriff. The common council consists of the sheriffs' peers, and of the representatives of the guilds triennially elected, who are 96 in number, and who, in default of election by the guilds, may be chosen by the lord mayor and aldermen from each of the guilds so neglecting. The officers of the corporation are a recorder, who must be a barrister of six years' standing, but is not required to be a freeman; he is elected by the lord mayor and aldermen, with the approbation of the common council, subject to the approval of the lord-lieutenant and privy council, holds his office during good behaviour, and is permitted by the act of the 21st and 22nd of Geo. III., in case of sickness or absence, to appoint a deputy, who also, by the 39th of Geo. III., must be a barrister of six years' standing: two coroners, elected from the aldermen by the lord mayor and a majority of that body alone: a president of the court of conscience, who is the ex-lord mayor during the year after his office expires, and may appoint any alderman to officiate for him: two town-clerks, who are also clerks of the peace, either freemen or not, and elected for life in the same manner as the recorder, and subject to the approval of the privy council: a marshal, who must be a freeman, and is similarly elected, nominally for one year, but generally re-elected on its expiration: water bailiffs, elected in the same manner as the marshal, and who give security by two sureties for £1000: serjeants-at-mace, similarly elected, and who give two sureties for £250 each; and several inferior officers. The freedom of the city is obtained either by gift of the aldermen and common-councilmen in general assembly, or by admission to the freedom of one of the guilds, and afterwards to that of the city, by favour of the corporation. Freemen of the guilds, either by birth, servitude, or marriage, can only be admitted as freemen at large by the common council, who have power to reject them after passing through the guilds; hence the freedom of the guilds entitles them only to the privilege of carrying on their respective trades, but not to that of voting at elections for the city representatives in parliament. There are 25 guilds, the first of which is the Trinity guild or guild of Merchants, which returns 31 representatives out of the 96; the others, called minor guilds, are those of the Tailors, Smiths, Barber-Surgeons, Bakers, Butchers, Carpenters, Shoemakers, Saddlers, Cooks, Tanners, Tallowchandlers, Glovers and Skinners, Weavers, Shearmen and Dyers, Goldsmiths, Coopers, Feltmakers, Cutlers, Bricklayers, Hosiers, Curriers, Brewers, Joiners, and Apothecaries. Only six of the guilds have halls; the others meet either in one of these or in a private building. The Merchants' Hall, on Aston's Quay, opposite Wellington bridge, is a new building of granite, two stories high, with little architectural ornament. The Tailors' Hall, in Back-lane, built in 1710, is ornamented with portraits of Chas. II., Dean Swift, and St. Homobon, a tailor of Cremona, canonized in 1316 for his piety and charity. The Weavers' Hall, on the Coombe, is a venerable brick building, two stories high, with a pedestrian statue of Geo. II. over the entrance, and in the Hall a portrait of the same king woven in tapestry, and one of a member of the family of La Touche, who had greatly encouraged the manufacture. The Carpenters' Hall is in Audoen's Arch, the Goldsmiths' in Golden-lane, and the Cutlers' in Capel-street.

The city returns two members to the Imperial parliament; the right of election, formerly vested in the corporation, freemen, and 40s. freeholders, has been extended to the £10 householders, and £20 and £10 leaseholders for the respective terms of 14 and 20 years, by the act of the 2nd of Wm. IV., cap. 88. The number of voters registered at the first general election under that act was 7041, of which number, 5126 voted. The limits of the city, for electoral purposes, include an area of 3538 statute acres, the boundaries of which are minutely detailed in the Appendix; the number of freemen is about 3500, of whom 2500 are resident and 1000 non-resident, and the number of £10 houses is 16,000: the sheriffs are the returning officers. The corporation holds general courts of quarter assembly at Christmas, Easter, Midsummer, and Michaelmas, which are occasionally adjourned, and post assemblies sometimes for particular purposes. As a justice of the peace, the lord mayor presides at the city quarter sessions, and always attends on the first day to open the court, accompanied by some of the aldermen, it being necessary that two at least of that body should be present with the lord mayor or recorder to form a quorum. The lord mayor's and sheriffs' courts are held on the Thursday after the first day of the sessions; each has cognizance of personal actions to any amount above £2; the process is by attachment of the defendant's goods. The lord mayor's court, in which he is the sole judge, is held every Thursday either at the city sessions-house, where it is an open court, or in the Mansion-house, where it may be private; it has summary jurisdiction, and takes cognizance of complaints, nuisances, informations, &c. The court of conscience, for determining causes and recovering debts not exceeding £2 late currency, is held daily before the president in the city assembly-house in William-street. The police establishment, as regulated by the Duke of Wellington, when chief secretary for Ireland, was under the control of a chief magistrate, aided by eleven others, three of whom sat daily at one of the offices of the four divisions, according to which the city was arranged: to each office a chief constable and petty constables were attached. The police force, consisting of a horse patrol of 29 men, a foot patrol of 169, 26 watch constables, and 539 watchmen, was maintained at an expense of about £40,000 per ann. By an act passed in 1836 the police of the metropolis is placed under two magistrates appointed by the lord-lieutenant, and the boundaries of their jurisdiction have been determined to be the rivers Dodder and Tolka to the south and north, and Knockmaroon hill to the west, which boundary may be extended according to the discretion of the lord-lieutenant and privy council to any place within five miles of Dublin castle; by whom the number of divisional offices may be reduced and also that of the magistrates, provided there be two to each office. The city is to be assessed for the payment of the establishment by a rate not exceeding 8*d*. in the pound, according to the valuation made under the act of the 5th of Geo. IV.

The *Mansion-house,* the residence of the lord mayor during his year of office, is externally a plain edifice of brick, on a detached and receding site on the south side of Dawson-street; the interior contains some large apartments fitted up in an antiquated style. On the left hand of the entrance-hall is the "Gilt Room," a small apartment in which is a portrait of Wm. III., by Gubbins; this room opens into the drawing-room, which is 50 feet long: the walls are hung with portraits of Earl Whitworth, the Earls of Hardwicke and Westmoreland, John Foster, the last speaker of the Irish House of Commons, and Alderman Alexander. Beyond this is the ball-room, used also for civic dinners, 55 feet long and wainscoted with Irish oak; in this room are placed the two city swords, the mace, the cap of maintenance and the gold collar of S S, presented by Wm. III., to replace that presented by Chas. II.; it also contains portraits of Chas. II., Geo. II., the Duke of Cumberland, and the late Duke of Richmond. A door from the ball-room opens into a noble rotundo, 90 feet in diameter, round which is continued a corridor 5 feet wide; the walls are painted in imitation of tapestry, and the room is covered with a dome; in the centre is a lantern, by which the apartment is lighted; it was built in 1821 expressly for the reception of George IV., who honoured the corporation with his presence at dinner. On the right of the entrance-hall are the Exchequer-room, wainscoted with Irish oak, and hung with portraits of the Duke of Bolton, the Earl of Buckingham, the Marquess of Buckingham, and the Earl of Harcourt; and the sheriffs' room, 40 feet long, in which are portraits of the Duke of Northumberland, Lord Townsend, John Duke of Bedford, and Aldermen Sankey, Manders, and Thorpe, the last of whom is distinguished by the title of "the good lord mayor." An equestrian statue of Geo. I., which was formerly on Essex bridge, is placed in the lawn at the side of the mansion house; and at the extremity of the court in which the rotundo is built are colossal statues of Chas. II. and Wm. III. The *City Assembly-house,* purchased by the corporation from the artists of Dublin, by whom it was built for an exhibition-room, is a plain but commodious structure in William-street, and contains several good rooms; in the circular room the common council holds its meetings; the board of aldermen meets in another apartment; and under the common council room is a circular apartment in which the court of conscience is held.

The *Sessions-house,* in Green-street, opened for business in 1797, is ornamented in front with a central pediment and cornice supported by six engaged columns rising from a broad platform, to which is an ascent by a flight of steps extending along the whole front of the building, and on each side of the centre are the doors of entrance to the court-rooms; in another front, corresponding with this, in Halston-street, are the entrances to the apartments occupied by the agents during contested elections. The interior is spacious, lofty, and well arranged; the ceiling is supported by Ionic columns. In this building are held the court of quarter sessions, the court of oyer and terminer, the lord mayor's and sheriffs' court, and the recorder's court. The principal prison for malefactors of all classes is *Newgate,* situated near the sessions-house, in Green street. It is a square building, flanked at each angle by a round tower with loop-hole windows. The interior is divided into two nearly equal portions by a broad passage with high walls on each side, having iron gates at intervals, through the gratings of which visitors may converse with the prisoners; the cells are neither sufficiently numerous nor large, nor is the prison well adapted for due classification. A chapel attached to it is attended by three chaplains; one of the Established Church, one of the R. C. and one of the Presbyterian religion. The *Sheriffs' Prison,* in Green-street, was built in 1794, and occupies three sides of a quadrangle with an area in the centre, which is used as a ball-court; it is visited by the chaplains of Newgate and a medical inspector. The *City Marshalsea,* a brick building attached to the preceding, is designed for prisoners committed from the lord mayor's court for debts under £10, and from the court of conscience. The *Smithfield Penitentiary* is appropriated to the confinement of juvenile convicts not exceeding 19 years of age; it is visited by three chaplains, and inspected by the divisional magistrates; an efficient classification is observed, and all the prisoners are regularly employed. The *Richmond Bridewell,* on the Circular road, erected by the city at an expense of £40,000, is a spacious structure enclosed by walls flanked with towers at the angles, and is entered by a massive gateway; between the outer wall and the main building is a wide space, intended for a rope-walk; the interior consists of two spacious quadrangles, the sides of which are all occupied by buildings; the cells, which are on the first floor, open into corridors with entrances at each end; the rooms in the second floor are used as work-rooms; the male and female prisoners occupy distinct portions of the prison; the prisoners not sentenced to the tread-mill are employed in profitable labour, and a portion of their earnings is paid to them on their discharge; they are visited by a Protestant and a R. C. chaplain, a physician, surgeon, and apothecary. A great improvement in the city prisons is now in progress. Attached to the city are the manor or liberty of St. Sepulchre, belonging to the Archbishop of Dublin; the manor of Grangegorman or Glasnevin, belonging to the dean of Christ-Church; the manor of Thomas-Court and Donore, belonging to the Earl of Meath; and the liberty of the deanery of St. Patrick. The *Liberty of St. Sepulchre* extends over a part of the city, including the parishes of St. Patrick, St. Nicholas Without, and St. Kevin; also over a large tract of the county of Dublin to the south-east of the city, as far as the Wicklow boundary, including a small portion of the latter county and of Kildare, bordering on that of Dublin. The court is held at Longlane, in the county of Dublin, before the archbishop's seneschal, and has a very extensive criminal as well as civil jurisdiction, but exercises only the latter: the court-house and prison for the whole archbishoprick are situated there. It has a civil bill jurisdiction to any amount, extended to the Dublin manor courts in 1826. At the record side the proceedings are either by action against the body, for sums under £20 by service and above it by arrest; or, for sums above £10, by attachment against the goods. The court at the record side sits every Tuesday and Friday; the civil bill court, generally on alternate Wednesdays, except in the law terms, when it stands adjourned. At this court, in which a jury is always impannelled and sworn, sums to any amount may be recovered at a trifling expense. The jurisdiction of the *Manor Court of Glasnevin* is of great extent, comprising the baronies of Coolock, Castleknock, and Half-Rathdown, in the county of Dublin, and the lordship of St. Mary's abbey, which includes portions of the city and county. The seneschal sits in Dublin every Friday, and at Kingstown on alternate Fridays for the convenience of that town and the surrounding parishes within his jurisdiction. Causes are tried before a jury, and debts to any amount are recoverable at a small expense; from 900 to 1000 causes are heard annually. *Thomas-Court and Donore Manor-Court* has a jurisdiction extending over the barony of Donore, and that part of the liberty of Thomas-Court which is within the city: the civil bill court, in which debts to any amount are recoverable, is held every Wednesday in the courthouse in Thomas-Court, a plain building erected in 1160; a record court is also held there every Wednesday and Saturday.

VICE-REGAL GOVERNMENT.

Dublin is the seat of the Vice-regal government, consisting of a lord-lieutenant and privy council, assisted by a chief secretary, under-secretary, and a large establishment of inferior officers and under-clerks both for state and the despatch of business. The official residence of the lord-lieutenant is *Dublin Castle,* first appropriated to that purpose in the reign of Elizabeth; but his usual residence is the Vice-regal Lodge, in the Phoenix Park. The buildings of the Castle form two quadrangles, called the Upper and Lower Yards. The Upper, 280 feet by 130, contains the lord-lieutenant's apartments, which occupy the whole of the south and part of the east sides; the council-chamber and offices connected with it; the apartments and offices of the chief secretary, and of several of the officers of the household; and the apartments of the master of the ceremonies, and of the aides de camp of the viceroy. The entrance into this court is on the north side by a massive gateway towards the east end, ornamented by a figure of Justice above the arch; and towards the west end is a corresponditig gateway, which is not used, ornamented by a figure of Fortitude; both by Van Nost. The approach to the vice-regal apartments is under a colonnade on the south side, leading into a large hall, and thence by a fine staircase to the state apartments, containing the presence chamber and the ball-room; in the former is the throne of gilt carved work, under a canopy of crimson velvet richly ornamented with gold lace; the latter, which, since the institution of the order of St. Patrick, has been called St. Patrick's Hall, has its walls decorated with paintings, and the ceiling, which is panelled in three compartments, has in the centre a full-length portrait of George III., supported by Liberty and Justice, with various allegorical devices. Between the gateways, on the north side of the court, are the apartments of the dean of the chapel royal and the chamberlain, a range of building ornamented with Ionic columns rising from a rusticated basement and supporting a cornice and pediment, above which is the Bedford Tower, embellished with Corinthian pillars and surmounted by a lofty dome, from the summit of which the royal standard is displayed on days of state. In the eastern side of the Upper Yard, is the council-chamber, a large but plain apartment, in which the lord-lieutenants are publicly sworn into office, and where the privy council holds its sittings. The privy council consists of the lord-primate, the lord-chancellor, the chief justices, and a number of prelates, noblemen, public functionaries, and others nominated by the King. This body exercises a judicial authority, especially in ecclesiastical matters, as a court of final resort, the duties of which are discharged by a committee selected from among the legal functionaries who are members of it. The Lower Yard is an irregular area, 250 feet long and 220 feet wide; in it are the treasury buildings, of antiquated style and rapidly decaying; the ordnance department, a modern brick building; and the office of the quartermaster-general, besides which are the stables, riding house, and the official residence of the master of the horse. To the east of the Record Tower is the Castle chapel, rebuilt at an expense of £42,000, principally after a design by Johnston, and opened in 1814; it is an elegant structure, in the later style of English architecture. The interior is lighted on each side by six windows of elegant design, enriched with tracery and embellished with stained glass: the east window, which is of large dimensions and of beautiful design, is of stained glass, representing our Saviour before Pilate, and the four Evangelists in compartments, with an exquisite group of Faith, Hope, and Charity; it was purchased on the continent and presented to the chapel by Lord Whitworth, during his vice-royalty.

The Phoenix Park, situated westward of the city, and north of the Liffey, is 7 miles in circumference, comprising an area of 1759 acres enclosed by a stone wall. Its name is derived from the Irish term *Finniske,* "a spring of clear water," now corrupted into Phoenix. A lofty fluted Corinthian pillar resting on a massive pedestal, and having on the abacus a phoenix rising from the flames, was erected near the lord-lieutenant's lodge by the Earl of Chesterfield, when chief governor. *The Vice-regal Lodge* was purchased from Mr. Clements, by whom it was built, and was originally a plain mansion of brick. Lord Hardwicke, in 1802, added the wings, in one of which is the great dining-hall; the Duke of Richmond, in 1808, built the north portico of the Doric order, and the entrance lodges from the Dublin road and Lord

Whitworth added the south front, which has a pediment supported by four Ionic columns of Portland stone, from a design by Johnston, and the whole of the façade was afterwards altered to correspond with it: the demesne attached to the lodge comprises 612 acres. The Wellington memorial occupies an elevated position: it consists of a massive truncated obelisk, 205 feet high from the ground, resting on a square pedestal 24 feet high, based on a platform 480 feet in circuit, and rising by steps to the height of 120 feet. On each side of the pedestal are sunken panels intended to receive sculptures in alto relievo, representing the principal victories of the duke; and on each side of the obelisk are enumerated all his battles, from his first career in India to the victory at Waterloo. In front of the eastern side of the pedestal rises another of small proportions, for an equestrian statue of the duke after his decease. It has been so far completed at an expense of £20,000. The park contains residences for the ranger, the principal secretary of state, the under secretary at war, and the under secretary of the civil department. The Powder magazine, erected in 1738, is a square fort, with half bastions at the angles, surrounded by a dry ditch, and entered by a drawbridge; in the interior are the magazines, which are bomb-proof and well secured against accidental fire. It is defended by ten 24-pounders. Near the Vice-regal Lodge a level space of about 50 acres, cleared of trees, is used as a place of exercise and reviews for the troops of the garrison. The park also contains the buildings of the Hibernian school for soldiers' children, the buildings erected by the Ordnance for the trigonometrical survey of Ireland, the Military Infirmary, and the garden of the Zoological society. Near one of the entrances to the Vice-regal Lodge, in a wooded glen, is a chalybeate spa surrounded with pleasure grounds, and furnished with seats for invalids, fitted up at the expense of the Duchess Dowager of Richmond for the accommodation of the public.

The military department is under the control of the commander of the forces, under whom are the departments of the adjutant-general, quarter-master-general, royal artillery, engineers, commissariat and medical staff. The garrison is under the more immediate command of the general officer commanding the eastern district of Ireland, the head-quarters of which is in the city. The commander of the forces resides in the Royal Hospital, Kilmainham, of which he is master by virtue of his office. This hospital was founded for superannuated and maimed soldiers, in 1679, by royal charter, on the site of the dissolved priory of St. John of Jerusalem, at an expense of £23,559. The building consists of a quadrangle, 306 feet by 208 on the outside, enclosing an area of 210 feet square. On the north side is the dining-hall, 100 feet by 50, the walls of which are appropriately ornamented with guns, pikes, and swords, and with standards taken from the Spaniards. The chapel is a plain but venerable structure: the east window, ornamented with stained glass, is very large, and beneath it is the communion table, of highly wrought Irish oak. The remainder of the quadrangle, round which is a covered walk, is appropriated to the use of the inmates. The present establishment is for 5 captains, an adjutant, and 200 soldiers selected from the out pensioners, whose number is about 20,000. The building is surrounded by a space of ground laid out in lawns and avenues well planted: its principal approach is from the military road. The garrison of the city is quartered in several barracks. The largest and oldest are the Royal Barracks, situated on an eminence overlooking the Liffey, between the city and the principal gate of the Phoenix Park: the chief entrances are by two gates from Barrack-street. They are adapted for 10 field officers, 83 officers, 2003 non-commissioned officers and privates, and 460 horses, with an hospital for 240 patients. The buildings are divided into five squares, under the designation of royal, palatine, cavalry, stable, and clock squares. The barracks in South Great George's street are adapted for 17 officers of infantry and 324 privates. The Richmond barracks, near Golden Bridge, on the bank of the Grand Canal, have accommodation for 76 officers of infantry and 1602 non-commissioned officers and privates, and an hospital for 100 patients. The Porto Bello cavalry barracks, on the Grand Canal, are adapted for 27 officers and 520 men, with stabling for 540 horses, and an hospital for 40 patients. The barracks in the Phoenix Park, for infantry, have accommodation for 10 officers and 250 non-commissioned officers and men. Connected with the powder magazine are accommodations for one officer of artillery and 18 men. The Island bridge barracks, for artillery, are adapted for 23 officers and 547 men, with stabling for 185 horses, and an hospital for 48 patients. The Recruiting Depôt at Beggar's Bush, beyond Sir Patrick Dun's Hospital, consists of a fort enclosed with a wall, and four bastions with defences for musketry, and affords accommodation for 122 officers and 360 privates, with an hospital for 39 patients. The Pigeon-house fort is situated on the south wall, midway between Ringsend and the Lighthouse, and comprises a magazine, arsenal, and custom-house, the whole enclosed with strong fortifications, and garrisoned by 16 officers of foot and artillery and 201 men, with stabling for 13 horses, and an hospital for 17 men. Adjoining the fort is a basin, 900 feet by 450, intended for a packet station; but since the formation of Howth and Kingstown harbours it has not been used. The Military Infirmary, designed for sick and wounded soldiers who cannot be properly treated in the regimental hospital, is in the Phoenix Park, near its principal entrance.

COURTS OF JUSTICE.

The supreme courts of judicature consist of the Chancery, in which the lord-chancellor presides, assisted by the Master of the Rolls, who holds a subordinate court; the King's Bench, which is under the superintendence of a chief justice and three puisne judges; the Common Pleas, under a similar superintendence of four judges; and the Exchequer, which contains two departments, one for the management of the revenue, the other a court both of equity and law, in which a chief baron and three puisne barons preside. The courts are held in a magnificent structure, commonly called the Four Courts, situated on the north side of the river, having Richmond and Whitworth bridges at its eastern and western extremities; it consists of a central pile, 140 feet square, containing the courts, and two wings, in which are most of the offices connected with the despatch of legal business: these, with the centre, form two quadrangles. The front of the building consists of a boldly projecting central portico of six Corinthian columns on a platform, to which is an ascent by five steps, and supporting a highly enriched cornice surmounted by a triangular pediment, having on the apex a statue of Moses, and at the ends those of Justice and of Mercy. Through this portico is the principal entrance into the great circular hall, opposite to which is a passage to apartments connected with the courts, and on each side are others leading to the two quadrangles. In the intervals between these four passages are the entrances to the four chief courts; the Chancery on the north-west, the King's Bench on the north-east, the Common Pleas on the south-east, and the Exchequer on the south-west. The

Rolls' Court is held in an apartment in the northern part of the central building, between the Courts of Chancery and King's Bench, where also are other apartments used as a law library and a coffee-room. The eastern wing, which forms the northern and eastern sides of one quadrangle, is appropriated to the offices belonging to the Common Pleas and some of those of the Chancery, the remainder of which, with the King's Bench and Exchequer offices, are in the northern and western sides of the other wing. A new building, for a Rolls' Court and a Nisi Prius Court, has been erected between the northern side of the main building and Pill-lane, on a piece of ground purchased for the purpose of isolating the courts, in order to diminish the risk of fire, and to provide additional accommodation for the augmentation of legal proceedings. This stately and sumptuous structure was begun by Mr. Thomas Cooley, architect, and completed by Mr. Gandon, at an expense of about £200,000, and the whole of the sculpture was executed by Mr. Edward Smith, a native artist.

INNS OF COURTS.

The King's Inns are situated on a piece of elevated ground of about three acres, formerly called the Primate's Garden, at the northern end of Henrietta-street, the tenure of which having been deemed doubtful, as being held under the Dean and Chapter of Christ-Church, was secured to the society by act of parliament. The structure consists of a centre and two wings, each with a back return; the principal front has a northern aspect, looking towards the rear of the houses on Constitution Hill, but the more usual approach for purposes of business is at the rear through Henrietta-street. The centre, which is crowned with an elegant octagonal cupola and dome, forms a lofty arched gateway, with a door on each side, leading into a confined area between the wings, the northern of which contains the dining-hall, and the southern, the Prerogative and Consistorial Courts, and the repository for the registration of deeds; The Prerogative Court is established for the trial of all testamentary cases where the testator has bequeathed property in more than one diocese. Its jurisdiction is vested in the Lord-Primate, under the acts of the 28th of Hen. VIII. and 2nd of Eliz., which gives him power to appoint the judge or commissary, who ranks next after the judges of the supreme courts. In the Consistorial Court are decided all cases of ecclesiastical jurisdiction of the province of Dublin. The library of the King's Inns is kept in a separate building, erected in Henrietta-street in 1827, at an expense of £20,000, after designs by Mr. Darley: the upper story is a spacious apartment, with recesses for the books and a gallery continued all round; it contains a very extensive collection, which was partly the property of Christopher Robinson, Esq., senior puisne judge of the Court of King's Bench; the law books were chiefly selected by Earl Camden, Lord-Chancellor. The library was entitled to one of the eleven copies of new publications appropriated to the public institutions under the late copyright act, which right has been lately commuted for an equivalent in money. The lower part of the building contains accommodations for the librarian. Bankrupt cases were tried before commissioners, appointed by the lord-chancellor, of whom there were 25, arranged in five sets who presided alternately; the court was held in an upper apartment of the Royal Exchange. By a late act the duties have been transferred to a single judge, under the title of Commissioner of Bankruptcies. The court for the relief of insolvent debtors was placed by an act of the 2nd of Geo. IV. under the jurisdiction of two commissioners, to be appointed by the lord-lieutenant, who hold their court in North Strand-street, with which is connected a suite of offices on Lower Ormond Quay. Prisoners under processes from the courts of justice and insolvent debtors are confined in the Four Courts Marshalsea, a large building in Marshalsea-lane, off Thomas-street: the prison has two court-yards, two chapels, several common halls and a ball-court. The Law Club was instituted in 1791 by a number of the most respectable solicitors and attorneys: the clubhouse is a plain building in Dame-street. The Law Society was formed in 1830; it proposes to form a law library, and to erect a common hall for the purposes of the society: the meetings are at present held in chambers on the King's Inns' Quay. The Law Students' Society, instituted in 1830, consists exclusively of law students and barristers.

ECCLESIASTICAL STATE.

Archiepiscopal See of Dublin and Glendalough. – The See of Dublin comprehended both the dioceses of Dublin and Glendalough until the arrival of the Danes, who having settled themselves in the plain country on each side of the Liffey, on their conversion to Christianity established a separate bishop, who derived his spiritual authority from the Archbishop of Canterbury and acknowledged him as his superior. Donat, the first bishop of Dublin chosen by the Danes, built the conventual and cathedral church of the Holy Trinity, usually called Christ-Church, about the year 1038. His successor, Patrick, on his election by the people of Dublin, was sent to England to be consecrated by Lanfranc, Archbishop of Canterbury. Gregory, the third in succession after Patrick, on proceeding to England on a similar mission, carried with him a letter from his flock, in which notice is taken of the animosity of the Irish bishops in consequence of their acknowledgment of the jurisdiction of an English prelate. In 1152 the see was raised to an archbishoprick by Cardiual Paparo, the Pope's legate, who invested Gregory with one of the four archiepiscopal palls brought from Rome. Laurence O'Toole was the first archbishop who did not go to England for consecration; the ceremony in his case was performed in Christ-Church by Gelasius, Archbishop of Armagh; and the custom of having recourse to Canterbury was never afterwards resumed. Archbishop Laurence proceeded to Rome in 1179, where he assisted at the second council of Lateran, and obtained a bull confirming that which had decreed the dioceses of Glendalough, Kildare, Ferns, Leighlin, and Ossory, to be suffragan to the metropolitan see of Dublin. On the death of Laurence, Hen. II. bestowed the archbishoprick on John Comyn, an Englishman, and granted him the temporalities with power to hold manor courts. The archbishops henceforward were lords of parliament in right of the barony of Coillach. On Comyn's consecration, Pope Lucius III. invested the see with sole supreme ecclesiastical authority within the province, whence originated the long continued controversy between the archbishops of Armagh and Dublin, which is fully detailed in the account of the former see. In the archiepiscopal investiture granted by Cardinal Paparo, the dioceses of Dublin and Glendalough are considered to be, strictly speaking, a single see; but in compliance with the wishes of the inhabitants of the mountain districts, which contained the latter, it was allowed to retain its name and a separate subordinate existence. But King John, in 1185, granted to Comyn the reversion of this bishoprick on its next avoidance, and the charter to this effect was confirmed by Matthew O'Heney, archbishop of Cashel, the Pope's legate, at a synod held in Dublin in 1192. But though this union was legally effected about the year 1214, the mountain clans, who were still unamenable to English law, long continued to appoint their own bishops of Glendalough. Henry de Loundres, the next archbishop, appears to have exercised the privileges of a peer of parliament in England, perhaps in right of the manor of Penkridge in Staffordshire, granted to the see by Hugh Hussey, founder of the Galtrim family in Ireland, and which long formed a peculiar of the diocese. The same prelate raised the collegiate church of St. Patrick, which had been erected by his predecessor, to the dignity of a cathedral, in consequence of which the diocese continues to have two cathedral churches. This circumstance afterwards gave rise to a violent contest between the two chapters as to the right of electing an archbishop. The dispute was terminated by an agreement that the archbishop should be consecrated and enthroned in Christ-Church, which, as being the more ancient, should have the precedency; and that the crozier, mitre, and ring of every archbishop, in whatever place he died, should be deposited in it, but that both churches should be cathedral and metropolitan. There have been always two archdeaconries in the united diocese of Dublin and Glendalough, whose jurisdictions may have been formerly coterminous with their respective sees; but the long and intimate union of these, and the little use made of the archidiaconal functions, render it nearly impossible to define their respective limits with any degree of accuracy.

The records of Christ-Church inform us that it owes its foundation to Sitric, the son of Anlaffe, king of Dublin, who, about the year 1038, gave to Donat, bishop of that see, a place where arches or vaults were built, on which to erect a church to the honour of the Blessed Trinity, to whom the building was accordingly dedicated. It was originally the conventual church of a monastery of secular canons unattached to any of the cenobitical orders, who were changed by Laurence O'Toole, in 1163, to canons regular of the order of Arras, a branch of the Augustinians. Sitric originally endowed this establishment with some small tracts on the sea coast of the present county of Dublin; and these possessions were greatly extended after the arrival of the English, when the successive augmentations of its revenue raised it to the rank of one of the most important priories in the island. Its privileges were confirmed by Henry II. and his successors;

its priors were spiritual peers of parliament. This convent had anciently an endowed cell in the diocese of Armagh.

In 1541, Henry VIII. changed the monastic establishment into a dean and chapter, confirming its ancient estates and immunities, and making Payneswick, the last prior, its first dean on the new foundation, which consisted of a dean, chanter, chancellor, treasurer, and six vicars choral. Archbishop Brown, in 1544, erected in this church the three prebends of St. Michael's, St. Michan's, and St. John's; and from the time of these alterations it has generally borne the name of Christ-Church, instead of that of the Holy Trinity. King Edward VI. added six priests and two choristers or singing-boys, to whom he assigned a pension of £45. 6. 8. per annum, payable out of the exchequer during pleasure. Queen Mary confirmed this pension, and granted it in perpetuity. James I. made some further alterations, and ordained that the archdeacon of Dublin should have a stall in the choir, and a voice and seat in the chapter in all capitular acts relating to the church. Welbore Ellis, the eleventh dean, installed in 1705, was subsequently made Bishop of Kildare, from which period the deanery has continued to be held in commendam with that bishoprick. The gross annual revenue of the deanery, on an average of three years ending Dec. 31st, 1831, was £5314. 5. 11½. The cathedral establishment consists at present, therefore, of the dean (who is the Bishop of Kildare, and is guardian of the temporalities of the see during its vacancy on the death or avoidance of the archbishop), chanter, chancellor, treasurer, archdeacon, and the three above-named prebendaries, under whom are six vicars choral, six stipendiaries or choirmen, and six singing boys and a registrar. The advowsons of the Dean and Chapter are (besides the three prebends already mentioned) the rectories of St. Mary, St. Paul, and St. Thomas, and the vicarage of Balscaddan, all in Dublin diocese; the alternate presentation to the rectory of St. George, Dublin, and the fourth turn to the union of Baronstown, in the county of Louth. For the repairs of the building and the payment of the inferior officers there is an economy fund, amounting on an average of three years ending 31st of Dec., 1831, to £2386. 8. 6. per ann., arising mostly from rents, tithes, and the dividends on about £10,000 funded property, including also the above-named pension.

The *Ecclesiastical province of Dublin,* over which the Archbishop presides, comprehends the dioceses of Dublin and Glendalough, Kildare,

Ossory, Ferns, and Leighlin. It is entirely included in the civil province of Leinster, and is estimated to comprise an area of 1,827,250 acres. Under the Church Temporalities' Act (3rd and 4th of Wm. IV., c. 37), on the next vacancy in the bishoprick of Kildare, that see is to be permanently united with Dublin and Glendalough; and in like manner the bishoprick of Ossory is to be permanently united with Ferns and Leighlin. The act also provides that, on the next avoidance of the see of Cashel, that archbishoprick is to be reduced to the rank of a bishoprick, and, together, with all its dependent sees, is to be suffragan to the Archbishop of Dublin, whose jurisdiction will then extend over the whole of Munster, the greater part of Leinster, and part of Galway in Connaught.

The *Diocese of Dublin and Glendalough* extends over all the county of Dublin, together with parts of Queen's county, Wicklow, Kildare, and Wexford; and contains an estimated area of 477,950 acres, of which 142,050 are in Dublin, 600 in Queen's county, 257,400 in Wicklow, 75,000 in Kildare, and 2900 in Wexford. The lands belonging to the united sees amount to 34,040 statute acres, of which 23,926 are profitable land; and the gross income, on an average of three years ending Dec. 31st, 1831, was £9230. 12. 9. It comprises 95 benefices, exclusively of chapelries; of these, 39 are unions of two or more parishes, and 56 are single parishes or parts of parishes; 11 of them are in the gift of the Crown, 39 in lay and corporation patronage, 5 in joint or alternate presentation, and the remainder in the patronage of the Archbishop, or incumbents. The parishes or districts are 180: there are 124 churches, and 9 other buildings in which divine worship is performed, and 50 glebe-houses. The diocesan school is endowed with 10 acres of land and £100 late currency for the master.

In the R. C. divisions the Archbishop of Dublin is primate of Ireland, and his three suffragan bishops are those of Kildare and Leighlin, Ossory, and Ferns: he is styled only Archbishop of Dublin, and not of Dublin and Glendalough, as in the Established Church. The R. C. diocese of Dublin comprises 48 parochial districts, of which 9 are in the city; and contains 121 chapels, served by 153 clergymen, 48 of whom are parish priests and 105 coadjutors or curates. The Archbishop's parish is St. Mary's, in which is the R. C. cathedral, called the Metropolitan Church, or Church of the Conception. The chapter consists of the same number and denomination of officers as the chapter of St. Patrick's Cathedral, but the dean and precentor are styled vicars general.

The *Cathedral of Christ-Church* is a long cruciform building, composed of a nave with a north aisle, transepts, and choir, with a central tower. The southern transept, measuring ninety feet by twenty-five, is entered by a Norman doorway in good preservation: the tower is a low massive pile, terminating in a pointed roof. The whole of the building has recently been repaired and several improvements made, at an expense of upwards of £8000 from the economy fund. The choir is separated from the nave by an elegant skreen, above which is the organ gallery, and decorated with a noble eastern window of stained glass, representing the armorial bearings of the members of the chapter, and having its lower part ornamented with an enriched border of openwork above the altar. The ceiling is intersected with quadrangular mouldings, with heavy bosses at the points of intersection serving to conceal a deviation from the straight line of direction between the entrance and the altar window, which is an irremediable defect in the original construction: a handsome border of tracery work goes round the walls. There are several remarkable monuments, the greater number of which are placed against the blank south wall of the nave. Among them are one of Strongbow, and of his wife Eva, or of his son, mutilated by the fall of the roof, and placed in its present situation by the Lord-Deputy Sidney, in 1570; a very beautiful monument of Thomas Prior, an early and zealous promoter of the Dublin Society; one of Lord Chancellor Bowes; another of Lord Chancellor Lifford and a fourth of Robert, Earl of Kildare, who died in 1743; besides those of several successive bishops of Kildare. A very fine monument has been lately erected to the memory of Nathaniel Sneyd, Esq., who was shot by a lunatic while walking in Westmoreland-street. Various eminent prelates of the see of Dublin have been interred within the walls of this church.

ST. PATRICK'S.

John Comyn, archbishop of Dublin, having erected a collegiate church for 13 prebendaries, in the southern suburbs of the city, on the site of an ancient parochial church, said to have been founded by St. Patrick in 448, dedicated it to God, the Blessed Virgin, and St. Patrick, and endowed it amply. Henry de Loundres, his successor, raised it to the dignity of a cathedral, consisting of a dean, precentor, chancellor, and treasurer, with thirteen prebendaries, increased its temporalities, and authorised the members to hear all pleas of their parishioners in their prebendal and economy churches. From a taxation in 1227 the number of prebendaries appears to have been increased to 22, three of whom were added by Bishop Ferings. The controversy which arose between this cathedral and that of Christ-Church, as to the right of electing the archbishop, has been noticed in the account of the latter cathedral. Among other privileges granted to the canons of this church by Henry VIII., was a dispensation from parochial residence on any other benefice, on condition of maintaining hospitality in the cathedral, but the establishment was soon after dissolved by the same monarch in 1546, together with the monastic institutions. Edward VI. disposed of the church and its appendages for a parish church, a seat for the courts of justice, a grammar school or literary college, and an hospital; the deanery was assigned for the archbishop's residence, and the lord-deputy took possession of the archiepiscopal palace; but this arrangement was revoked by Queen Mary, who at the beginning of her reign restored the cathedral to all its former privileges and possessions, by a charter commonly called the Charter of Restitution.

At present the chapter consists of a dean, precentor, chancellor, treasurer, the archdeacons of Dublin and Glendalough, and the prebendaries of Cullen, Swords, Kilmactalway, Yago, St. Audeon's, Clonmethan, Wicklow, Timothan, Mallahidart, Castleknock, Tipper, Tassagard, Dunlavan, Maynooth, Howth, Rathmichael, Monmohenock, Stagonil, Tipperkevin, and Donoughmore in Omaile. The dignity of dean has always been elective in the chapter, on the congé d'elire of the archbishop, except in cases of the promotion of the former dean to a bishoprick, the vacancy of the archiepiscopal see, or the neglect of the chapter, in which cases the appointment belongs of right to the Crown. The powers of the chapter in this regard were twice infringed upon, but they have been restored by their perseverance. By the original charter and the statute of the 14th of Edw. IV., the dean was constituted the immediate ordinary and prelate of the church of St. Patrick, and exercises episcopal jurisdiction throughout the liberties and economy thereof: he has a spiritual court in which his official or commissary, and a temporal court in which his seneschal general presides; and grants marriage licences, probate of wills, &c. The gross yearly revenue of the deanery, on an average of three years ending Dec. 31st, 1831, amounted to £1997. 8. 1. By the Church Temporalities Act the dean of St. Patrick's is to be dean of Christ-Church also; on the next avoidance of that deanery, he will be dean of Christ-Church without installation or induction. The dean and chapter have the right of presentation to the parishes of St. Bridget, St. Nicholas Within, and St. Nicholas Without. The dean, in right of his dignity, presents to the vicarage of Kilberry, and to the curacies of Malahide and Crumlin; the precentor and treasurer have the alternate presentation of the vicarage of Lusk, and the archdeacon of Dublin that of the perpetual cure of Booterstown, and three turns out of four of the united cures of Kilternan and Kilgobbin. The gross amount of the Economy fund, on an average of three years ending the 29th of Sept., 1831, was £2076. 2. 11. The archdeacon of Dublin had a stall in the chapter of the cathedral of Christ-Church, and a voice in the election of the archbishop, previously to his possessing the same in that of St. Patrick; but the archdeacon of Glendalough had neither of these rights until about the year 1267, when a new prebend was erected and annexed to the office. An additional corporation of six minor canons (since reduced to four) and six choristers was established in 1431 by Archbishop Talbot, on account of the devastations of the lands of the prebends having rendered them insufficient for the service of the church: the first in rank he styled sub-dean, and the second succentor: he endowed the entire body with the tithes of Swords, except such portions as were especially allotted to the prebendary and perpetual vicar; and vested the appointment and dismissal of the minor canons in the dean and chapter, and of the choristers in the precentor. This arrangement was sanctioned by Henry VI. and Pope Eugenius IV., who fixed the rank of the minor canons between that of prebendaries and vicars choral. In 1520 the minor canons and choristers were made a body corporate by charter. Archbishop Henry de Loundres, at the time he established the four dignitaries, instituted also the college of vicars choral, for whose common support he granted the church of Keneth (now Kinneagh), to which various endowments were subsequently added. The head of this college, styled sub-dean, or dean's vicar, enjoyed very considerable authority, possessing even a seat in the chapter, as also did the next vicar, called the sub-chanter, or chanter's vicar. They were incorporated by Richard II., and received their last charter from Charles I., who fixed their number at twelve, of whom five at least were to be priests, and the dean's vicar was to have a superior salary, and extensive power over the rest: the salary of the twelve vicars is directed by this charter to be apportioned by the dean and chapter, of whom the former enjoys the nomination to all vacancies; but out of the body thus appointed, the chanter, chancellor, and treasurer choose their respective vicars, as also does the Archdeacon of Dublin. The charter likewise secures to the Archbishop his ancient visitorial power forms the college into a body corporate; confirms their ancient possessions and binds them to pay a master of the choristers and two singing boys in addition to four choristers.

The Cathedral of St. Patrick is a venerable cruciform pile, 300 feet in length, of which the nave occupies 130 feet, the choir 90, and St. Mary's chapel 55: the transept extends 157 feet in length. The nave, the entrance to which is by a beautifully arched and deeply receding doorway, is 30 feet in width, with two aisles, each 14 feet wide, separated from it by octagonal pillars supporting plain Gothic arches of dissimilar arrangement but imposing appearance: it is lofty, and is lighted by a magnificent window at the western end, over the main entrance. In the south end of the transept is the chapter-house; the entire northern end is occupied by the parish church of St. Nicholas. The monuments in this cathedral are numerous: among the most remarkable in the nave are those of Archbishops Smith and Marsh, and that of the Earl of Cavan, who died in 1778; and on two pillars on the south side are tablets to the memory of Dean Swift and of Mrs. Johnson, the celebrated Stella. The oldest monument is a mutilated gravestone to the memory of Archbishop Tregury, who died in 1471. In the choir are many monuments: that of the first Earl of Cork, and several members of his family, which is placed on the right side of the altar, is an unsightly pile of black stone of antiquated sculpture, with ornaments of wood, painted and gilt, exhibiting sixteen unconnected figures, representing as many individuals of the family. Similar in style are the smaller monuments, on the opposite side, of Thomas Jones, Archbishop of Dublin, and Roger Jones, Viscount Ranelagh, near which is a plain slab to the memory of Duke Schomberg, with a very caustic inscription from the pen of Swift.

The foundation of a university in Dublin was at first attempted by John Leck, archbishop of the see, who in 1311 obtained a bull from Pope Clement V. for its foundation, but it was not accomplished till 1320, when his successor, Alexander de Bicknor, having procured a confirmation of the former bull from Pope John XXII., established a school of learning in St. Patrick's cathedral, for which he framed statutes, and over which he appointed William Rodiart, then dean of St. Patrick's, chancellor. Edw. III., in 1358, granted to the scholars his letters of protection; and in 1364 confirmed a grant of land from Lionel, Duke of Clarence, to found a divinity lecture in the university; but, for want of sufficient funds, the establishment gradually declined, though it appears to have lingered till the dissolution of the cathedral establishment, in the reign of Henry VIII. In 1568, a motion was made in the Irish parliament for its re-establishment, towards which Sir Henry Sidney, then lord-deputy, offered to settle on it lands of the yearly value of £20 and £100 in money. In 1584, Sir John Perrott, lord-deputy, had it in contemplation to re-establish the university by appropriating to its support the revenues of the cathedral of St. Patrick; but in this attempt he was strenuously opposed by Dr. Adam Loftus, Archbishop of Dublin, who made application to Queen Elizabeth and to the lord-treasurer of England for the protection of his cathedral; and also prevailed upon the mayor and citizens of Dublin to give the dissolved monastery of All Saints or All Hallows, on Hoggin (now College) Green, which had been granted to them by Henry VIII., as a site for the intended building. In 1591, letters patent were issued for the erection of the present establishment, to be styled "Collegium Sanctae et Individuae Trinitatis juxta Dublin, a Serenissima Reginâ Elizabethâ fundatum;" to be a corporate body; under the title of the Provost, Fellows, and Scholars of the College of the holy and Indivis-ible Trinity, with power to possess lands to the yearly value of £400, to have a common seal, and to be for ever exempt from local taxes. The provost and fellows were authorised by it to make laws, statutes, and ordinances for the government of the college, with liberty to select from those of Oxford or Cambridge, at their option; and to grant the degrees of bachelor, master, and doctor in all arts and faculties, pro-vided that all fellows should vacate their fellowships after seven years occupancy from the time of their taking the degree of master of arts. The first students were admitted in 1593. The funds of the college were so much diminished by the breaking out of the Tyrone rebellion, that the establishment must have been dissolved, had not the queen, in 1601, made the college a further grant of £200 per annum, till it should regain its possessions; and James I. granted it a revenue of £388. 15. English currency, and endowed it with many valuable lands and advowsons in Ulster; he also granted it the privilege of returning two representatives to parliament. The prosperity of the college was much retarded by internal dissensions, to which the election of the provosts frequently gave rise, and from the want of a more definite constitution to remedy this evil. In 1627 a new code of statutes was framed by Dr. Bedell, afterwards bishop of Kilmore; and in 1633 Archbishop Laud, then chancellor of the university, drew up a more complete code, founded on that of Bedell, which, together with a new charter, was enforced by royal authority, though not without considerable opposition. By this charter the power of electing the provost, and of enacting and repealing statutes, was vested in the Crown; the fellowships were distinguished into senior and junior, and made tenable for life; the extension of the number of fellows from three to sixteen, and of scholars from three to seventy, which had been previously made, was rendered permanent; and the government of the college was vested solely in the provost and the seven senior fellows, with power to enact by-laws, to be confirmed by the visitors. No subsequent alterations have taken place in the constitution of the college, except an increase in the number of junior fellows. By the Act of Settlement, the chief governor of Ireland, with the consent of the privy council, was empowered to erect another college to be of the university of Dublin, and to be called the King's College, and to raise out of the lands vested in the king by that act a sum not exceeding £2000 per ann. for its endowment. This clause has never been acted upon; and Trinity College differs in its constitution from those of Oxford and Cambridge, by combining in its own government the full privileges and powers of a university, the provost and senior fellows constituting the only senate or university convocation, and possessing the same power of electing officers and conferring degrees. A new fellowship was founded, in 1698, out of lands bequeathed to the college by Dr. John Richardson bishop of Ardagh, who had been a fellow. Three others were added in

1724, on the foundation of Erasmus Smith; and five additional fellow-ships were founded, to be endowed out of the increased revenues of the university, two of them in 1762, and three in 1808. The *Senate*, or *Congregation of the University*, by which degrees are publicly conferred, consists of all masters of arts and resident doctors in the three facul-ties, having their names on the college books, and who are liable to a fine for non-attendance. The *Caput Senatus Academici* consists of the vice-chancellor, the provost, or vice-provost, and by election of these, with the consent of the congregation, of the senior master non-regent, resident in the college: they have each a negative voice to prevent any grace for the conferring of a degree from being proposed to the sen-ate. Every grace must first be granted privately by the provost and sen-ior fellows, before it can be proposed to the caput or the senate. There are now two regular days for conferring degrees; namely, Shrove-Tues-day and the Tuesday nearest to the 8th of July, whether before or after. The Board, formed by the provost and senior fellows, meets generally every Saturday to transact all business relating to the internal manage-ment of the college.

The following are the principal university and college officers: the chancellor, at present his royal highness the Duke of Cumberland; the vice-chancellor, nominated by the chancellor, at present the Rt. Hon. and Most Rev. Lord J. G. De La Poer Beresford, Archbishop of Armagh, who may appoint a pro-vice-chancellor; the provost, who, except by dispensation from the Crown, must be a doctor or bach-elor in divinity, and thirty years of age, at present Bartholomew Lloyd, D. D.; the vice-provost, elected annually by the provost and senior fellows, but who is generally the senior of the senior fellows, and re-elected for many successive years; two proctors, chosen annu-ally, one from the senior and one from the junior fellows, the former being moderator in philosophy for the masters, and the latter for the bachelors of arts; a dean and a junior dean, chosen annually, the for-mer from the senior and the latter from the junior fellows, and whose duty it is to superintend the morals of the students, and enforce their attendance on college duties; a senior lecturer, chosen annually from the senior fellows, to superintend the attendance of the students at lectures and examinations, and to keep a record of their merits; a censor, created in 1728, whose office is to impose literary exercises in lieu of pecuniary fines upon such students as may have incurred academic censure; a librarian and junior librarian; a librarian of the lending library; a registrar; a registrar of chambers; a bursar and junior bursar; a registrar of the university electors, appointed in 1832 for keeping the register of persons qualified to vote for the university members of parliament; an auditor; six university preachers; and four morning lecturers.

The professorships are seventeen in number. The *Regius Professorship of Divinity,* originally founded in St. Patrick's cathedral, and held in 1607 by Dr. James Ussher, afterwards Archbishop of Armagh, was more amply endowed in 1674, by Charles II., out of lands given to the college by the Act of Settlement; in 1761 it was made a regius professorship by statute of George III.; and by another, in 1814, its endowment was augmented, and the office made tenable for life. The professor is elected by the provost and senior fellows from the fellows who are doctors of divinity, and vacates his fellowship on his appointment; he acts as moderator in disputations for degrees in divinity, has to preach four times in the year in defence of the Christian religion before the university, to read publicly during the year four prelections in divinity, besides lectures twice every week during term, and to hold an annual examination of the divinity students; he has four assistants. A lectureship in divinity was founded by Archbishop King in 1718, and was formerly elected to annually from the senior fellows; but this office has been recently separated from a fellowship, and is now held with one of the college livings: its duties also have been considerably increased, and more intimately connected with the education of such students as are preparing for holy orders. Archbishop King's lecturer has now five assistants. Students in divinity must attend with diligence the lectures and examinations of this lecturer and his assistants during the first year of their course, and during the second, the lectures of the Regius Professor and his assistants; without this two years' course of study, no student can obtain the certificates necessary for admission to holy orders. The *Regius Professorship of Greek,* previously held by a lecturer under the statute of Charles I., was founded in 1761 by statute of George III.; the professor is annually elected, and has two assistants. Two *Professorships of Modern Languages,* one for the French and German, and one for the Italian and Spanish, were formed in 1777 by a royal grant of £200 each per ann. The *Professorships of Hebrew, Oratory, History, Mathematics, and Natural Philosophy* were founded by act of parliament, and endowed by Erasmus Smith; the professors are chosen from among the fellows by the provost and senior fellows, with the approbation of the governors of Erasmus Smith's schools; a lectureship in Mathematics was founded in the middle of the 17th century by Arthur, Earl of Donegal, who endowed it with £10 per annum. The *Regius Professorship of Civil and Canon Law* was founded in 1668, by letters patent of Charles II., and endowed out of revenues granted to the university by the Act of Settlement; the professor acts also as moderator in all disputations for degrees in law. The *Regius Professorship of Feudal and English Law* was founded in 1761, by statute of George III.; the professor is elected by the provost and senior fellows, either for life or for a term of years; he must be a barrister of at least two years' standing, and, if a fellow of the college, may hold the appointment for life, resigning his fellowship. The *Regius Professorship of Physic* originated in a statute appointing one of the fellows of the university to devote himself to the study of physic; but since the Restoration, the regius professor of physic and the medical fellow have been regarded as distinct, and, except in two instances, have never been united in the same person. The *Professorships of Anatomy, Chymistry and Botany,* originally lectureships established about the year 1710, were founded by an act of the 25th of George III. for the establishment of a complete school of physic in Ireland, in conjunction with three other professorships on the foundation of Sir Patrick Dun's hospital; the professors are elected for seven years, at the end of which time they may be re-elected; they deliver periodical lectures in the theatre of the college. The *Lectureship in Natural History* was founded by the provost and senior fellows in 1816: the lecturer, who is also curator of the museum, delivers lectures on such parts of natural history, including geology and mineralogy, as the provost and senior fellows may appoint. The *Professorship of Astronomy* was founded in 1774, by Dr. Francis Andrews, provost of the college, who bequeathed £3000 for the erection of an observatory, and £250 per annum for the salary of such professor and assistants as the provost and senior fellows should appoint; a statute was obtained, in 1791, for regulating the duties of the professor, who is thereby constituted astronomer-royal for Ireland, and has an assistant, appointed by himself; he resides constantly in the observatory, from which he can never be absent more than 62 days in the year, without leave of the provost or vice-provost. The *Professorship of Political Economy* was founded in 1832, by Dr. Whately, Archbishop of Dublin, upon the principle of the Drummond professorship at Oxford; the professor, who must be at least a master of arts or bachelor in civil law, and a graduate of Dublin, Oxford, or Cambridge, is elected for five years: his duty is to deliver lectures in that science to such graduates and undergraduates as may be recommended to him by their tutors, and to print one lecture annually. A *Professorship of Moral Philosophy* has been recently founded, and annexed to one of the college livings.

The *members of the university on the foundation* at present consist of the provost, seven senior fellows, eighteen junior fellows, and seventy scholars: the junior fellows are elected as vacancies occur, on Trinity Monday; candidates must have taken at least the degree of bachelor of arts; they are examined on the four last days of the week preceding the election. Only three of the fellows are allowed to be members of lay professions, one of medicine, and two of law, without a dispensation from the Crown; all the rest must devote themselves to the church, and are bound by oath, on their marriage, to vacate their fellowships. The *benefices in the gift of the college* are 21 in number, and are situated in the dioceses of Armagh, Clogher, Down, Derry, Raphoe, and Kilmore; 17 of them became forfeited to the Crown by the rebellion of O'Nial, and were bestowed on the college by James I.; many of them are of considerable value, and on the death of an incumbent are offered to the clerical fellows in rotation. These benefices, by letters patent of James I., are Arboe, Ardtrea, Clogherney, Clonfeacle, Clonoe, and Desertcreight, in the diocese of Armagh; Aghalurcher, Cleenish, Derryvullen, and Enniskillen, in the diocese of Clogher; Killileagh, in the diocese of Down; Ardstraw, Cappagh, and Drumragh, in the diocese of Derry; Clondehorky, Clondevadock, Conwall, Kilmacrenan, Ramochy, and Tullyaghnish, in the diocese of Raphoe; and Killesandra, in the diocese of Kilmore. The *terms of the university* were formerly four in the year, and as altered by Archbishop Laud corresponded nearly to those of Oxford; but by a statute obtained in 1833 they were reduced to three only; Michaelmas, Hilary, and Trinity; but if Easter fall within the limits of Hilary or Trinity term, the term for that year is continued for an additional week. These terms may be kept by answering at examinations held for the purpose, at the beginning of each; but residence, either in the college or in the city, is indispensable for students in divinity, law, and medicine, as terms in these faculties can only be kept by regular attendance on the lectures of the university professors. Members of the university are not required to subscribe to the articles, or to attend the duties, of the church of England, if they profess to have conscientious objections, except on their obtaining a fellowship or scholarship, or on admission to a degree in divinity. By charter of James I. *the university returned two members to the Irish parliament* till the Union; after which time it returned only one member to the Imperial parliament, till the recent Reform act, since which it has returned two. The right of election, which was originally vested solely in the provost, fellows, and scholars, has, by the same act, been extended to all members of the age of 21 years, who had obtained, or should hereafter obtain, a fellowship, scholarship, or the degree of Master of Arts, and whose names should be on the college books: members thus qualified, who had removed their names from the books, were allowed six months to restore them, on paying a fee of £2, and such as continued their names, merely to qualify them to vote, pay annually to the college the sum of £1, or a composition of £5 in lieu of annual payment. The number of names restored under this provision was 3005, and at present the constituency amounts to 3135. The provost is the returning officer.

The *buildings of the university,* which, from their extent and magnificence, form one of the principal ornaments of the city, consist of three spacious quadrangles, erected chiefly after designs by Sir William Chambers. The principal front, which occupies the whole of the eastern side of College-green, is 380 feet long, built of Portland stone, and consists of a projecting centre, ornamented with four three-quarter Corinthian columns supporting an enriched cornice and pediment, under which is the principal entrance; and at each extremity of the façade is a projecting pile of square building, decorated with duplicated pilasters of the same order, between which is a noble Venetian window, enriched with festoons of flowers and fruit in high relief; and above the cornice, which extends along the whole of the front, rises an attic surmounted by a balustrade. The entrance is by an octangular vestibule, the ceiling of which is formed of groined arches: it leads into the first quadrangle, called Parliament-square, from its having been rebuilt chiefly by the munificence of Parliament, which granted at different times £40,000 for the purpose. This quadrangle, which is 316 feet in length and 212 in breadth, contains, besides apartments for the fellows and students, the chapel, the theatre for examinations, and the refectory. The *chapel*, which is on the north side, is ornamented in front by a handsome portico of four Corinthian columns, supporting a rich cornice surmounted by a pediment; the interior is 80 feet in length, exclusively of a semicircular recess of 20 feet radius, 40 feet broad, and 44 feet in height; the front of the organ gallery is richly ornamented with carved oak. The *theatre,* on the south side, has a front corresponding exactly with that of the chapel, and is of the same dimensions; the walls are decorated with pilasters of the Composite order, rising from a rustic basement; between the pilasters are whole-length portraits of Queen Elizabeth, the foundress, and of the following eminent persons educated in the college; Primate Ussher, Archbishop King, Bishop Berkeley, William Molyneux, Dean Swift, Dr. Baldwin, and John Foster, Speaker of the Irish House of Commons: there is also a fine monument of black and white marble and porphyry, executed at Rome by Hewetson, a native of Ireland, at an expense of £2000, erected to the memory of Dr. Baldwin, formerly provost, who died in 1758, and bequeathed £80,000 to the university. The *refectory* is a neat building, ornamented with four Ionic pilasters supporting a cornice and pediment over the entrance; a spacious ante-hall opens into the dining-hall, in which are portraits of Henry Flood, Lord Chief Justice Downes, Lord Avonmore, Hussey Burgh, Lord Kilwarden, Henry Grattan, the Prince of Wales (father of Geo. III.), Cox, Archbishop of Cashel, and Provost Baldwin. Over the ante-hall an elegant apartment has been recently fitted up for the *Philosophy school,* and furnished with a valuable collection of philosophical and astronomical instruments; and in it are delivered the public lectures of the professors of natural philosophy and astronomy. The second quadrangle, called the *Library-square,* is 265 feet in length and 214 feet in breadth. Three sides of it are occupied by uniform ranges of brick building, containing apartments for the students; these are now the oldest buildings in the college and are fast verging to decay. The fourth side is formed by the *library,* a very fine building of granite, the basement story of which forms a piazza extending the whole length of the square, above which are two stories surmounted by an enriched entablature and crowned with a balustrade. It consists of a centre and two pavilions at the extremities: in the western pavilion are the grand staircase, the Law school, and the librarian's apartment; from the landing-place large folding doors open into the library, a magnificent gallery, 210 feet in length, 41 feet in breadth, and 40 feet high; between the windows on both sides are partitions of oak projecting at right angles from the side walls, and forming recesses in which the books are arranged; the partitions terminate in fluted Corinthian columns of carved oak, supporting a broad cornice, surmounted by a balustrade of oak richly carved, and forming a handsome front to a gallery which is continued round the whole of the room. From the gallery rises a series of Corinthian pilasters between a range of upper windows, supporting a broad entablature and cornice; at the bases of the lower range of pilasters are pedestals supporting busts, finely executed in white marble, of the most eminent of the ancient and modern philosophers, poets, orators, and men of learning, including several distinguished members of the university. At the extremity of this room is an apartment, in a transverse direction, 52 feet in length, fitted up in similar style, and containing the Fagel library, over which, and communicating with the gallery, is the apartment for MSS., containing records illustrative of Irish and English history of great value, works in the Greek, Arabic, and Persian languages, and some richly illuminated bibles and missals: the magnificent collection comprises upwards of 100,000 volumes. To the north of the Library-square is the third quadrangle, of modern structure, but with few pretensions to architectural elegance. It is wholly appropriated to chambers for the students, which occupy two of its sides, the other two being formed by the rear of the northern range of the Library-square and by one side of the dining-hall. A temporary building near its centre contains the great bell, formerly suspended in a steeple which made part of the ancient chapel of the college; it was intended by the original design of the first or principal quadrangle to be erected in a dome over the gateway. The old chapel and belfrey occupied the vacant space between the first and second quadrangles. An additional square, to contain suites of apartments for students, is laid out and the buildings of one side of it commenced, eastward of the Library-square, part of which is to be taken down when the new range of buildings is finished. The *University Museum*, a handsome apartment 60 feet long and 40 feet wide, is immediately over the vestibule of the entrance from College Green; it comprises, under the superintendence of a curator, several collections of minerals, of which there are more than 9000 specimens. The

131

Printing-office, founded by Dr. Stearne, Bishop of Clogher, is a handsome structure with an elegant portico of the Doric order, and is situated on the east of the Library-square. To the south of the library is a fine garden for the fellows; and to the east of the College buildings is the Park, comprising about 120 acres, planted and tastefully laid out for the use of the students. Beyond the park are the *Chymical Laboratory* and the *School of Anatomy:* this range of building, which is 115 feet in length and 50 feet in breadth, contains a chymical laboratory and lecture-room, with apartments for the professor, a dissecting-room extending the whole length of the building, and an anatomical lecture-room, 30 feet square; an anatomical museum, 30 feet long and 28 feet wide, in which was a valuable collection of preparations of human, comparative and morbid anatomy, the largest and by much the most valuable part of which, being the private collection of Dr. Macartney, the present professor, has been sold by him to the university of Cambridge. The *Provost's house,* a spacious and handsome edifice, is to the south of the west front of the university, and is skreened from Grafton-street by a high wall with a massive gateway in the centre. The *College Botanic Gardens* are situated in the south-eastern extremity of the city, near Ball's bridge, and comprised originally about four acres, to which two more have been lately added; they are enclosed towards the public road into the city by a dwarf wall of granite surmounted by a very high iron palisade, were first laid out in 1807, and contain an extensive collection of plants well arranged and kept in excellent order. The *College Observatory* is situated on Dunsink-hill, in Castleknock parish, about 4 miles to the north-west of the city. The building fronts to the east, and consists of a centre and two receding wings, the former surmounted by a dome which covers the equatorial room, and is moveable, having an aperture two feet six inches wide, which can be directed to any part of the horizon; around the dome is a platform, which commands an extensive and varied prospect. The first professor was Dr. Ussher, senior fellow of Dublin college, under whose direction the building was erected, and who was succeeded, on his death in 1792, by the late learned and ingenious Dr. Brinkley, afterwards Bishop of Cloyne; after whose death, in 1835, the present astronomer-royal of Ireland, Sir William Rowan Hamilton, was appointed.

The Metropolitan parishes are all in the diocese of Dublin
St. Andrew's was formerly united to St. Werburgh's, but the union having been dissolved in 1660, it was by act of parliament erected into a
separate parish, and in 1707 the present parish of St. Mark was by
another act formed out of it. It contains 7870 inhabitants: the number
of houses valued at £5 and upwards is 731, the total annual value
being £46,022. The rectory, the annual income of which is £346. 8.
3½ forms the corps of the precentorship of St. Patrick's cathedral: the
vicarage is in the gift of the Lord-Chancellor, the Archbishop of
Dublin, the three Chief Judges, and the Master of the Rolls; the
amount of minister's money is: £529. 15. 1. The church, situated in St.
Andrew's street, opposite Church-lane, was commenced in 1793, and
completed in 1807, at an expense of £22,000. It is of elliptical form,
80 feet by 60, whence it has acquired the popular name of the Round
Church: over the principal entrance, which is at the extremity of the
lesser axis of the ellipsis, is a statue of St. Andrew bearing his cross; and
at the opposite end is the communion table, reading desk, pulpit, and
organ loft, with galleries for children on each side of it. The parochial
school for boys and girls is supported by an annual sermon and the
rent of the lands of Phrompstown. An alms-house for 28 widows,
founded in 1726 by Dr. Travers, is supported by the weekly collections
in the church.

    St. Anne's parish was formed out of the united parishes of St.
Stephen, St. Peter, and St. Bride, and made a separate parish in 1707.
It contains 8363 inhabitants; the number of houses valued at £5 and
upwards is 785, the total annual value being £56,812. 10. The living
is a vicarage, in the patronage of the Archbishop of Dublin; the amount
of minister's money is £588. 18. 5. The church, situated in Dawson-
street, opposite Anne-street, was designed from a church in Rome, but
remains unfinished; the front consists of a portal with Doric half
columns and smaller side entrances surmounted by ornamented windows, above which the gable of the building is seen. The interior is
spacious and handsome; the galleries, which surround it on three sides,
are supported by Ionic pillars of carved oak: it was thoroughly repaired
in 1835, towards which the Ecelesiastical Commissioners granted
£736.5.6. There is a parochial school for boys, who are clothed, fed,

educated, and apprenticed; also one for girls, an infants' school, and the model school of the Kildare-place Society. An alms house for widows is supported by the Sunday collections. The remains of the celebrated authoress, Mrs. Hemans, were deposited in the vault beneath the church in 1835. Judge Downes was also buried in this church.

St. Audeon's, or *Owen's,* was originally a chapel dedicated to the Blessed Virgin and enlarged by the family of Fitz-Eustace of Portlester; afterwards it was given as a parish church to the priory of Grace Dieu by John Comyn; but in 1467 it was made a prebend with cure of souls in the cathedral of St. Patrick, by Archbishop Tregury. The parish contains 4599 inhabitants, and 426 houses valued at £5 and upwards, the total annual value being; £19,399. The rectory or prebend is of the annual value of £243. 1. 4., and the minister's money amounts to £220. 12. 11. The present church consists only of the western end of the ancient edifice, which comprised a nave and collateral aisle, at the end of which is a modern steeple with a ring of bells; the rest of it is now in ruins. The eastern extremity still presents a fine specimen of the pointed style, and there are many curious old monuments, among which is one of Lord Portlester and his lady, erected in 1455: it is the burial-place of several ancient families. The Ecclesiastical Commissioners have granted £162. 0. 11. for the repairs of this church. There is a parochial school for boys, who are clothed, partly dieted, and apprenticed; also a school for girls, who are partly clothed; an infants' school, a Sunday school, and a female orphan school.

St. Bridget's or *St. Bride's* parish was formed out of those of St. Bride, St. Stephen, and St. Michael de la Pole, and after having belonged to Christ-Church was annexed to St. Patrick's in 1186. It contains 12,543 inhabitants; the number of houses valued at £5 and upwards is 732, and the total annual value is £23,377. 10. The living is a perpetual curacy, in the patronage of the Dean and Chapter of St. Patrick's; the minister's money amounts to £286. 4. I., and the gross income is £405. 13. 10. The church, a very plain building, situated in the street to which it gives name, was erected in 1684: it was repaired in 1827 at an expense of between £300 and £400, by parish assessment; and the Ecclesiastical Commissioners have since granted £158. 5. 9. for its further repair. Among the monuments are those of Mr. and Mrs. Pleasants, distinguished for their munificent charitable donations and bequests. The Episcopal chapel of the Molyneux Asylum, in Peter-street, is in this parish. There is a parochial boarding school for boys, a parochial day school, a boarding school for orphans, a day and an infants' school, and a Sunday school. The school in Stephen-street is supported by the interest of a legacy of £3900 from Ralph Macklin, Esq. Two almshouses for 20 widows and 12 old men are maintained by a bequest of Mr. Pleasants; and several large legacies have been bequeathed to the parish. There is a chalybeate spa near the church.

St. Catherine's anciently formed part of the parish of St. James, but was separated from it by an act of parliament in 1710. It contains 23,237 inhabitants, and 1264 houses of the value of £5 and upwards, the total annual value being £31,921. The living is a vicarage, in the patronage of the Earl of Meath; the minister's money amounts to £395. 3. 10. The church, which had been a chapel to St. Thomas the Martyr, was rebuilt in its present form in 1769: it is situated on the south side of Thomas-street, and is built of mountain granite, in the Doric style: four semi-columns, with their entablature, enriched by triglyphs, support a noble pediment in the centre, and on each side the entablature is continued the entire length, and supported at each extremity by coupled pilasters: above the entablature, at each side of the pediment, is a stone balustrade. Between the centre columns is a handsome Ionic arched door, and the other intermediate spaces are occupied by a double range of windows. The interior is elegantly simple: eight Ionic columns support the galleries, above which the same number of Corinthian pilasters rise to the roof. At the west end of the building is an unfinished belfry. The Ecclesiastical Commissioners have granted £126 for its repair. In the interior is a tablet to the memory of Dr. Whitelaw, the historian of Dublin, who was 25 years vicar of this parish, and died in 1813; and another to that of William Mylne, engineer, who constructed the waterworks of Dublin: underneath is the family vault of the Earl of Meath. A free Episcopal church has been opened in Swift's-alley, in a building purchased from the Baptist society in 1835, and consecrated by the archbishop: it is under the management of eight trustees, one-half of whom must be clergymen of the Established Church. Another is in progress at Harold Cross, in this parish. There are a parochial boarding school for girls, a parochial day school for boys and girls, a school on Erasmus Smith's foundation, three national schools, an evening school, an infants' school, and two Sunday schools. There are two almshouses for widows, one supported by the parish and the other by a member of the La Touche family.

St. George's parish originally formed part of that of St. Mary, and though not strictly within the liberties of the city, it has been included in the new electoral boundary under the Reform act. It contains 14,692 inhabitants, and 1261 houses valued at £5 and upwards, the total annual value being £63,900. The living is a rectory, in the alternate patronage of the Dean and Chapter of Christ-Church and the representatives of the late Lord Blessington; the minister's money amounts to £628. 5. 9., and the gross income is £800. The church, erected in 1802 in Hardwicke-place, after a design by F. Johnston, and at an expense of £90,000, presents a front consisting of a central projecting portico of four fluted Doric columns resting on an elevated platform supporting a bold entablature (the frieze and cornice of which are carried entirely round the building) surmounted by a triangular pediment over which rises the steeple of four ornamented stories, terminating in a light and graceful spire tapering to a height of 200 feet from the ground. The interior is fitted up in a chaste and elegant style, and a projecting building at the east end contains the vestry-room and parish school. The Ecclesiastical Commissioners have granted £1512. 12. 5. for its repair. There are three other Episcopal places of worship: St. George's chapel, commonly called Little St. George's, in Lower Temple-street, was founded by an endowment, by Archbishop King, of £49 per ann., out of two houses in Great Britain-street, the property of Sir John Eccles, to support a lecturer; it consists of a plain building with a square tower, surrounded by a cemetery, and is a donative, in the gift of A. Eccles, Esq. The free church in Great Charles-street was originally a Methodist place of worship, and was purchased, about 1826, for its present purpose, and consecrated by the Archbishop of Dublin, in whom the appointment of the minister is vested; it is a plain neat structure. The Episcopal chapel of the female penitentiary, on the north circular road, is the third. There are three parochial schools, a boarding school for girls, a day school for both sexes, and an infants' school, also a day school for both sexes endowed with a bequest by Miss Kellett.

Grangegorman parish, situated partly within the new electoral boundary, north of the city, and partly in the county of Dublin, was formed out of those parts of the parishes of St. Michan, St. Paul, and

St. George, which were in the manor of Grangegorman. It contains 7382 inhabitants, and 472 houses valued at £5 and upwards, the total annual value being £6102. The living is a perpetual curacy, in the patronage of the Prebendaries and Vicars choral of the cathedral of Christ-Church. The church was erected by a grant from the Board of First Fruits, in 1830. Within the parish are the House of Industry, the Richmond Penitentiary, the Lunatic Asylum for the district of Dublin, and the female orphan school, to the last-named of which an Episcopal chapel is attached. There are two day schools for both sexes, one of which is attached to the House of Industry, a female orphan school, and a day and infants' school, connected with the R. C. chapel. The total number of pupils in the day schools is 493.

St. James's parish contains 13,197 inhabitants, and 625 houses valued at £5 and upwards, the total annual value being £13,176. The living is a vicarage, in the patronage of the Earl of Meath; the minister's money amounts to £109. 1. 4. The church is a low and very plain building; owing to the small accommodation it affords to the numerous parishioners, it is the intention of the Ecclesiastical Commissioners to erect a new one. The cemetery is very large and situated on the north side of a hill sloping down towards the river. The episcopal chapels of the Royal and Foundling Hospitals are in this parish; and there is a chapel of ease at Golden-Bridge, chiefly for the use of Richmond barracks. There are parochial schools for boys and girls, three national schools, and an infants' school.

St. John's parish contains 4351 inhabitants, and 291 houses valued at £5 and upwards, the total annual value being £9846.10. It was erected into a prebend with cure of souls in the cathedral of Christ-Church. in 1554, and is in the gift of the Dean and Chapter; the minister's money amounts to £118. 9. 3., and the gross income of the prebendary is £398. 2. 8. The church, situated at the corner of John's-lane, was rebuilt in 1773: it presents to Fishamble-street a neat front adorned with four Doric columns supporting a pediment, and approached by a broad flight of steps: in this front is the chief entrance to the body of the church and one to each of the galleries. In 1836 it underwent a thorough repair, for which a grant of £879. 9. 7. was wade by the Ecclesiastical Commissioners. There are parochial schools for boys and girls, two national schools for boys and girls, a Sunday school, and an evening school for adult males.

St. Luke's parish contains 6605 inhabitants, and 337 houses valued at £5 and upwards, the total annual value being £7654. The living is a vicarage, in the diocese of Dublin, and in the patronage of the Dean and Chapter of Christ-Church; the minister's money is £92.7. 8., and the gross income £171. 17. 4. The church, erected in 1708, when the parish, which had been a part of that of St. Nicholas, was formed, is approached by an avenue of trees from the Coombe, and is a plain structure entered by a large doorway between rusticated columns: it was re-roofed in 1835 by a grant of £1029. 13. 6. from the Ecclesiastical Commissioners. There are parochial schools for boys and girls, in which some of the children are clothed and some dieted; also an infants' school and a national school, all supported by charity sermons and some small bequests.

St. Mark's parish was severed from that of St. Andrew by act of parliament in 1707: it contains 14,811 inhabitants, and 1076 houses valued at £5 and upwards, the total annual value being £38,592. The living is a vicarage, in the joint patronage of the Lord-Chancellor, the Archbishop of Dublin, the three Chief Judges, and the Master of the Rolls; the minister's money is £330. 3. 3. The church is situated in Mark-street, adjacent to Brunswick-street: it was built in 1729, and is a large building perfectly plain; the interior is very neat and commodious. The Ecclesiastical Commissioners have granted £165. 13. 5. for repairing it. The Mariners' church, built in Forbes-street in 1832, and the Episcopal chapel belonging to the marine school, are in this parish; as locally is Trinity College, which is extra-parochial. There are parochial, day, and female schools, one on the foundation of Erasmus Smith, the marine school for sailors' orphans, a female orphan school, and an infants' school.

St. Mary's, orginally part of St. Michan's parish, and separated from it in 1697, contains 25,305 inhabitants, and 2018 houses valued at £5 and upwards, the total annual value being £91,895. The living is a rectory, in the gift of the Dean and Chapter of Christ-Church: the minister's money amounts to £974. 16. 6., and the gross income is £1127. The church is a large building, in Stafford-street, possessing little architectural beauty. Its chief entrance is a large gate with Ionic columns on each side, surmounted by a square belfry. In the interior are many monumental tablets, among the more remarkable of which is one to the memory of Edw. Tennison, Bishop of Ossory; one to that of Dr. Robt.

Law; one to that of Mr. Wm. Watson, founder of the Society for Discountenancing Vice; and one lately erected to the Hon. T. B. Vandeleur,
third justice of the King's Bench, Ireland. In the crowded cemetery are
the tombs of Dr. Marlay, Bishop of Waterford, and uncle to the late
Henry Grattan; Mrs. Mercer, the foundress of Mercer's Hospital; and
Mr. Simpson, the founder of Simpson's Hospital. The Board of First
Fruits, in 1831, granted a loan of £1615 for the repair of the church,
and in 1836 the Ecclesiastical Commissioners granted £205. 3. 11. for
the same purpose. St. Mary's chapel of ease, built on a plot of ground
in Mountjoy-street, presented to the parish by the Earl of Mountjoy, is
a very elegant specimen of the modern Gothic, from a design of Mr.
Semple; it has a light tapering spire surrounded by minarets of similar
shape. It was opened in 1830 as a free church, and has lately received a
grant of £445. 13. 0. for its repair from the Ecclesiastical Commissioners. The Episcopal chapel of the Lying-in Hospital and the Bethesda
Episcopal chapel are in this parish; the latter was erected in 1786, at the
sole expense of Wm. Smyth, Esq., nephew of the Archbishop of that
name: he appointed two clergymen to officiate, and, in 1787, annexed
to it an asylum for female orphans, in which about 24 children are
entirely supported. A penitentiary adjoins it, which was opened in 1794
for the reception of females discharged from the Lock Hospital. Here
are parochial schools for boys and girls, who are totally provided for; a
free school for both sexes, an infants' school, and schools for boys and
girls in connection with the Scots' Church. A female almshouse in
Denmark-street was founded by Tristram Fostrick, Esq., in 1789. Mrs.
Mary Damer, in 1753, bequeathed £1765, and Richard Cave, Esq., in
1830, £1600 to the parish for charitable uses.

St. Michael's parish was created a prebend with cure of souls in
Christ-Church cathedral, in 1554, by Archbishop Browne: it contains
2288 inhabitants, and 112 houses valued at £5 and upwards, the total
annual value being £3670. The rectory or prebend is in the gift of the
Dean and Chapter of Christ-Church; the minister's money amounts
to £50. 5. 11., and the gross income is £250. 8. The church stands at
the corner of Michael's-hill and High-street, and is a small building in
the pointed style of architecture. The tower, which is without a spire,
is ancient and of large dimensions, very disproportionate to the small
structure of which it now forms the vestibule. There is a parochial
school; 20 of the children are clothed.

St. Michan's parish was also erected into a prebend of Christ-Church, with cure of souls, by Archbishop Browne, in 1554, and comprehended the whole of Dublin north of the Liffey until 1697, when the parishes of St. Mary and St. Paul were severed from it. It contains 23,918 inhabitants, and 1464 houses valued at £5 and upwards, the total annual value being £43,568. 10. The prebend is in the patronage of the Dean and Chapter of Christ-Church; the minister's money is £488. 15. 7., and the gross income, £719. 7. 6. The church, situated in Church-street, is one of the oldest in the city, being supposed to have been founded by the Ostmen previously to the erection of Christ-Church and to have been originally the cathedral church of the diocese. It is a very spacious cruciform structure, with a square tower, erected at a comparatively modern period, although the whole has an appearance of great antiquity. It was re-roofed and thoroughly repaired in 1828, at a cost of about £1500, defrayed by parish cess, since which time the Ecclesiastical Commissioners have granted £230. 19. 1. for its further repair. On one side of the communion table is an ancient figure of a bishop or an abbot; there is also a monumental tablet to the memory of the celebrated Dr. Lucas. There are a parochial school for girls, a day school for girls, and an infants' school, four day schools for boys, and two for girls, and a Sunday school.

St. Nicholas Within included also the parishes of St. Nicholas Without and St. Luke until 1707, when they were formed into separate parishes. It contains 1845 inhabitants, and 103 houses valued at £5 and upwards, the total annual value being £3929. 10. The living is a perpetual curacy, in the patronage of the Dean and Chapter of St. Patrick's; the minister's money is £3. 0. 7., and the gross income £125. The church, an unsightly edifice, situated in Nicholas-street, has been taken down and is to be rebuilt under the directions of the Ecclesiastical Commissioners, till which time divine service is performed in the school-room. There is a lectureship attached to it, which is maintained by the rent of lands in the county of Louth. There is a parochial school for 12 boys, who are clothed, educated, and apprenticed: it is supported by the rent of two houses, amounting to £36 per annum, and an annual charity sermon.

St. Nicholas Without, formed into a parish in 1707, contains 12,391 inhabitants, and 871 houses valued at £5 and upwards, the total annual value being £226.8, 10. 1. The living is a perpetual curacy, in the patronage of the Dean and Chapter of St. Patrick's; the minister's money is £207. 12. 6., and the gross income £264. 10. The church, which was dedicated to St. Myra, and occupied the north transept of St. Patrick's cathedral, having fallen into decay, has been restored, and still forms part of that building. The Ecclesiastical Commissioners have granted £432. 7. 7. for its repair. There are parochial schools for boys, girls, and infants, and two Sunday schools.

St. Paul's, which, previously to the year 1697, formed part of St. Michan's parish, contains 10,570 inhabitants, and 786 houses valued at £5 and upwards, the total annual value being £21,632. The living is a rectory, in the patronage of the Dean and Chapter of Christ-Church; the minister's money is £255. 4. 1., and the gross income £386. 9. 4. The church, situated in North King-street, was rebuilt in 1824, and is now a neat edifice in the Gothic style, with a small but elegant spire. The cemetery is the usual place of interment for the garrison of Dublin: it contains a monument to the memory of Lieut. Col. Lyde Brown, of the 21st Fusileers; a mural tablet to that of three privates of the same regiment, who were killed in the insurrection of 1803; and a mausoleum for the family of Col. Ormsby. The chapel of the King's or Blue-coat Hospital is in this parish. There are parochial schools for boys and girls, an infants' school, and a Sunday school. The late Lord Netterville bequeathed £9000 to this and the adjoining parish of St. Michan for a dispensary and hospital, which is also supported by subscription.

St. Peter's parish, erected by order of council in 1680, is the largest in the city, comprising the ancient parishes of St. Peter and St. Kevin, and a portion of that of St. Stephen: it contains 27,176 inhabitants, and 2260 houses valued at £5 and upwards, the total annual value being £124,865. 10. It is a vicarage, united to the rectories of Tawney, Rath-farnham, Donnybrook, and district of Booterstown, together forming the corps of the archdeaconry of Dublin, in the patronage of the Arch-bishop; the minister's money is £1086. 15. 4., and the gross annual income is £2768, out of which there are 12 curates to be paid. The church, situated in Aungier-street, is a very large unornamented build-ing, in the form of the letter T: the Ecclesiastical Commissioners have granted £735. 0. 6. for its repair. In the attached cemetery are interred the remains of many persons of rank; those of the celebrated John Fitzgibbon, Earl of Clare, lie here under a plain tombstone; Maturin, the poet, who was curate of the parish, is also buried here. There are within its limits three chapels of case, one in Kevin-street, one in Upper Mount-street, Merrion-square, and a third at Rathmines; and within the parish are Sandford Episcopal chapel at Cullenswood, and an Episcopal chapel in Upper Baggot-street. The church or chapel of *St. Kevin* is a plain edifice, in the form of the letter T, situated to the south of Kevin-street; it appears to have been erected on the site of an ancient chapel dedicated to St. Kevin. The chapel in Upper Mount-street, dedicated to *St. Stephen,* is an elegant structure. The portico is of the Ionic order; over the pediment rises the belfry tower, of octangular form, covered with a cupola, the apex of which is 100 feet high. The Episcopal church in Upper Baggot-street, with a female penitentiary attached, was erected in 1835 by subscription, at a cost of upwards of £6000: the exterior is plain, but the interior is exceedingly handsome; it will accommodate 1200, and has from 300 to 400 free seats: the appointment of the chaplain is in nine trustees. The Episcopal chapel of the Magdalen Asylum, in Leeson-street, is also in this parish. There are parochial schools for boys, girls, and infants; schools at Sandford chapel for boys, girls, and infants; a Methodist female orphan school; St. Stephen's male and female day school in Mount-street; Bride-street parochial female school; day schools at Hatch-street and Cuff-lane; two in Whitefriar-street; two at Rathmines and Miltown; two other infants' schools and five Sunday schools. There is also a parochial dispensary, and a loan fund established in 1813.

St. Thomas's parish was separated from St. Mary's, in 1749, by act of parliament: it contains 20,881 inhabitants, and 1373 houses valued at £5 and the total annual value being £65,537. 10. The living is a rectory, in the patronage of the Dean and Chapter of Christ-Church; the minister's money is £684. 12. 1. and the gross income £922. 1. 10. The church, erected in 1758, presents a front to Marlborough-street, opposite to Gloucester-street, composed of two pilasters and two three-quarter columns of the Composite order, supporting an entablature and enclosing ornamented niches, and, in the centre, a Corinthian doorway, with an angular pediment: on each side of this façade is a half-pediment, supported by a Corinthian pilaster at the extremity, and a half-pilaster in the return: an intended pediment over the centre has not been erected. The Ecclesiastical Commissioners have granted £915. 17. 9. for the improvement of the building. The

Episcopal chapel of the Feinaglian institution at Luxemburgh, for the use of the pupils, but open also to their friends, is in this parish. A parochial school for girls is supported by a bequest of £75. 1. 3. per ann. and voluntary contributions; there are also a day school for boys and girls, a national school, and a Sunday school. The buildings of the Board of National Education and a savings' bank are in this parish.

St. Werburgh's parish contains 3384 inhabitants, and 214 houses valued at £5 and upwards, the total annual value being £11,602. 10. It is a rectory, united to the rectory of Finglass and the chapelries of St. Margaret and Ward, together forming the corps of the chancellorship of the cathedral of St. Patrick, in the gift of the Archbishop; the minister's money is £200. 2., and the gross income £680. The church was erected in 1759. The front is composed of a basement story ornamented with six Ionic pilasters with an entablature, and a grand entrance of the same order. The second story, which is diminished, is adorned with four Corinthian pilasters, coupled, enclosing a large window, and supporting a pediment, above which rises a square tower of Composite architecture, terminating with urns placed at the angles. An elegant spire which formerly surmounted the whole was taken down in 1810, on account of its dangerous state; and, for the same reason, the entire tower was taken down in 1835. The Ecclesiastical Commissioners have granted £1140. 16. 11. for the restoration of the tower and the general repairs of the building. The Lord-Lieutenant of Ireland, attends here to qualify on his coming into office, the castle of Dublin being situated in the parish. The east window of stained glass is considered the handsomest in Dublin and cost about £600: the subject is the Presentation. In the interior are several neat monuments, and on the exterior, in the wall of the church, are some very ancient sculptured figures, evidently belonging to an older building. In the vaults are deposited the remains of Sir James Ware, the antiquary, Lord Edward Fitzgerald, and Edwin, the actor. The vice-regal chapel, Dublin Castle, is within the precincts of this parish. There is a parochial boarding school for girls, and parochial day schools for boys and girls, a day school for girls, and a Sunday school. James Southwell, Esq., in 1729, bequeathed £1250, the interest to be applied for various purposes: he also bequeathed £380 for a ring of bells, and a fund to place boys in the Blue-coat school.

ROMAN CATHOLIC PAROCHIAL DISTRICTS, PLACES OF WORSHIP, CONVENTS, AND CHARITIES CONNECTED THEREWITH.

The city is divided into nine R. C. parishes or ecclesiastical districts: St Mary's, St. Michan's, St. Paul's, St. Andrew's, St. Audeon's, St. Catherine's, St. James's, St. Michael's and John's, and St. Nicholas's: the first three are on the north side of the Liffey. The ecclesiastical duties are executed by nine parochial priests and 52 other officiating clergymen.

The parish of *St. Mary* is the mensal of the archbishop, and comprises the Protestant parish of St. Thomas, and the principal parts of those of St. Mary and St. George: the parochial duties are performed by the Archbishop, seven officiating clergymen, and one assistant. The chapel, a spacious and magnificent building, commenced in 1815 and not yet completed, is dedicated to the Blessed Virgin Mary, and is usually styled the Church of the Conception. The front to Marlborough-street will, when finished, consist of a portico of six fluted Doric columns, supporting an entablature ornamented with triglyphs, and surmounted by a pediment. The interior is divided into a nave and side aisles by two splendid colonnades; the west end forms a circular termination, under which is the principal altar of white marble, detached from the walls and enclosed by a circular railing; in the centre of each aisle is a quadrangular recess. The total expense of completing the structure is estimated at £50,000. Besides the above, there are the chapel of St. Francis Xavier, Upper Gardiner-street; a chapel belonging to the Dominican friary, Denmark-street; and a chapel belonging to the convent of Carmelite nuns, North William-street. The chapel of St. Francis Xavier is attended by the priest of the order of "Jesuits," established here in 1817: the inmates consist of a superior and five priests, who have a classical school in Hardwicke-street. The building is cruciform and of the ancient Ionic order, with a lofty portico in the centre; and at each side are receding wings forming vestibules, crowned with domes supported by columns of the Ionic order; the interior is highly decorated, and the organ, which is considered to be one of the finest in Ireland, was built for the great musical festival at Westminster. The chapel in Denmark-street, dedicated to St. Dominic, belongs to the order of Dominicans, consisting of a prior and five friars; in connection with this is St. Patrick's Juvenile Society. The chapel in North William-street belongs to the convent of the

order of Carmelites: the inmates consist of a superioress and a sisterhood of 15. The chapel is a neat building, in the later style of English
architecture; a school, in which 20 girls are educated, clothed, and
wholly provided for, is attached to the institution. The Sisters of Charity have an establishment in Upper Gardiner-street, consisting of a
superioress and a sisterhood of 14, who superintend the education of
200 girls. The principal establishment of the Christian Doctrine Con-
fraternity, consisting of a director and two assistants, is in North Rich-
mond-street, where they support a model school for the novices for
the other houses of the society; they also instruct 550 children in the
parochial chapel and 130 in Denmark-street, every Sunday. The con-
fraternity instruct children in all the other parochial and in most of
the friary chapels: the total number of children under their tuition
amounts to 987 males and 3942 females. There are two national
schools, one in Gloucester-place, and the other in King's Inns-street;
an almshouse in North William-street for twenty-three widows, which
is supported by subscription; and the Metropolitan Orphan Society, in
which 99 children are supported, chiefly by penny weekly subscriptions of the working classes. The Asylum for Female Penitents, founded
in 1833, affords shelter to 30 inmates; another in Mecklenburgh-street,
founded in the same year, supports 35; a third in Dominick-street supports 34, and there is another in Marlborough-street; in all of them the
penitents are employed in needlework, washing, and similar useful
occupations.

St. Michan's parish comprises parts of the Protestant parishes of St.
Mary, St. George, St. Michan, St. Paul, and Glasnevin. The duty is performed by a parish priest and six officiating clergymen. The chapel in
North Anne-street is a splendid edifice, built entirely of granite; it is in
the later English style, with three finely arched entrances in the front,
which terminate above in a sharply pointed gable, embattled and surmounted with a cross; the interior is richly ornamented with sculpture, and the ceiling is elaborately groined, the intersecting arches
springing from heads of saints finely sculptured; the altar is embellished
with paintings of the Virgin and Child, and of St. Francis, copied from
Guido. There is another chapel on George's-hill, belonging to the
convent of the Presentation order, the inmates of which, consisting of
a superioress and ten sisters, superintend a school, at which about 300
female children are instructed, 50 of whom are clothed, and from 16

to 20 are also boarded. The institution is chiefly supported by the profits of the work done by the children. The chapel, which is exceedingly neat, is open every morning. There is a day boys' school of about 300 pupils; also an establishment for 12 orphans who are totally provided for and when of a proper age apprenticed; the institution is supported by subscriptions. The Orphan Society of St. Vincent a Paulo was founded in 1826, in which 40 orphan children are wholly provided for, and 45 by the Society for Destitute Orphans under the tutelage of the Blessed Virgin Mary of Mount-Carmel. The Society of St. John the Evangelist, for promoting the exercise of spiritual and corporal works of mercy, is in North King-street, and has a good library in connection with it. In Paradise-row is the Josephian Orphan Society, in which 36 orphans are totally provided for; and in the same street is the House of Reception for aged females, containing 18 inmates.

St. Paul's parish comprises the Protestant parish of Grangegorman, the principal part of St. Paul's, and parts of St. Michan's and Glasnevin. The duty is performed by a parish priest and six officiating clergymen. The chapel on Arran-quay having been found to be too small, another, near the entrance of the old building, is now completed with the exception of the portico and steeple: the interior is richly ornamented; behind the altar is a painting in fresco, on which the light is thrown after the manner of the *"lumiére mystérieuse"* in some of the churches of Paris. The whole cost of the erection of the building will be about £10,000, which will be wholly defrayed by voluntary subscription. There is a chapel of ease at Phibsborough, a neat Gothic structure, but too small for the increasing congregation: beneath are male and female free school-rooms, and apartments for an orphan society, and over the sacristy a residence for the clergyman and a lending library belonging to a branch society of St. John the Evangelist. The chapel of St. Francis, in Church-street, belongs to the friary of the Capuchins, the community of which consists of a guardian and six friars. The chapel is a large plain building; the altars are adorned with paintings of the Crucifixion, the Virgin and Child, and St. Francis: a free school for boys is connected with it. There is a school in Queen-street, in which about 250 boys and 150 girls are instructed; also a national boys' and girls' school connected with the chapel at Phibsborough. The convent of the Sisters of Charity, in Stanhope-street, consists of a local superioress and a sisterhood of twenty, who support a house of refuge, in which 50 industrious young women of good character are sheltered; the institution derives much of its support from the work executed by the inmates. St. Stephen's Cholera Orphan Society was first established in 1828, as a general orphan institution, but in 1830, owing to the ravages of the cholera, it assumed its present name and character.

St. Andrew's parish comprises nearly the whole of the Protestant parishes of St. Andrew, St. Mark, and St. Anne, and part of that of St. Peter. The duty is performed by a parish priest and seven officiating clergymen. The chapel, in Westland-row, was commenced in 1832, and finished in 1837: its form is that of a Roman cross; the length being 160 feet, the transept 150, the breadth and height 50 each. The walls of the interior are in compartments formed by Grecian Doric pilasters. The great altar consists of four pillars of scagliola, supporting a pediment copied from the Lantern of Demosthenes at Athens. The tabernacle is in imitation of the triumphal arch of Titus in Rome, and is surmounted by a group in white Italian marble, by Hogan, representing the Ascension; on each side of the great altar are smaller altars of Egyptian marble; several good paintings have lately been brought from Rome, and hung up over and at the sides of the altar. The portico in front consists of two pillars and four pilasters in the Grecian Doric style, prolonged at each end by a parochial house, thus presenting a façade of 160 feet in length. The cost of erection, which is defrayed by subscription, amounted to £18,000. In Clarendon-street is the chapel of St. Teresa belonging to the order of the Discalced Carmelites, the inmates of which consist of a provincial, a prior, and six friars. It is a spacious building of plain exterior: in front of the altar is a fine statue of a Dead Christ in Italian marble, by Hogan. Attached to the convent is an almshouse for widows, and the Society of St. Joseph, for promoting the exercise of spiritual and corporal works of mercy. There is a parochial school attended by upwards of 3100 female children: it is in connection with the National Board of Education. Within the parish there are the following religious institutions; the House of Mercy, Baggot-street, the inmates of which consist of a superioress and a sisterhood of 15, who maintain a day school of about 300 children, visit the sick poor, and receive under their protection distressed women of good character; their house is a plain large building of three stories. In Stephen's-green East is St. Vincent's Hospital, containing 60 beds, and a dispensary, founded by the sisters of charity: a superioress and sisterhood of six preside over it. The Asylum for Female Penitents, in Townsend-street, is superintended by a superioress and a sisterhood of three, and affords shelter and the means of reformation to 41 penitents. The Andrean Orphans' Friend Society was revived in 1832, and supports 28 children by weekly penny subscriptions; the Orphan Society of St. John of the Cross is supported in like manner.

St. Audeon's, the smallest R. C. parish in the city, comprises the whole of the Protestant parish of the same name. The chapel, situated off Bridge-street, is in bad repair and too small for the congregation; a considerable sum has been already subscribed towards its re-erection. There is a male and female school in which 20 of each sex are clothed; also the Malachian Orphan Society for destitute children. John Power, Esq., in 1835, erected in Cook-street a building for 24 aged and destitute widows, at an expense of about £700; it is supported by subscriptions and an annual charity sermon.

St. Catherine's comprises nearly the whole of the Protestant parish of the same name. The duty is performed by a parish priest and seven officiating clergymen. The chapel was erected in Meath-street, in 1780: it is a very spacious octagon building of brick, with a gallery along five of its sides, the altar being in the centre of the other three. Near it is a school, erected in 1823 by subscription, and attended by upwards of 400 children of each sex: there are also Sunday schools. A chapel in John's-lane belongs to the Augustinian friary of St. John; the inmates consist of a prior and four friars. The chapel, a spacious structure, occupies part of the site of the priory of St. John the Baptist, which was founded in the year 1188 by A. Du Palmer; and in connection with it is a female orphan school, also an asylum for old and destitute men, in Rainsford-street. To this convent belonged the Rev. Wm. Gahan, author of many pious works.

St. James's parish comprises nearly the whole of the Protestant parish of the same name. The duty is performed by a parish priest, who is also chaplain to the county gaol of Kilmainham, and by four officiating clergymen. The chapel, which is situated at James-gate, is about to be taken down and a new building erected. There is a chapel at Dolphin's Barn for the accommodation of that populous district; and also a nunnery of the Carmelite order, consisting of a superioress and a sisterhood of 16, established in 1834, in the same neighbourhood, attached to which is a free school for girls. There is a National school for boys and girls; also St. James' and St. Joseph's Orphan Society, which maintains 50 children. The Catholic cemetery, Golden-Bridge described under that head, is in this parish.

St. Michael's and *St. John's* parish comprises the Protestant parishes of St. Michael, St. John, St. Nicholas Within, and St. Werburgh, and parts of those of St. Peter, St. Andrew, and St. Bride. The duty is performed by a parish priest and five officiating clergymen. The chapel, situated in Exchange-street and erected in 1815, has two fronts of hewn stone in the later English style: the exterior is of elegant design, and in the interior, which is richly embellished, are three altars; over each respectively are paintings of the Crucifixion, of St. John the Evangelist by Del Frate, and of St. Michael trampling on Satan, a copy from Guido; its fine organ, made by Lawless, cost £800. It contains a handsome monument to Dr. Betagh, a celebrated preacher, who died in 1811, and another to the Rev. Dr. Anglen; at one end are six confessionals of elegant design and beautiful workmanship. The chapel was erected between 1813 and 1816, at a cost of nearly £10,000, which was defrayed by subscription. Attached to it is a house for the residence of the clergymen, containing 20 spacious apartments with a corridor to each story; the cost of its erection was about £2000, and it was completed in the short space of two months and eight days. A chapel in Whitefriar-street belongs to the order of Calced Carmelites; the inmates are a provincial, a prior, and six friars, whose residence is in an adjoining house in Aungier-street. The chapel has its front to Whitefriar-street: the interior presents a beautiful architectural view; the right side has a range of large windows, and the left is ornamented with corresponding niches, filled with statues of eminent saints; the ceiling is coved and divided into rectangular compartments; its erection cost £4000. It stands on the site of a Carmelite church founded in 1274, upon land granted by Sir Robert Bagot. The remains of St. Valentinus, martyr, have been translated from Rome by order of Pope Gregory XVI., and are deposited in this chapel in a suitable vase. Another, which is a cruciform structure, situated on Merchants'-quay, belongs to the order of Franciscans; the inmates are a prior and six friars. It is dedicated to St. Francis of Assisium, but is more generally known by the name of Adam and Eve, from an ancient chapel of that name on the site of which the present building was erected. When finished it will exhibit the ceiling divided into enriched panels; the interior ornamented with pilasters, supporting an enriched cornice of granite, over which the windows are placed; there are three elegant and commodious galleries, capable of holding 1500 persons; the altar will be constructed in the most florid style of Corinthian architecture: an Ionic portico is to front the river. In Smock-alley are parochial schools for both sexes, in connection with the National Board of Education, at which 600 children attend; also an evening and Sunday school, and two orphan schools, one for boys and the other for girls, 20 of each, who are wholly provided for and apprenticed; all these are supported by subscription, a grant from the National Board an annual sermon, and the profits of an annual bazaar. A society was founded in Smock-alley in 1817, called "The Society of St. John the Evangelist," for administering to the spiritual and temporal wants of the sick, and for the suppressing abuses at wakes; a library is in connection with it. Near Tullow is the establishment of the Orphan Society of St. Francis of Assisium, founded in 1817, in which 24 children are supported. St. Peter's, St. Patrick's, St. Bonaventure's, and the county and city Cholera Orphan Societies are all in this parish; they are chiefly supported by subscriptions and sermons; as is also the Catholic Society for Ireland, for the gratuitous distribution of religious books, established in 1836.

The parish of *St. Nicholas* comprises the Protestant parishes of St. Nicholas Without, the city part of St. Nicholas Within, St. Luke, St. Kevin, the entire of the Liberties of Christ-Church and St. Patrick, and parts of the parishes of St. Peter and St. Bride. The duty is performed by a parish priest and six officiating clergymen. The chapel is built on the site of a Franciscan friary, erected in 1235 on a piece of ground granted by Ralph le Porter. It has a square tower, ornamented on each face with coupled Corinthian pilasters and terminating with a figure of Faith. The interior is exquisitely finished: the great altar, which is of Italian marble, was executed at Rome; over it is a group representing a "Dead Christ on the lap of Mary," by Hogan, and two relievos, "The Last Supper" and "The Marriage of Joseph and Mary," from Raphael. A monastery of the order of the Religious Brothers of the Christian Schools, in Mills-street, consists of a superior and two monks, who superintend a free school for boys. There is also a national school for boys, in which 450 are educated and 50 of them clothed; and an Orphan Institution. A convent of the order of the Institute of the Blessed Virgin Mary, in Harcourt-street, commonly called the

Loretto convent, consists of a local superioress and a sisterhood of three, who educate about 40 girls.

PROTESTANT DISSENTERS.

There are four Presbyterian meeting-houses, situated respectively in Capel-street, Ushers-quay, Eustace-street, and Great Strand-street, all of the first class; the two former maintain the doctrines of the church of Scotland, and the two latter are Unitarian. Each congregation supports a school and maintains the poor of their own persuasion. That in Capel-street is possessed of a legacy called "Campbell's fund," being the interest of £500, which is distributed among four blind men; and another of the same amount, called Fenner's funds, for the relief of six widows. Those of Strand-street and Eustace-street have each a respectable collection of books for the use of the ministers and con-gregation, to which others can have access on very liberal terms. Dr. John Leland, author of several theological works, was one of the min-isters of the Eustace-street congregation for 50 years. There are three congregations of Independents, whose places of worship are in D'Olier street, York-street, and King's Inns-street, the last named of which has a theological institution, or college, the object of which is to afford the means of theological instruction, according to the tenets of the Westminster and Savoy articles of faith and the doctrinal articles of the Church of England, to such young men as appear to have a call to the sacred ministry; and connected with York-street chapel are a day and Sunday school, a Dorcas and Benevolent institution, and a con-gregational, missionary, and a city mission, association. The Methodist congregations, the first of which was formed in 1746 by Mr. Wesley himself, have their places of worship in Whitefriar-street, Abbey-street, Cork-street, Hendrick-street, South Great George's-street, and Langr-ishe-place; a congregation also meets in the Weavers' hall on the Coombe. There are two Baptist congregations, one of which has a meeting-house in Lower Abbey-street, which presents a Grecian front of considerable architectural elegance; the other meets in an apartment called the Apollo Saloon, in Grafton-street. A Moravian congregation, formed in 1750, has a meeting-house in Bishop-street; and in the same street is a residentiary-house of the same sect, in which a number of the female members live in community. There is a church for German

Lutherans in Poolbeg-street, the only one in Ireland. The Society of Friends, or Quakers, have a meeting-house in Eustace-street, fitted up with great neatness, and another in Meath-street, also a cemetery in Cork-street. The Jews have a synagogue in Stafford-street, and a cemetery near Ballybough bridge.

FREE SCHOOLS.

The King's Hospital, or Free School of Chas. II., commonly called *the Blue-coat Hospital,* was founded in 1670 by the corporation, and established by royal charter, for the reception of reduced citizens and the education of their children, to which latter object, for want of more extensive funds, it has necessarily been limited. It maintains, clothes, educates, and apprentices 100 boys, who receive a solid English and mercantile education, and such of them as are intended for the sea service are instructed in navigation. The building, erected at an expense of £21,000, consists of a centre and two wings; the centre has an Ionic portico supporting a pediment, with an unfinished cupola, and contains apartments for the principal officers: the annual income is about £4000. A Society for instructing the children of the poor in the English language and in the Protestant religion was incorporated by royal charter in 1730, under the title of the Incorporated Society for promoting English Protestant schools in Ireland, but is more generally known by that of *the Charter School Society.* It was originally maintained by donations, subscriptions, and bequests of money and lands, and subsequently by large grants of public money; but these were discontinued some years since and the society left to its own resources. At the time of this change there were forty schools under its direction, two of which were in Dublin; the number is now reduced to eight. Two schools, supported by the funds of Erasmus Smith's bequest, have been established in Dublin, one on the Coombe, the other in St. Mark's parish. *The Hibernian Soldiers' School,* situated in the Phoenix Park, was established in 1769 for the maintenance, clothing, and instruction of the children of the soldiers. In addition to the usual branches of an English education the boys are taught the trades of tailors and shoemakers, and the girls are instructed in needlework; both, when of proper age, are apprenticed to handicraft trades, schools, and, by a new charter in 1808, the governors are empowered to place such children in the regular army, as private soldiers, as are desirous of entering into that service. The buildings consist of a centre and two wings, 300 feet in length and three stories high; there are extensive work-rooms for the children, and a farm of 13 acres is attached to the school, which is partly cultivated by the boys, whose time is divided between employment and recreation, in which athletic sports are encouraged: the school is supported by parliamentary grants and private donations: the average annual expenditure is about £4500: the number of children is about 200, of which one-third are girls. *The Hibernian Marine School* was established by charter about the year 1777, for the maintenance of children of decayed seamen in the navy and merchants' service; the number of boys in this school is 180, who, when of proper age, are placed in the navy, or apprenticed to masters of merchantmen: the building, situated on Sir John Rogerson's Quay, consists of a centre and two wings; it is supported by parliamentary grants and private benefactions. The Society for the Education of the Poor of Ireland, usually called the *Kildare-place Society,* was founded in 1811. Its object was the diffusion of a well-ordered and economical system of primary instruction throughout the country, without any interference with the religious opinions of the pupils, and the publication of cheap elementary books. It was almost wholly supported by large grants of public money, and built an extensive model school for males and females, with other accommodations for offices and stores in Kildare-place. The grants of public money have been withdrawn, and the society now proceeds on a more confined scale by voluntary contributions only. *The Association for Discountenancing Vice,* formed in 1792, and incorporated by statute in 1800, also founded and assisted schools, in which education should be conducted upon Protestant principles, and likewise received large parliamentary grants, which were withdrawn at the same time as those to the Kildare-place Society. To supply the place of these institutions, a *Board of National Education* has been formed for the education of children of all religious persuasions. The commissioners, who were appointed by the lord-lieutenant, are the Duke of Leinster; the Protestant and Roman Catholic Archbishops of Dublin; the Rev. Dr. Sadleir, senior fellow of T. C. D.; Rev. James Carlile, minister of the Scotch Church; the Rt. Hon. Anthony R. Blake, Chief Remembrancer of the Court of Exchequer; and

Robert Holmes, Esq., Barrister. They transact their business in a large establishment in Marlborough-street, formerly the town residence of the Marquess of Waterford, at the rear of which three model schools have been built, and a building is now being erected for a lecture-room, museum, &c., with apartments for the secretary and inspector: it is chiefly supported by parliamentary grants. *The Dublin Free School* was opened in School-street in 1808, for the instruction of poor children of both sexes, on the system of Joseph Lancaster: it is supported wholly by private subscription and a small weekly stipend from the pupils, and is used both as a day and Sunday school. *The Sunday School Society* was established in 1809, and up to January 1835 had in connection with it 2813 schools attended by 20,596 gratuitious teachers and 214,462 pupils. There are several highly respectable schools on a new system. "The Feinaiglean" which takes its name from professor Von Feinagle native of Germany, who introduced it. The principal is the Luxemburgh, formerly Aldborough House which was purchased from Lord Aldborough, who had expended upwards of £40,000 on its erection, and £15,000 raised in shares was laid out on it to adapt it for the purpose.

INFIRMARIES FOR MEDICAL AND SURGICAL CASES.

Sir Patrick Dun's Hospital, in Canal-street, was founded for the relief of the sick, maimed, or wounded, and as an appendage to the School of Physic for extending the sphere of medical practice, by a fund arising from the produce of estates bequeathed by the founder to the College of Physicians. The institution is under the direction of a board of governors. The medical department consists of two physicians in ordinary, one extraordinary, a surgeon, and an apothecary; and the house department, of a treasurer, registrar, providore, and matron. Lectures are delivered twice every week, during the medical season, by the professors of the school of physic in rotation in the theatre, and clinical lectures are also given at the bedside of the patient. The building, which is capable of receiving 100 patients, was commenced in 1803, and completed at an expense of £40,000, of which sum, £9000 was granted by parliament, and the remainder was defrayed from the proceeds of the estates, and by subscription. The building consists of a centre and two projecting wings: the ground floor of the centre contains apartments for the matron and apothecary, the pupils' waiting-room, and the theatre; and in the upper story are the board-room of the College of Physicians, the library, and the museum; the wings contain the wards for the patients. Patients who are not objects of charity are admitted on pay-ing £1. 10. per month during their continuance in the hospital; the average annual income is upwards of £3000.

Steevens' Hospital, near Kilmainham, was founded by a bequest of Dr. Steevens, who, in 1710, bequeathed his estate, amounting to £600 per annum for that purpose; the hospital was opened in 1733. The building forms a quadrangle, having a piazza round the interior of the lower story, and a covered gallery round that above it; attached to it is a small chapel: the board-room contains a medical library. The resi-dent officers are a surgeon, apothecary, Protestant chaplain, steward, and matron. The funds, aided by grants of public money, support 220 beds; this is the largest infirmary in Dublin. *Meath Hospital,* originally in Meath-street, was removed to the Coombe, and ultimately to its present site in Long-lane, Kevin-street; it is now the infirmary for the county. It contains a detached ward for fever cases, a fine theatre for operations, and a spacious lecture-room. *Mercer's Hospital,* founded in 1734 by Mrs. Mary Mercer, is a large stone building, situated between Mercer-street and Stephen-street, containing 55 beds. A theatre for operations was added to it in 1831. *The Charitable Infirmary*, Jervis-street, was the first institution of the kind in the city: the building, a plain brick structure, erected in 1800, can accommodate 60 patients. *Whitworth Hospital* was erected in 1818, on the bank of the Royal Canal, near Drumcondra; it has a ward appropriated for a class of patients who can contribute towards their own maintenance in it. *The City of Dublin Hospital,* in Upper Baggot-street, has accommodations for 52 patients: it is also the principal institution for diseases of the eye. *The United Hospital of St. Mark's and St. Anne's* was opened in Mark-street in 1808, and contains 10 beds; an establishment for vaccination is attached to it. *The Maison de Santé,* George's-place, Dorset-street, is intended for those who, though unable to defray the expense of med-ical advice at home, are in circumstances to prevent them from seek-ing admission into a public hospital; the subscription paid by a patient is a guinea per week. The Netterville and the Royal Military Hospi-tals are noticed under preceding heads.

LUNATICS.

The Richmond District Lunatic Asylum, which was erected in 1830 into a district asylum for the county and city of Dublin, the counties of Meath, Wicklow, and Louth, and the town of Drogheda, occupies a rectangular area of 420 feet by 372, on the western side of the House of Industry. The building forms a hollow square of three stories: the inmates are arranged in four classes of each sex, each under the charge of a keeper, whose apartment commands a view of the gallery in which the patients are confined: there are separate airing-grounds for every class. The total number of patients on the 1st of Jan., 1836, was 277, of whom 130 were males and 147 females; the expenditure for the same year was £4180. 16. In *the House of Industry* there is a department for incurable lunatics, idiots, and epileptic patients, in which those capable of any exertion are employed suitably to their unhappy circumstances. *St. Patrick's* or *Swift's Hospital,* for the reception of lunatics and idiots, was founded by the celebrated Dean Swift, who bequeathed his property, amounting to £10,000, for this purpose. The building, situated near Steevens's Hospital, was opened in 1757, and has also apartments, rated at different prices, for those whose friends can contribute either wholly or partially to their maintenance. A large garden is attached to it, in which some of the patients are employed with considerable advantage to their intellectual improvement. The Society of Friends maintain a small asylum near Donnybrook, for lunatics of their own body.

THE LYING-IN HOSPITAL AND OTHER BENEVOLENT INSTITUTIONS.

The Lying-in Hospital, in Great Britain-street, was originally a small private infirmary, opened in 1745 by Dr. Bartholomew Mosse; but the benefit resulting from it having attracted other contributors, the first stone of the present building was laid in 1750: the doctor, after expending the whole of his property in forwarding the institution, obtained from parliament two successive grants of £6000 each. In 1756 the governors were incorporated by charter, the preamble of which states the threefold object of the institution to be the providing for "destitute females in their confinement, the providing a supply of well-qualified male and female practitioners throughout the country, and the prevention of child murder;" and in the following year the hospital was opened for the admission of patients. The institution is under the direction of a board of 60 governors. The details of management are superintended by a master, always a resident and a medical practitioner, elected for seven years, and deriving his emolument from the number of his pupils, among whom eight females educated for the practice of midwifery are paid for by Government; he delivers four courses of lectures annually, and at the end of six months the students are examined before the assistants, who are appointed for three years, and if duly qualified receive a certificate. The income for the year ending March 31st, 1836, was £4770, arising mainly from the exertions of its managers. The number of cases annually admitted is about 2500. The building consists of a centre and two projecting pavilions connected with it by curved colonnades; the whole of the façade extends 125 feet in length; the principal entrance leads into a spacious hall, and a broad flight of steps leads from the hall to the chapel. The western pavilion forms an entrance to the porter's lodge, and the eastern to the rotundo; in the rear is a spacious lawn enclosed by an iron palisade, forming the interior of Rutland-square. The rotundo comprises a suite of spacious and elegant rooms appropriated to purposes of amusement; the entrance from Sackville-street leads into a waiting-room for servants, and communicates with a vestibule adjoining the great room, which is a circle of 80 feet diameter; the orchestra is of elegant design. On the east and west are respectively a spacious tea-room and card-room; and on the north is a vestibule leading to the ball-room, which is 86 feet long and 40 feet wide. Above this room is another of equal dimensions, though less ornamented; and on the same floor are two smaller apartments, which are let for exhibitions. The new rooms, built in 1786 and facing Cavendish-row, are fronted with a rusticated basement, from which rise four three-quarter columns of the Doric order, supporting a triangular pediment, in the tympanum of which are the arms of Ireland, the crest of the Duke of Rutland, and the star of the Order of St. Patrick; these rooms are elegantly fitted up and well adapted to the same uses: all the profits arising from them are appropriated to the support of the hospital.

The other institutions of a similar description are in Townsend-street; in Bishop-street, called the Anglesey Hospital; on the Coombe, in the building which was the Meath Hospital; in South Cumberland-street; and on Ellis's-quay, called the Western Lying-in Hospital. An institution is attached to Mercer's hospital, for the relief of lying-in women at their own dwellings.

The infirmaries for special complaints not already noticed are the *Fever Hospital* and *House of Recovery,* Cork-street, which was opened in 1804. It consists of two parallel brick buildings, 80 feet by 30, three stories high, connected by a colonnade of 116 feet. The eastern range is used for fever, the western for convalescent patients; an additional building, much larger than any of the former, was added in 1814, by which the hospital was rendered capable of containing 240 beds. The expenditure is chiefly defrayed by a parliamentary grant; the subscriptions and funded property amount to about £1000 per annum. From the opening of the establishment to the end of March, 1835, the number of patients amounted to 104,759. *The Hardwicke Fever Hospital,* attached to the House of Industry, contains 144 beds. *The Westmorland Lock Hospital* was opened in 1792, for the reception of venereal patients of both sexes, and was originally designed for the reception of 300 inmates; but afterwards the number of beds was reduced to 150, to which females only are admissible. The building, situated in Townsend-street, consists of a centre, in which are the officers' apartments, and two wings, with additional buildings for the reception of patients; the centre and wings project a little, and the former has a plain pediment. *A Vaccine Institution* was opened in 1804, in Sackville-street, for the gratuitous vaccination of the poor, and for supplying all parts of the country with genuine matter of infection. There is an *infirmary for ophthalmic affections* in North Cumberland-street, and another in Cuffe-street, one for cutaneous diseases in Moore-street, one for the diseases of children in Pitt-street, and another in North Frederic-street. *Dispensaries* are numerous, and generally attached to hospitals and infirmaries. Among those unattached are that in Cole's-lane, for St. Mary's parish, where the poor are also in special cases attended at their own lodgings; the Dublin General Dispensary, Fleet-street; St. Thomas's Dispensary, Marlborough-green; St. Peter's Parochial Dispensary, Montague-street; South Eastern General Dispensary, Grand Canal-street, near Sir P. Dun's Hospital, to which is attached a Nourishment and Clothing society; the Sick Poor Institution, in a great measure similar, in Meath-street; St. George's Dispensary, Dorset-street; and the Charitable Institution, Kildare-street.

The associations for the relief and protection of orphans and destitute children are numerous. *The Foundling Hospital,* a very extensive establishment in James-street, for the reception of infants of this description from all parts of Ireland, for many years afforded an asylum to 2000 deserted children within its walls, and to nearly 5000 who were kept at nurse in the country till of age to be admitted into the central establishment; these children were clothed, maintained, educated, and apprenticed from the funds of the hospital, which were assisted by annual parliamentary grants of from £20,000 to £30,000. The internal departments were wholly closed by order of government on the 31st of March, 1835, and all the children who are not apprenticed, amounting to 2541, are at present settled with nurses in the country. There are also about 2800 apprentices serving their time as servants and to trades, who are still under the superintendence of the governors. The buildings, which are very extensive, contain schoolrooms for both sexes, dormitories, a chapel, and accommodations for several resident officers, and attached to it is a large garden, in the cultivation of which the older inmates assist. In addition to the Blue Coat, Royal Hibernian, and Royal Marine Institutions, already noticed under the heads of their respective public establishments, the following are peculiarly worthy of notice:- *The Female Orphan House* was commenced in 1790 by Mrs. Edw. Tighe and Mrs. Este, and, owing in a great measure to the advocacy of the celebrated Dean Kirwan, who preached a succession of sermons for its support, was opened in the present buildings on the North Circular Road, which contain ample accommodations for 160 children and a large episcopal chapel. The candidates for admission must be destitute both of father and mother, and between the age of five and ten; the inmates receive an education suited to fit them for the higher class of domestic servants. Its funds are aided by a parliamentary grant equal to the sum voluntarily contributed. *The Freemasons' Orphan School,* under the patronage of the Grand Lodge of Ireland, provides for the orphan daughters of deceased members of the Society. *Pleasants' Asylum,* Camden-street, opened in 1818 by means of a bequest of the late T. Pleasants, Esq., receives 20 Protestant female orphans, who are maintained and educated till they arrive at years of maturity, when they are entitled to a respectable portion on marrying a Protestant, approved of by the trustees. The special objects of *the Protestant Orphan Society,* founded in 1828, and *the Protestant Orphan Union,* formed subsequently, appear from their names; the latter owes its origin to the ravages of the cholera, which also gave rise to three other societies for the reception of children of every religious persuasion, who had been deprived of their parents by that dreadful scourge. Most of the places of worship in Dublin have boarding-schools attached to them for boys or girls, or both, into which orphans are admitted in preference. In this department of charitable institutions may be included *the Asylum for the Deaf and Dumb* at Claremont, near Glasnevin, which, from small beginnings, is now adapted to the reception of more than 100 inmates, who are wholly maintained, clothed, and instructed; the boys, after school hours, are occupied in gardening, farming, and other mechanical works; and the girls in needlework, housewifery, laundry work, and in the management of the dairy; a printing-press has been purchased for the instruction of some of the boys in that business, and for the printing of lessons adapted to the use of the pupils. The building contains separate schoolrooms for male and female pupils: attached to it are about 19 acres of land. This institution is wholly supported by subscription and private benefactions; it has various branch establishments in different parts of the country.

AGED AND IMPOTENT.

The House of Industry was established by act of parliament in 1773, for the indiscriminate reception of paupers from every part; but it has since been limited to destitute paupers of the county and city, and to the relief of certain classes of diseases. The establishment occupies 11 acres, on which are two squares of buildings; one for the aged and infirm, the other for the insane together with detached infirmaries for fever, chronic, medical, and surgical cases, and a dispensary. The total number of aged and impotent poor that have been admitted is 426,175, of whom 1874 are now in the institution. It is under the superintendence of a resident governor and seven visitors appointed by the lord-lieutenant, and is maintained by an annual grant of public money. *Simpson's Hospital,* in Great Britain-street, for blind and gouty men, was opened in 1781, by means of a bequest of a citizen of that name, who had himself laboured under a complication of these complaints. It is a large plain building, with a small plot of ground in the rear for the accommodation of the inmates: its interior is divided into 24 wards, containing about 70 beds, but the number supported is about 50. The annual income of the hospital averages £2700. *The Hospital for Incurables* was opened in Fleet-street, in 1744, by a musical society, the members of which applied the profits of concerts to this benevolent purpose. In 1790, by means of a bequest of £4000 by Theobald Wolfe, Esq., the institution was removed into its present building near Donnybrook, originally erected for an infirmary for small-pox patients. The governors were incorporated in 1800. The house, a substantial plain building, can accommodate 70 patients; the ground belonging to it, 14 acres, is let so advantageously, as to leave the institution rent-free. *The Old Men's Asylum,* in Russell-place, North Circular Road, was instituted in 1810 for 124 reduced old men of good character. *St. Patrick's Asylum for Old Men,* in Rainsford-street, maintains 17 inmates, the majority of whom are upwards of 80 years of age each. The literary teachers, carpenters, printers, and vintners have each an asylum or fund for the relief of decayed members of their respective bodies. *The Scottish Society of St. Andrew* is formed for the relief of distressed natives of that country while in Dublin. *The Richmond National Institution for the Industrious Blind,* in Sackville-street, affords instruction to 40 male inmates in weaving, basket-making, netting, and some other similar kinds of handicraft, and has a sale-room for the disposal of the manufactured articles. *The Molyneux Asylum* for blind females was opened in 1815, on a similar principle, in the former family mansion of Sir Capel Molyneux in Peter-street, which had been for some years employed as a circus for equestrian exhibitions. Attached to it is an Episcopal chapel. There are several asylums for destitute aged women, mostly attached to some of the places of worship. There are two places for the reception of females of virtuous character during the pressure of temporary want of employment, one in Baggot-street, under the superintendence of Protestant ladies; the other in Stanhope-street, under that of an R. C. nunnery.

FEMALE PENITENTIARIES.

The Magdalen Asylum in Leeson-street, was founded by Lady Denny in 1766; the house is adapted for the reception of 60 inmates, and the average number in the asylum is 50; after a probation of three years they are either restored to their families, or provided with the means of honest subsistence; they are employed during the time of their continuance in the asylum in profitable industry, and receive one-fourth of their earnings during their residence, and the remainder on their leaving the house: the institution has received considerable benefactions from the Latouche family. *The Lock Penitentiary* was opened in 1794 by Mr. John Walker, as a penitentiary for the special reception and employment of females discharged from the Lock Hospital; there are generally about 30 in the asylum, who are employed in needlework and other female occupations. *The Dublin Female Penitentiary,* in the North Circular Road, was opened in 1813: the house is large and commodious; there are about 35 females on the establishment. *The Asylum in Upper Baggot-street* affords shelter to 30 inmates. Each of these has a Protestant Episcopalian place of worship attached to it. The R. C. asylums of a similar character are situated respectively in Townsend-street, containing 41 penitents and superintended by the Sisters of Charity; in Mecklenburgh-street, which receives 35; in Dominick-street, late Bow-street, where 34 are sheltered; in Marlborough-street, late James's-street, which supports 45; besides St. Mary's Asylum, Drumcondra-road, in which the average number is 30. The origin of several of these institutions was attended with circumstances of peculiar interest. A house of shelter for the temporary reception of females discharged from prison is on the Circular road, Harcourt-street. The Lock Hospital has a department in which 12 females, who had been patients, are employed in washing for the establishment, under the superintendence of a matron, and are entirely supported in the house.

GENERAL DISTRESS.

The Mendicity Association, formed in 1818, has for its object the suppression of street-begging, by supplying relief to destitute paupers, chiefly by means of employment. A large building on Ussher's Island, formerly the town residence of the Earl of Moira, and having a large space of ground attached to it, is fitted up for the purposes of the institution. The paupers are provided with food and apartments to work in, but not with lodging, and are divided into seven classes; first, those able to work at profitable employment, who receive full wages for their work; 2ndly, those whose earnings are not adequate to their entire support, who receive wages at a lower rate; 3rdly, those unable to perform full work; 4thly, the infirm; 5thly, children above six years of age, who are educated and instructed in useful employments; and lastly, children under six years of age, who are taken care of while their parents are at work: a dispensary is attached to the building and the sick are visited at their own lodgings. The institution is under the superintendence of 60 gentlemen elected annually. *The Sick and Indigent Roomkeepers' Society,* formed in 1790, gives temporary relief in money to the destitute poor at their own lodgings. At a general meeting held at the Royal Exchange, once a month, the amount of the relief to be given during the ensuing month is fixed, which is distributed by four committees for the Barrack, Workhouse, Rotundo, and Stephen's Green divisions of the city, which sit weekly. *The Strangers' Friend Society,* formed in the same year as the preceding institution, has similar objects, and is conducted on the same principle of temporary domestic relief. *The Benevolent Strangers' Friend Society,* of like character, is of later formation. *The Charitable Association,* formed in 1806, is designed for the relief of distressed persons of every description, except street beggars: relief is administered at the dwellings of the pauper. A loan fund is attached to the institution.

EMINENT MEN.

The following eminent persons were born in the city in the years attached to their names: Richard Stanyhurst, historian, 1545; Wm. Bathe, an eminent writer, 1564; Henry Fitzsimons, an eminent writer, 1569; James Ussher, the celebrated prelate, 1580; Sir James Ware, the antiquary, 1594; Arthur Annesley, Earl of Annesley, 1614; Henry Lutterel, an engraver, 1650; Nahum Tate, a poet, 1652; Wm. Molyneux, mathematician, astronomer, and patriot, 1656; Thomas Southerne, a dramatic poet, 1659; James Butler, Duke of Ormonde, 1665; Jonathan Swift, Dean of St. Patrick's, 1667; Marmaduke Coghill, Chancellor of the Exchequer in Ireland, 1673; Dr. Robert Clayton, a celebrated prelate, 1695; Wm. Robertson, a learned divine, 1705; Thos. Frye, the first manufacturer of porcelain in England, 1710; James McArdill, engraver, 1710; Mary Barber, authoress, 1712; John Gast, an eminent divine, 1715; Springer Barry, a celebrated actor, 1719; Thos. Leland, historian, 1722; Rev. Mervyn Archdall, an antiquary, 1723; Geo. Barrett, painter, 1728; Francis Gentleman, a dramatic writer, 1728; John Cunningham, a poet, 1729; Edm. Chandler, Bishop of Durham, 1730; Nathaniel Hone, portrait painter, 1730; Isaac Bickerstalt, dramatist, 1732; Andrew Caldwell, compiler of parliamentary debates, 1732; Hugh Hamilton, painter, 1734; James Caulfeild, first Earl of Charlemont, 1738; Sir Philip Francis, author and statesman, 1740; Edward Malone, critic and antiquary, 1741; John Fitzgibbon, Earl of Clare, 1749; Henry Grattan, statesman, orator, and patriot, 1751; Wm. Mossop, medalist, 1754 John Hickey, sculptor, 1756; Joseph Cooper Walker, antiquary, 1761; Geo. McAllister, painter on glass, 1786. The birth-dates of the following natives of Dublin have not been ascertained: Edward Borlase, historian; Thomas Dogget, a celebrated actor; Robert Molesworth, Viscount Molesworth; Charles Byrne, miniature painter; Zach. Crofton, a celebrated divine; and Wm. Halliday, Irish grammarian. Dublin gave the title of Earl to His Royal Highness the late Duke of Kent.

DUNDRUM, a village, in the parish of Taney, half barony of Rathdown, county of Dublin, and province of Leinster, 3½ miles (S.) from Dublin, on the road to Enniskerry; containing 680 inhabitants. This village, in which are a number of very pretty cottages, is pleasantly situated on a sheltered declivity near the base of the fine mountain range that extends along the south side of the county. It is a favourite place of resort for invalids from Dublin, for whom the mildness of its climate and the purity of the air are peculiarly favourable; and is noted for numerous herds of goats, which, browsing among the mountain pastures, afford milk of very excellent quality. An office for the twopenny post from Dublin has been established in the village, in which are a chapel belonging to the R. C. union of Booterstown, a school, and a dispensary. The environs abound with pleasing and strikingly diversified scenery and are embellished with numerous gentlemen's seats and elegant villas, most of which are situated in tastefully ornamented grounds and command fine views of the bay of Dublin and the country adjacent. Of those in the more immediate neighbourhood the principal are Wickham, the seat of W. Farran, Esq., a handsome residence containing a richly stored museum of natural curiosities; Sweetmount, of W. Nolan, Esq.; Dundrum House, of J.

Walshe, Esq.; Churchtown, of W. Corbet, Esq.; Churchtown House, of D. Lynch, Esq.; Sweetmount Villa, of J. Burke, Esq.; and Sweetmount House, of M. Ryan, Esq. The ruins of Dundrum castle consist of one tower covered with ivy.

DUNLAVAN, a market and post-town, and a parish, partly in the barony of Uppercross, county of Dublin, but chiefly in the lower half-barony of Talbotstown, county of Wicklow, and province of Leinster, 7½ miles (N.) from Baltinglass, and 21 (S.W.) from Dublin on the old road from Blessington to Timolin; containing 2528 inhabitants, of which number, 1068 are in the town. This place is situated on the confines of the counties of Wicklow, Dublin, and Kildare. The town, which is the property of the Tynte family, is built on an eminence surrounded by higher grounds, and consists of two streets, one of which branches off at right angles, from the centre of the other. It contains about 180 houses, of which several are well built, is amply supplied with water from springs, and is considered a healthy place of residence. The market, chiefly for corn and potatoes, is on Wednesday; and fairs for cattle are held on March 1st, May 19th, the second Friday in July, Aug. 21st, the third Tuesday in October, and Dec. 1st. The market-house, in the centre of the principal street, and said to have been erected at an expense of £1200, by the Rt. Hon. R. Tynte, was, in 1835, thoroughly repaired, and one end of it fitted up as a court-house, by Lady Tynte; it is a handsome building of hewn stone, with four projecting porticoes, and crowned in the centre by a dome. During the disturbances of 1798, it was fortified and garrisoned for the protection of many families that fled to this town from the insurgents, who were in the neighbourhood. A chief constabulary police force has been stationed in the town, and petty sessions are held on alternate Wednesdays.

The parish comprises 6565 statute acres, as applotted under the tithe act; the lands are chiefly under tillage, the soil is fertile, and the system of agriculture is improving. There is very little waste land, and scarcely any bog. Some quarries of stone and slate are worked chiefly for building, but both are of inferior quality. A splendid mansion and out-offices have been lately built at a very great expense by Lady Tynte, on part of the estate called Loughmogue, now Tynte Park; and her grandson and heir, Mr. Tynte, who resides with her, has considerably improved the grounds by planting and fencing. The living is a rectory and vicarage, in the diocese of Dublin and Glendalough, united episcopally and by act of council to the rectory and vicarage of Uske and the vicarages of Rathsallagh and Friendstown, and, in 1833, by act of council, to the curacy of Tubber, together constituting the union and the corps of the prebend of Dunlavan in the cathedral church of St. Patrick, in the patronage of the Archbishop. It appears, from a terrier in the registry, that anciently the vicarage was endowed with one third of the tithes, but since 1732 the vicarage and prebend have been held together. The tithes amount to £340. 9. 10½., and of the whole benefice to £472. 0. 9½. The glebe-house was built by a gift of £100, and a loan of £900 from the late Board of First Fruits, in 1812; the glebe comprises 18 acres. The church, a neat edifice in the later English style, was erected in 1816, by a loan of £1300 from the same Board, and enlarged in 1835, by a grant of £460 from the Ecclesiastical Commissioners. In the R. C. divisions the parish is the head of a union, comprising also the parishes of Donard and Donaghmore; the chapel is a neat cruciform edifice, erected on a site presented by Lady Tynte Caldwell, and her daughter Elizabeth, as appears from a tablet over the entrance; there are chapels also at Donard and Donaghmore. About 130 children are taught in two public schools, of which one is supported by Mrs. Pennefather; and there are six private schools, in which are about 230 children, a Sunday school, and a dispensary. Mr. Powell, of Tubber, about 40 years since, bequeathed £200, directing the interest to be appropriated to the apprenticing of one Protestant child of this parish, and one of the parish of Tubber; but payment has of late been withheld. On the townland of Tomant are two Danish raths, commanding extensive views, and an ancient churchyard, near which is a well, supposed to be efficacious in various disorders but probably owes its celebrity to its being a fine cold spring; there is also a rath at Milltown. Dean Swift was for some time incumbent of this parish.

DUNLEARY, county of Dublin. —See KINGSTOWN.

EGMONT. —See CHURCHTOWN.

ESKER, a parish, in the barony of Newcastle, county of Dublin, and province of Leinster, ¾ of a mile (E.) from Lucan; containing 1075 inhabitants. This place constitutes one of the four manors in the county which formerly belonged to the Crown. By an inquisition taken in the 15th of Henry VII. (1499), John Brownunsinge was found seized in fee of eight messuages, eight gardens, and 35 acres of land in Esker and Ballyowen, held of the Crown at an annual rent, which he bequeathed to the church of Esker, "in pure and perpetual alms." There are quarries of good building stone in the parish. The gentlemen's seats are Esker Lodge, the residence of Major Wills; Esker, of J. Cash, Esq.; St. Helen, of W. Gorman, Esq.; Esker Cottage, of J. Spring, Esq.; Esker House, of G. Clarke, Esq.; Ballyowen Lodge, of J. Cathrew, Esq.; Finstown Lodge, of S. Bell, Esq.; and the Glebehouse, of the Rev. W. Stewart. The parish is in the diocese of Dublin: the rectory forms part of the union and corps of the deanery of St. Patrick's, and the vicarage part of the union of Leixlip, under which head the tithes are stated. In the R. C. divisions it is part of the union or district of Palmerstown, Clondalkin, and Lucan. About ten boys are educated in a private classical school. The ruined church forms a conspicuous and picturesque object, appearing, from its extensive remains, to have been originally a large structure. In the vicinity are the ruins of the ancient castellated mansion of Ballyowen.

FINGLAS, a parish, partly in the barony of Nethercross, and partly in that of Coolock, county of Dublin, and province of Leinster, 3 miles (N.) from Dublin Castle, on the mail coach road to Ashbourne, and on a small stream which falls into the Tolka at Finglas bridge; containing 2110 inhabitants, of which number, 840 are in the village. In the reign of Hen. II, Strongbow, aided by Milo de Cogan and Raymond le Gros, with 500 men, routed the Irish army consisting of several thousands, and nearly took King O'Conor prisoner. On June 18th, 1649, the Marquess of Ormonde, with the royal army, encamped here, previous to the fatal action of Rathmines; and on July 5th, 1690, King William, after the victory of the Boyne, here took up a position and mustered his army, amounting to more than thirty thousand effective men; and hence a detachment, under the Duke of Ormonde, marched to take possession of Dublin. The manor was long vested in the Archbishop of Dublin: Fulk de Saundford, one of the prelates of this see, died here in 1271, and Archbishop Fitz-Simon, also, in 1511. The parish comprises 4663 statute acres, chiefly pasture: there are good quarries of limestone and stone for building. The Royal Canal passes through the townlands of Ballybogan and Cabra. An extensive cotton-mill was here burnt down in 1828, the ruins of which remain. A large tannery has existed at Finglas Wood for nearly two centuries, and is still carried on by J. Savage, Esq., one of the same family as the original proprietor: the residence is very ancient, and it is reported that Jas. II. slept one night there. By the 4th of Geo. I. a grant was made to the Archbishop of Dublin of markets on Tuesdays and Saturdays, fairs on April 25th and Sept. 29th, and a court of pie-poudre during the markets, by paying 6*s.* 8*d.* per ann. to the Crown. A noted pleasure fair is held here on the 1st of May. This is a station for the city of Dublin police; and in the vicinity are three private lunatic asylums. The seats are Jamestown, the residence of Mrs. Shew; Tolka Lodge, of J. W. Bayley, Esq.; Kilrisk, of J. Green. Esq.; Newtown, of Barnett Shew, Esq.; Belle Vue, of W. Gregory Esq.; Farnham House, of J. Duncan, Esq.; St. Helena, of W. Harty, Esq., M. D.; Drogheda Lodge, of M. Farrell, Esq.; Ashfield, of Capt. Bluett, R. N.; Springmount, of C. White, Esq.; Elms, of Jolin T. Logan, Esq., M. D., St. Margaret's, of Mrs. Stock; Cabra House, of J. Plunkett, Esq.; Riversdale, of C. Stewart, Esq.; Rose Hill, of N. Doyle, Esq.; Tolka Park, of J. Newman, Esq.; Tolka View, of the Rev. Dr. Ledlie; Rosemount, of Capt. Walsh; Little Jamestown, of Edw. Mangan, Esq.; Rosemount, of M. Rooney, Esq.; and Cardiffe Bridge, of J. Newman, Esq. The living is a vicarage, in the diocese of Dublin, united to the curacy of Ballycoolane, and in the patronage of the Archbishop: the rectory, with the curacy of St. Werburgh's, Dublin, and the chapelries of St. Margaret's, Artaine, and the Ward, constitutes the corps of the chancellorship of St. Patrick's cathedral, Dublin. The tithes amount to £740. 5. 10., of which £462. 2. 5. is payable to the chancellor, and the remainder to the vicar. The glebe-house was erected, in 1826, by aid of a gift of £550, and a loan of £450, from the late Board of First Fruits; there is a glebe of 16 acres of profitable land, divided into three portions, two of which are at a great distance from the parsonage. The church, a plain substantial building, stands on the site of an abbey said to have been founded by St. Canice, or, as some think by St. Patrick, the former having been the first abbot: several of the early saints were interred here, and there are monuments to members of the families of Flower and

Bridges, and one to Dr. Chaloner Cobbe, an eminent divine. This place gives name to a rural deanery, extending over Finglas and its chapelries, Castleknock, Clonsillagh, Chapelizod, Glasnevin, Coolock, Raheny, Clontarf, and Clonturk, or Drumcondra. In the R. C. divisions the parish is the head of a union or district, comprising Finglas, St. Margaret's, the Ward, Killeek, and Chapel-Midway, in which are two chapels, in Finglas and at St. Margaret's. The parochial schools are aided by the chancellor of St. Patrick's and the vicar; an infants' school was established in 1835; and there are two national schools, and a dispensary. Lands producing about £41 per ann., of which £32 are expended on the schools, have been left in trust to the vicar and churchwardens for the benefit of the poor and for other pious purposes. Here are two strong ramparts, one of which, at the rear of the glebe-house, is called King William's rampart. In the grounds of J. Savage, Esq., coins of the reigns of Jas. II. and Wm. and Mary have been found. Here is a well, dedicated to St. Patrick, slightly chalybeate, and once much celebrated: and there is an ancient cross in the churchyard. The vicarage was held for the few later years of his life by Dr. T. Parnell, the intimate associate of Swift, Addison, Pope, and other distinguished literary characters.

GARRISTOWN, a parish, in the barony of Balrothery, county of Dublin, and province of Leinster, 4 miles (N.W.) from Ashbourne; containing 2081 inhabitants, of which number, 741 are in the village of Garristown, and 218 in that of Baldwinstown. It is a constabulary police station, and has a dispensary. There is a windmill on a hill near the village, from which is an extensive prospect, commanding a view over fourteen counties. Good building stone and turf are obtained in the parish; and fairs are held on May 5th, Aug. 15th, and Nov. 1st. The living is a vicarage, in the diocese of Dublin, and in the gift of Lord Trimleston, in whom the rectory is impropriate: the vicarial tithes were valued at £50, and there is a glebe of 25 acres. The church is a plain building: the glebe-house, which was built in 1791, is in ruins. In the R. C. divisions the parish is united to Ballymadun; there is a chapel in each parish; that of Garristown was erected in 1828, and galleries were added to the chapel of Ballymadun in 1833. There is a national school, in which about 100 boys are instructed, and there are also two private schools.

GLASNEVIN, a parish and village, in the barony of Coolock, county of Dublin, and province of Leinster, 1½ mile (N.) from Dublin, on the road to Naul; containing 1001 inhabitants, of which number, 559 are in the village. This place, which is pleasantly situated on the northern bank of the river Tolka, was, early in the last century, the residence of many families of distinction, and of several of the most eminent literary characters of that age; and from its proximity to the metropolis it is still the residence of many highly respectable families. Among the more distinguished of its earlier inhabitants were the poet Tickell, Addison, Swift, Delany, Steele, Sheridan, and Parnell. The demesne of the first-named is now the site of the botanical gardens of the Royal Dublin Society, and a large apartment of the house is appropriated as the lecture-room of that institution. Delville, formerly the seat of the Rev. Dr. Delany, Dean of Down, and now the residence of S. Gordon, Esq., was the frequent resort of Dean Swift and other distinguished literary men of that day. It is pleasantly situated on the banks of the Tolka; on an eminence in the grounds is a temple decorated with paintings by Mrs. Delany, and a medallion bust of Mrs. Johnson, the "Stella" of Swift; beneath this building were found by a former proprietor the remains of a printing press, used by Swift in printing his satires on the Irish Parliament; the house and domestic chapel still retain their original character. On the opposite side of the Tolka is the celebrated seat and demesne of Mitchel, now the residence of the Bishop of Kildare; a little beyond it is Hampstead, formerly the residence of Sir Richard Steele, subsequently that of the late Judge Parsons, and now the seat of B. O'Gorman, Esq.; and in the contiguous parish of Finglas, was the residence of Parnell, formerly vicar of that parish. In the village are many handsome houses, of which the principal are those of Capt. J. A. Crawford, the Rev. W. C. Roberts, the Rev. R. Walsh (one of the editors of the History of Dublin), Capt. R. Smyth, W. Marrable, Esq., T. Howard, Esq., G. Alker, Esq., and Fairfield, the residence of the Rev. J. Hutton. The botanical gardens occupy more than 27 statute acres, laid out with great skill and a due regard to the illustration of that interesting study. The botanical department contains an extensive range of hothouses, occupying the summit of the higher ground in the centre of the garden, and including extensive collections of beautiful and rare plants, of which the various species of each large genus are appropriated as much as possible to separate houses. In front of the hothouses is the arboretum, in which herbaceous plants trees and shrubs are arranged according to the Linnaean system, and to the north arrangements are being made for a classification of similar plants according to their natural orders, on the system of Jussieu, with a division for medical plants, and for such as are peculiar to Ireland. The horticultural department occupies the western side of the garden, and contains divisions for exhibiting the rotatory system of cropping in the cultivation of culinary vegetables; collections of the most useful grasses, clovers, grain, &c., &c.; a selection of hardy fruits, and a collection of choice fruits, to illustrate the methods of pruning and training them. The ornamental department, including the aquarium and the banks of the Tolka, is being laid out as an American garden, with a view to exhibit the various features of landscape gardening, and also contains a division for the culture of specimens of all the agricultural roots. The gardens are under the superintendence of a professor, a curator, and a foreman; and the establishment consists of eight pupils, three apprentices, three labourers, and a porter. The professor's house and lecture-room are near the entrance of the gardens, and during the season from June to September, lectures are given three times every week, and are in general numerously attended; the gardens are also open to the public two days in the week from 12 o'clock till 4. A public cemetery was opened here in 1832, comprising 6 Irish acres, neatly laid out in the centre is a chapel for the funeral service, and the area is enclosed with walls, having at each angle a castellated watch tower: the profit of this cemetery will be appropriated to the education of poor children.

The parish, which comprises 983 statute acres, as applotted under the tithe act, and valued at £4499 per annum, is the head of an extensive manor belonging to the cathedral establishment of Christ-Church, Dublin, and frequently called Grangegorman, from its courts having been held formerly in a village of that name: courts leet and baron are regularly held, the former at Easter and Michael-mas, and the latter, in which debts to the amount of £2 are recoverable, every Friday. There is also a constabulary police station. The living is a rectory and curacy, in the diocese of Dublin, the rectory partly forming the corps of the precentorship, and partly that of the chancellorship of the cathedral of Christ-Church, and the curacy in the alternate patronage of the precentor and chancellor. The tithes amount to £184, half of which is payable to the curate. The church is a small structure, rebuilt in 1707, with the exception of the tower, which is overspread with ivy; the Ecclesiastical Commissioners have recently granted £207 for its repair: in the churchyard is a mural tablet to the memory of Dr. Delany. In the R. C. divisions the parish forms part of the union or district of Clontarf: a branch from the Carmelite convent of Clondalkin was established here in 1829, attached to which is a school. About 80 children are taught in two public schools, of which one, under the patronage of the Bishop of Kildare, was founded by Dr. Delany, who built the schoolhouse; and there is an infants' school, founded in 1834. Claremont, an extensive institution for deaf and dumb children, was founded in 1816, under the patronage of her present Majesty and the late Duke of Glouces-ter; the buildings are extensive, and the grounds comprise 18½ acres, subject to a rent of £220. 10. 9. The establishment contains school-rooms and dormitories for 100 children, as poor boarders and pupils, who must be not less than 8 nor more than 12 years old at their admission; it is under the management of a committee of subscribers, and is supported by donations and annual subscriptions, entitling the contributors to the nomination of children in proportion to their subscriptions; the master has accommodations also for children of the richer class, who pay £50 per annum. The Very Rev. Dr. Barret, Vice-Provost of Trinity College, bequeathed £70,000, and Sir Gilbert King, Bart., £7000, to trustees for charitable uses; from the former this institution received £2166. 6. 10. three and a half per cent. stock, and from the latter £332. 6. 1. There is also a private lunatic asylum, under the superintendence of Dr. Eustace, well arranged for the reception of patients. An almshouse for four poor Protestants was founded and endowed by Lord Forbes, in 1723; and there is a dis-pensary. A field, called the "Bloody Acre," is supposed to have been part of the site of the memorable battle of Clontarf.

GOLDENBRIDGE, a village, in the parish of St. James, barony of Newcastle, county of Dublin, and province of Leinster, 2 miles (W.) from Dublin, on the road to Naas: the population is included in the return for the parish. The Grand Canal passes close to the village, in which are paper, flour, and pearl barley mills. Near it, in an elevated and healthy situation, are the Richmond Infantry Barracks, consisting of two fronts with extensive courts open to the north and south; these are connected by a row of light and elegant houses, 300 yards in length. On the east and west fronts are two spacious areas, and in the centre a communication through a large portal surmounted by a cupola and spire. They occupy 14 Irish acres, and afford accommodation for 76 officers and 1600 privates; there is also stabling for 125 horses, and an hospital for 100 patients. A school-house was erected here in 1827 by subscription, aided by a grant of £250 from Government, which is used on Sundays as a chapel for the troops and the inhabitants of the neighbourhood. Near it is a Wesleyan Methodist meeting-house, and an infants' school was erected by subscription in 1835. Here is a cemetery, principally for Roman Catholics, which was purchased and enclosed by the late Catholic Association, at a cost of £1000; the first stone was laid in 1829. It contains about two Irish acres tastefully laid out, with an Ionic temple in the centre, in which the burial service may be performed for persons of every denomination. In two years from the time of its being opened it was nearly filled, about 12,000 persons having been interred within that period, and several handsome monuments erected. Waterloo Spa is in this village: the waters consist principally of sulphuretted hydrogen gas united with carbonic acid and magnesia, and are said to be beneficial in bilious and liver complaints, scrofula, and several other diseases.

GRALLAGH, a parish, in the barony of Balrothery, county of Dublin, and province of Leinster, 12 miles (N.) from Dublin; containing 236 inhabitants. The only seat is Tralee Lodge, the residence of R. Hyland, Esq. It is a vicarage, in the diocese of Dublin, forming part of the union of Hollywood: the rectory is impropriate in W. Dutton Pollard, Esq.; the tithes are included in the composition for Hollywood. In the R. C. divisions it is part of the union or district of Naul or Damestown. There are some remains of the church and in the churchyard is a holy well.

GRANGEGORMAN. —See City of Dublin.

HAROLD'S CROSS, a village, partly in the parish of St. Catherine, in the barony of Donore, and partly in the united parishes of St. Peter and St. Kevin, barony of Uppercross, county of Dublin, and province of Leinster, 1¼ mile (S.) from Dublin Castle, on the road to

Rathfarnham; containing 1101 inhabitants. This place was in ancient times the scene of repeated conflicts with the Danes; and in a house near it, on the road from Clanbrassil bridge, Robert Emmet, who had lodged there for some time under a fictitious name, after the insurrection of 1803, was apprehended by Major Sirr. The village contains 157 houses, chiefly built round a spacious green and along the roads leading on the west to Kimmage, and on the south to Rathfarnham. In the neighbourhood are some handsome villas, of which the chief are Mount Argus, that of J. Byrne, Esq.; and Greenmount, of J. Webb, Esq. On a branch of a river which rises above Castle Hill are some extensive mills; and in the neighbourhood is a very extensive cotton factory, called the Green Mount Mills, belonging to Messrs. Pim, and employing 150 persons. The machinery of these mills is driven by a steam-engine of 25 and a water-wheel of 20-horse power, giving motion to 100 power-looms and 6000 spindles; there are also a paper-mill and a flour-mill. In the village is a small monastery of discalced Carmelites, consisting of a prior and nine brethren, who support themselves by the exercise of several trades, and the profits of a school kept in the house. A convent of sisters of the order of St. Clare was removed hither from Dorset-street, Dublin, in 1804; the establishment consists of an abbess, 17 professed nuns, and 3 lay sisters; and attached to the convent is a very neat chapel, which is open to the public. Connected with this institution is a female orphan asylum, founded in 1803, and removed from Hendrick-street, Dublin, in 1806, when an appropriate building adjoining the convent was erected for its use. In this asylum 90 children are maintained, clothed, and instructed under the immediate care and superintendence of the sisters of St. Clare; it is supported by subscriptions, donations, and the produce of the industry of the children, who excel in the finer sorts of needlework. Near the entrance of Mount Jerome is a national school, established in 1834, which was previously a R. C. chapel. Mount Jerome, a beautifully picturesque demesne, adjoining the village, has lately been purchased by the Dublin Cemetery Company, formed under the provisions of an act of the 4th and 5th of Wm. IV., "for establishing a general cemetery in the neighbourhood of the city of Dublin." This cemetery comprises 25 acres of gently elevated ground, embellished with lawns and shrubberies, and wholly surrounded with lofty trees of venerable growth, giving it an air of seclusion and a solemnity of aspect peculiarly appropriate. Under the direction of the Company, who have a capital of £12,000 subscribed in £10 shares, provision will be made for the interment of persons of all religious denominations by recognised ministers of their respective congregations; and in order to facilitate the approaches from the south and south-east of the city, arrangements have been made with the Grand Canal Company for the improvement of the canal road from Portobello, and for exemption from toll of all carriages passing to or from the cemetery. The plan also embraces the erection of monuments and cenotaphs, and the construction of tombs and graves either by the company at a stipulated charge, or by individuals at their own expense; the whole is enclosed by a wall, and near the entrance a church is now being erected for the accommodation of the neighbourhood as a chapel of ease. Building stone of good quality is found in abundance in the vicinity, and the Grand Canal passes almost close to the village.

HOLLYWOOD, a parish, in the barony of Balrothery, county of Dublin, and province of Leinster, 4 miles (S.W.) from Balbriggan, on the road from Dublin by Naul to Drogheda; containing 1022 inhabitants. This parish, with respect to its agriculture, is in an unimproved state, though good limestone for burning exists near the ruins of its ancient church; there is also a quarry of black slate near Malahow. The principal seats are Malahow House, the residence of the Rev. T. Baker; and Malahow, of T. Cosgrave, Esq., from both of which are extensive views, and also from the R. C. parochial house at Damastown, embracing an extensive tract of country towards Dublin, backed by the Dublin and Wicklow mountains. The living is a vicarage, in the diocese of Dublin, episcopally united to the vicarages of Naul and Grallagh, and in the patronage of the Marquess of Drogheda; the rectory is impropriate in W. D. Pollard, Esq., and Capt. G. Pepper. The tithes amount to £229. 1. 9., of which £151.14. 4. is payable to the impropriators, and the remainder to the vicar; and the vicarial tithes of the whole union amount to £92. 8. 11. The glebe-house was built by a gift of £369 and a loan of the same amount from the late Board of First Fruits, in 1829; the glebe comprises 6 acres. In the R. C. divisions the parish forms part of the union or district of Naul or Damastown; the chapel at Damastown is a neat edifice, and near it is the parochial house for the R. C. clergyman, erected in

1833, at an expense of £500; there is a private school, in which are about 20 children. On levelling a hill near the ruins of the old church, in 1833, several urns containing ashes were found, about six feet below the surface. Near the spot is an extensive moat, or rath. There is a holy well, dedicated to St. Kennett.

HOLMPATRICK, a parish, in the barony of Balrothery, county of Dublin, and province of Leinster, 3½ miles (S.E.) from Balbriggan; containing, with the town of Skerries, 3109 inhabitants. This parish, which is situated on the eastern coast, derives its name from the island of Innis Patrick, about a mile from the shore, on which a monastery was founded by Sitric Mac Murchard towards the close of the 9th century. Moel Finian, Prince of the Bregii, became a monk in this establishment, of which he was made abbot; and in 1148 a great synod was held here by Gelasius, Archbishop of Armagh, assisted by Malachy O'Morgair, apostolic legate. Between the years 1213 and 1228 the establishment was removed from the island to the mainland, and a building erected on the coast at a short distance from the town of Skerries, where it continued to flourish till the dissolution, after which the site and possessions were granted by Queen Elizabeth to Sir Thomas Fitzwilliam. The mountain portions of the parish present an interesting variety of transition rocks, chiefly of green-stone (in some parts much mixed with calcareous matter), fine grauwacke, clay-slate, grauwacke slate, calcareous tufa, and limestone. The limestone rocks near Lough Shinny are worn into singular form by the action of the sea, which has broken the surface into bold undulations. Two small rocky islands, Colt and Shenex, form a group with Innis Patrick; and beyond these is the islet of Rockabill, or Cow and Calf. Innis Patrick consists of fine grauwacke alternating with granwacke-slate and clay-slate, with thin layers of limestone from half an inch to several feet in width, uniformly dipping southward; and on its western side is a horizontal section of the same material. The islands of Colt and Shenex are of similar composition, but Rockabill is of granite. At Milverton is a quarry of very fine building stone, frequently imbedded with fossils, which, when polished, is equal to marble and is often used for mantel-pieces. On Shenex and Red islands are martello towers, and at Skerries is a coast-guard station. There are nearly fifty wherries, of from 30 to 50 tons' burden each, belonging to Skerries:

they are engaged in the fishery, and have the benefit of a commodious harbour and pier, where coal brigs from the English side of the channel can unload, with an excellent roadstead and anchorage, where large vessels frequently take shelter in unfavourable weather. The manufacture of worked muslins is carried on in this town extensively, and gives employment to a great number of females. Milverton, the seat of G. Woods, Esq., is beautifully situated in a richly wooded demesne of 180 acres, commanding a fine view of the sea, with the town of Skerries in the foreground; within the demesne are the cemetery and some of the foundation of the church of St. Mavee, with a well dedicated to that saint. The only other seat is Hacketstown, the property of J. H. Hamilton, Esq., proprietor of the parish, and now the residence of his agent. There are two windmills and a water-mill for grinding corn; and fairs are held at Skerries on April 28th, and Aug. 10th, for cattle and pigs. The living is an impropriate curacy, in the diocese of Dublin, and in the patronage of J. H. Hamilton, Esq., in whom the rectory is impropriate, and who has endowed the curacy with £60 per ann., which is augmented with £40 per ann. from Primate Boulter's fund. The church is a neat edifice, adjoining the town. In the R. C. divisions the parish forms part of the union or district of Skerries; there are chapels in the town and at Milverton. A schoolhouse was built in 1834, at the expense of J. H. Hamilton, Esq.; and in the same year another was erected by a grant from the Commissioners of Education. There are some remains of a church on Innis Patrick, dedicated to St. Patrick.

HOWTH, a sea-port, post-town, and a parish, in the barony of Coolock, county of Dublin, and province of Leinster, 9 miles (N.E. by E.) from Dublin; containing 1706 inhabitants, of which number, 797 are in the town. This parish, which is situated on the northern shore of Dublin bay, was anciently called Ben-na-dair, from the number of oak trees by which the promontory was covered; and at one period had the name of Dun-Crimthan, from its being the residence of Crimthan, an Irish monarch, who distinguished himself by his powerful assistance in opposing the progress of the Roman arms in Britain. It was laid waste by the Danes in 819 O'Melaghlin, a native chieftain, in an expedition against those invaders, in 1012, ravaged the surrounding country; and Murtogh O'Brien, with his army from

Munster, obtained here, in 1086, a signal victory over the people of Leinster. In 1177, Sir Amorey Tristram and Sir John de Courcy landed here at the head of a large military force, and totally defeated the Danish inhabitants in a sanguinary battle at the bridge of Evora, over a mountain stream which falls into the sea near the Baily lighthouse. This victory secured to Sir Amorey the lordship of Howth, of which his descendants have continued in possession to the present day, under the name of St. Laurence, which Almaric, third baron, assumed in fulfilment of a vow previously to his victory over the Danes near Clontarf, in a battle fought on the festival of that saint. The territory of Howth was confirmed to Almaric de St. Laurence by King John, and is now the property of Thomas, 28th baron and 3rd Earl of Howth. In 1313, during the contested supremacy of the sees of Dublin and Armagh, Jorse, Archbishop of the latter see, came to this place, and privately by night carried his cross erect, as far as the priory of Grace Dieu, within the province of Dublin, in assertion of his precedency; but he was encountered by the family of the Archbishop of Dublin, who beat down his cross and drove him out of Leinster. In 1534, Lord Thomas Fitzgerald planted his cannon on the hill of Howth, to batter the ships entering the bay of Dublin with forces to reduce him to submission. In 1575, the celebrated Grana Uile or Granuwail, better known as Grace O'Malley, on her return from a visit to Queen Elizabeth, landed here and proceeded to the castle; but indignant at finding the gates closed, as was the custom of the family during dinner-time, she seized the young heir of St. Laurence, then at nurse near the shore and carried him prisoner to her own castle in Mayo, whence he was not released till after much negotiation, and only upon condition that when the family went to dinner the castle gates should be thrown open, and a cover laid for any stranger that might arrive; a custom which was scrupulously observed during the lifetime of the late Earl.

Previously to the formation of Kingstown harbour, this was the station for the Dublin Post-Office packets, and the most usual place of landing and embarkation between the English coast and Dublin; and on the 17th of August, 1821, his late Majesty Geo. IV. landed at the pier on his visit to Ireland. The town is built on the side of Howth hill, extending along the northern extremity of the hill; and consists of one principal street, and a few neat dwellings, and a spacious hotel of modern erection; the total number of houses, in 1831, was 154, inhabited principally by fishermen, who employ more than 50 boats in the fishery, chiefly for the supply of the Dublin market. The harbour, constructed at an expense of nearly half a million sterling, consists of two piers of stone; one extending 1503 feet in a right line from the shore, and continued in an obtusely angular direction 990 further to the north-west; and the other extending 2020 feet to the north-east, to meet the return of the former, leaving between their extremities an interval of 320 feet as an entrance into the harbour, which comprises an area of 52 statute acres. These piers consist of large masses of rock quarried from the hill above, resting on foundation blocks of red gritstone from the Runcorn quarries in Cheshire; they are faced on the sides with hewn granite from the opposite side of Dublin bay, and are from 170 to 200 feet broad at the base, 38 feet high, and from 80 to 85 feet wide on the summit. This great work was undertaken by Government under an Act of the 45th of Geo. III.; it was commenced in 1807, and completed in two years under the superintendence of the late John Rennie, Esq., affording employment to nearly 700 men. Nearly one-third of the harbour is dry at half ebb, and two-thirds at low water; in the deepest part, near the entrance, there is not more than 10 feet of water; it is therefore, as a safety harbour, ineffectual in bad weather for vessels drawing more than 9 feet of water, though it was valuable as a station for the Holyhead packets, to which it afforded a facility of sailing at all times. Since the application of steam to navigation, the passage from Howth harbour to Holyhead is effected in 7 hours on an average, whereas the packets often took 18 or 120 hours in crossing from the old station at the Pigeon House, in the mouth of the harbour, and during the winter season they were occasionally detained for several days. The entrance to the harbour, however, has been so much choked up by the drifting of the sand, that the government packets now sail from Kingstown, and the harbour is chiefly used by small vessels, and boats employed in the fishery. It is situated on the north side of the promontory in the sound between the island of Ireland's Eye and the mainland; on the east pier head is a lighthouse, displaying a red light, and on the western pier head are two small lights; at the upper end of the harbour is a martello tower, by keeping which between the two pier heads by day, or at night by keeping the lights between the S. and S. by W., the entrance is safely effected. The entrance into the Sound is through two channels, each about half a mile long, one at the eastern and the other at the western extremity of Ireland's Eye; the eastern channel is bounded on each side by ledges of rock, extending respectively from the south-eastern extremity of the island, and from the pier; and the western channel by a sand bank under Howth on one side, and a ledge of rocks extending from the north-western extremity of the island on the other.

The parish comprises about 1772 statute acres, consisting principally of eminences about 578 feet above the level of the sea, and forming a rocky peninsula which constitutes the northern boundary of Dublin bay. Its general aspect is that of rugged sterility; but from its elevation it affords many extensive and interesting views from the road to Dublin, which is one of the best roads in the country, extending from the city to the pier head. On the left are seen the mountains of Mourne stretching far into the sea, at a distance of about 40 miles; of a fine sweep of coast is the green island of Lambay; and immediately beneath, the picturesque island of Ireland's Eye, with the castle, park, town and harbour of Howth in the foreground. At a short distance is Puck rock, rising abruptly from the sea, and apparently wrested from the mainland by some convulsion, and cleft into two parts, near the summit of one of which is a representation of a human figure of colossal stature. From a bridle road leading to the summit of the bill is a fine panoramic view of the bay of Dublin, with the numerous seats and villas on its shores, backed with the Dublin and Wicklow mountains. In proceeding towards Sutton are seen the rocks called the Needles, the conical summit of Shell Martin, and, just below, the hill called Carroc-Mor, on which is a signal post communicating with the Pigeon-House in the bay. At the eastern extremity of the hill to which the road leads is the old lighthouse, now disused, its great elevation rendering it liable to be obscured by hanging mists; and on a small peninsulated rock at the southern extremity, called from its verdure the Green Bailey, a new lighthouse has been erected, displaying a bright fixed light with reflectors, 110 feet above the level of the sea, and visible at a distance of 17 nautical miles in clear weather. The promontory consists chiefly of clay-slate and quartz rock frequently alternating, and sometimes blending into an appearance of grauwacke; the strata display singular gradations of colour, from pale yellow to red and purple of a brownish hue, and from a greenish white to lavender. Porphyry is found on the south side, and limestone on the western side near the base; iron, copper, and lead ores have been found, with manganese and arsenic pyrites. Potters' clay of good quality abounds on the townland of Sutton. The blue limestone, which bears a fine polish, and the porphyry, which is white and red, are sent coastwise to Wicklow and Arklow, and in working the quarries, blue marl and Irish diamonds are frequently found. The Castle, the seat of the Earl of Howth, is an embattled structure, with a square tower at each end; opposite the left wing is a detached castellated edifice, forming a large archway. The hall, extending the whole length of the building, is decorated with ancient armour and weapons, among which is the two handed sword used by Sir Amorey Tristram in the battle of Howth; there are also many portraits, among which is one of Dean Swift, in his robes, in which is introduced, in a suppliant posture, that of Mr. Wood, whom he had by his satirical writings deprived of a patent for circulating a copper coinage in Ireland. All the state apartments are similarly spacious; and in one is a painting of the abduction of the young heir of St. Laurence by Grace O'Malley; the bed in which Wm. III. slept is still preserved. The demesne is richly wooded, and includes a spacious and well-stocked deer park; many parts present very beautiful views; and in the gardens are hedges of beech, 20 feet high and 6 feet thick. The other seats are Seafield, that of Col. Crogan; Sutton Abbey, of S. Kildahl, Esq., commanding a fine view of the city of Dublin, with the Wicklow and Dublin mountains; Sutton, of J. Sweetman, Esq.; Carrickbrack, of Mrs. G. Hannington, from which is a view of Dublin bay; Cliffs, of W. S. Bellingham, Esq.; and Rock Cottage, of W. Wilde, Esq. There is a coast-guard station, a branch from that of Baldoyle. The living is a rectory, in the diocese of Dublin, united to the vicarages of Baldoyle, and Kilbarrack, together forming the union and the corps of the prebend of Howth in the cathedral of St. Patrick, in the patronage of the Archbishop; the tithes amount to £231. The church, a neat edifice on an eminence at the entrance of the town, was erected by a gift of £800 and a loan of £600 from the late Board of First Fruits, in 1816. In the R. C. divisions the parish forms part of the union of Baldoyle and Howth; the chapel, near the centre of the town, is a neat edifice, erected within the last 20 years; and adjoining it is a school-room connected with the National Board, in which are about 150 children. A very neat school-house midway between Howth and Baldoyle has been erected for the accommodation of the children of both places, in which there are two good school-rooms, for males and females; it contains about 60 children, and is under the superintendence of the prebendary.

Nearly in the centre of the town are the venerable ruins of Howth abbey, originally founded on the island of Ireland's Eye, by St. Nessan, about the year 570, and in which was preserved the book of the four gospels, called the Garland of Howth, which was held in great veneration. The establishment was subsequently removed to this place, and the remains, within an area 189 feet long and 168 feet wide, enclosed by a wall surmounted with graduated battlements, are extensive and interesting. The enclosure, now a burial-ground, contains the ruins of two piles of building, called the Abbey and the College. The former, which appears to have been the church, has a lofty circular doorway at the west end, surmounted by a belfry, to which is an ascent by a staircase on the outside, and consisting, of a single massive wall with battlements pierced for the suspension of three bells; the nave, which is 93 feet long and 512 feet wide, is divided into two aisles of unequal length by a range of six pointed arches, of which three are smaller than the rest, and apparently of later erection than the walls; each of the aisles has an eastern window, and had a separate roof, the gables of which are standing; and at the west end of the south aisle, which is the shorter of the two, is the tower; there is a doorway on the south side, where was formerly a porch. Among the monuments is one of marble to Christopher, 13th baron of Howth, and his lady, whose effigies are still entire, erected in 1430, and decorated with sculptured emblems of the crucifixion, and coats of arms; there is also in this aisle an ancient monument without inscription, apparently to one of the abbots, ornamented with a crosier and cross fleury. This church was erected during the prelacy of Archbishop Luke, who succeeded to the see of Dublin in 1228, at the time the establishment was removed hither from Ireland's Eye; the bells of the ancient abbey were recently discovered in the vaults of the castle, where they had lain for more than 200 years, and are now carefully preserved in the hall. The College is on the south side of the enclosure, and consists of the hall, kitchen, and seven cells, of which some have been thatched and are inhabited by poor families. To the west of the castle are the ruins of a small oratory, with a bell turret over the entrance, dedicated to St. Fenton; they are situated at the base of an elevation, on the summit of which is a large cairn. In a hollow on the east side of the Hill of Howth are the remains of a cromlech, the table stone of which, 14 feet long, 12 feet wide, and about 6 feet thick, has fallen on one side, but is still supported on the other by upright stones, 7 feet high; it is by the peasantry called "Fin's Quoit," from a tradition that it was thrown into its present position by Fin M Coul. There are some petrifying springs: and ancient coins, spurs, bridles, and implements of war have been found in the parish.

INNIPATRICK, county of Dublin. —See HOLMPATRICK.

IRELAND'S EYE, a small island, in the parish of Howth, barony of Coolock, county of Dublin, and province of Leinster, 1 mile (N.) from the hill of Howth. This island, of which, according to Mr. Monck Mason, the proper name is "Hir-land-sie," was selected for the site of an abbey founded in 570 by St. Nessan, over which he presided till his death, and in which was preserved the book of the four Gospels, called the "Garland of Howth." The establishment was subsequently trans-ferred to the mainland, but there are still some remains of the preben-dal church and the conventual buildings on the south-west side of the island. It is situated opposite to the mouth of the harbour of Howth, and is about one mile in circumference; the surface is very irregular, rising in some parts into perpendicular masses of rugged rock, pre-senting a singular and picturesque appearance, and in others wrought into the form of arches by the action of the waves. The more level por-tions afford good pasturage for sheep and cattle; goshawks build among the rocks. On the north, east, and west sides the island down to the water's edge consists of quartz rock, and the eastern angle is a confused mass of clay-slate and quartz rock, the former of which predominates. Near the western extremity is a martello tower.

IRISHTOWN, county of Dublin. —See RINGSEND.

ISLAND BRIDGE, a village, in the parish of St. James, barony of Newcastle, county of Dublin, and province of Leinster, on the south-ern bank of the Liffey; the population is returned with the parish. A beautiful bridge crosses the Liffey at this place: it consists of one ellip-tical arch, 104 feet 10 inches in span, the key-stone of which is 24 feet above high water mark. The first stone was laid, in 1791, by Sarah, Countess of Westmoreland, after whom it is named Sarah Bridge. Here are very extensive artillery barracks, with an hospital, but it is intended to remove the artillery to the buildings of the Foundling Hospital, when the institution shall have been closed after the children now maintained in it are provided for elsewhere. Printworks were established in 1786, which have been greatly enlarged by the present proprietor, W. Henry, Esq., who has a handsome residence near them: they are on the banks of the Liffey, and furnish employment for between 500 and 600 persons. Here is also an extensive flour-mill belonging to Messrs. Manders and Co. Near the village is a spring, called St. John's well, at which a kind of festival of considerable antiquity is held on St. John's eve. It is much frequented by the working classes from the metropolis, for whom tents are pitched and the usual entertainments of patron days provided.

KILBARRACK, a parish, in the barony of Coolock, county of Dublin, and province of Leinster, 5½ miles (N.E.) from Dublin, on the road to Howth; containing 170 inhabitants. The Grand Northern Trunk railway from the metropolis to Drogheda will pass through this parish. It is a vicarage, in the diocese of Dublin, forming part of the union of Howth; the rectory is appropriate to the prebend of Howth in St. Patrick's cathedral, Dublin, and the tithes are included in the return for that parish. In the R. C. divisions it forms part of the union or district of Baldoyle and Howth. On the road to Howth are the ruins of the chapel of Mone, commonly called the Abbey of Kilbarrack, which formerly belonged to St. Mary's Abbey, Dublin: it is said to be of great antiquity, and to have been built on the strand near the great sand bank called the North Bull, for the assistance of shipwrecked mariners; the ancient cemetery, although unfenced and overgrown with weeds, is still occasionally used as a burial-ground.

KILBRIDE, a parish, in the barony of Uppercross, county of Dublin, and province of Leinster, 6 miles (S.W.) from Dublin. It is a vicarage, in the diocese of Dublin, and forms part of the union of Clondalkin. The church is in ruins. In the R. C. divisions it is united to Lucan, Palmerstown, and Clondalkin.

KILCREAGH, a parish, in the barony of Balrothery, county of Dublin, and province of Leinster, 2 miles (N.E.) from Swords; the population is included in the return for Donabate, into which this parish has merged. It is a vicarage, in the diocese of Dublin, incorporated with Donabate, and in the patronage of the Archbishop; the rectory is appropriate to the economy fund of St. Patrick's cathedral: the tithes are included with those of Donabate. The church, which was very small, is in ruins.

KILGOBBIN, or KILGOBBAN, a parish, in the half-barony of Rathdown, county of Dublin, and province of Leinster, 5½ miles (S. by E.) from Dublin, on the road to Bray; containing 1149 inhabitants. This parish comprises 3,290 statute acres; the system of agriculture is improving. Ballybrack and the principal part of the Three Rock mountains are within its limits; and there is an abundance of fine granite that is used for building, flagging, &c., and is chiefly sent to Dublin. Good turf is obtained from the mountains. There are several pretty villas, which, from their elevated situation, command extensive views, embracing the bay and city of Dublin, with a great expanse of sea and adjacent country: the principal are Fern Hill, the residence of J. McCasky, Esq.; Kilgobbin Cottage, of B. E. Lawless, Esq.; and Jamestown House, of J. Rorke, Esq. There is a constabulary police station in the village of Stepaside. It is a perpetual curacy, in the diocese of Dublin, forming part of the union of Kilternan: the tithes amount to £150. In the R. C. divisions it is part of the union or district of Sandyford or Glancullen. There is a school, aided by subscriptions and collections at an annual charity sermon, in which about 80 children are educated. Here are the remains of an ancient castle, erected by the family of Walsh, by which it was forfeited in the reign of Chas. I., and then passed to the Loftus family. The church, which is said to have been the first erected after the Reformation, stands near the castle, and has been disused since 1826, when one was built at Kilternan. Near it is an ancient cross, about eight feet high, and there is another in the Jamestown House demesne, in the vicinity of which was a holy well, dedicated to St. James. An urn, which is now in the museum of the Royal Irish Society, was discovered in the lawn of Kilgobbin Cottage.

KILL, or KILL of the GRANGE, a parish, in the half-barony of Rath-down, county of Dublin and province of Leinster, 5 miles (S.E.) from Dublin, on the road to Bray; containing 1305 inhabitants. This parish comprises 1551 statute acres, besides 257 at the Kill of the Grange of Clonkeen. Much of the land is in pasture, and the system of agriculture is improving. The mountain and sea views are very fine, and there are many seats, the chief of which are Newtown Park House, the residence of H. S. Close, Esq.; Belville, of Lieut.-Col. Cash; Killiney Castle, of P. Warren, Esq.; Carriglea, of the Rev. T. Goff; Stoneville, of Lieut.-Col. Pratt; Somerton, of S. Foote, Esq.; Newpark, of Willoughby Carter, Esq.; Ferney, of H. Scovell, Esq.; Newtown Park House, of R. Perry, Esq.; Barton Hall, of J. Hall, Esq.; Eversham, of W. Minchin, Esq.; Abiline and Naesgwydd, of T. Dixon, Esq.; Bellosguardo, of R. Powell, Esq.; Hollyville, of J. B. Stopford, Esq.; Stillorgan glebe, of the Rev. R. Greene; Newtown Park Cottage, of C. Doyne, Esq.; Anglesea, of C. Carleton, Esq.; Johnstown, of Capt. Whyte, R.N.; Woodpark, of D. Corneille, Esq.; Flower Grove, of the Rt. Hon. and Rev. Viscount Mountmorres Rochestown House, of J. Morgan, Esq.; Springfield, of P. Plunkett, Esq.; Granite Field, of Mrs. Spears; Rochestown Avenue, of B. Molloy, Esq.; Woodpark, of J. J. Kirk, Esq.; Rockland, of P. Lynch, Esq.; Rockland Park, of R. Brown, Esq.; Ashgrove, of J. Murphy, Esq.; Birch Grove, of G. Williamson, Esq.; and Kill Abbey, of R. Espinasse, Esq. This last seat was the country residence of the deans of Christ-Church, Dublin, and is part of the estate of Kill of the Grange of Clonkeen, but has been held by lease for above 120 years by the Espinasse family. The parish is in the diocese of Dublin, and is a curacy, forming part of the union of Monkstown; the rectory is part of the corps of the deanery of Christ-Church, Dublin. The tithes amount to £171. 15. 3., of which two-thirds are payable to the dean and one-third to the curate, who also receives £42. 2. 6. as the tithes of Kill of the Grange of Clonkeen. In the R. C. divisions it forms part of the union or district of Kingstown and Cabinteely. There is a parochial school near Comel's Court; and C. Doyne, Esq., has erected and supports an infants' school near his seat. The greater part of the village of Newtown Park is in this parish, as is also the village of Killiney, which is delightfully situated. Near it, on the summit of one of the Killiney hills, is an obelisk, commanding extremely beautiful views: it was erected by John Malpas, Esq., in 1742, principally to employ the neighbouring poor in a season of distress. Near Kill Abbey are the ruins of the old church, in many places covered with ivy; in the cemetery are the remains of an ancient cross, and there are remains of another at the entrance of the road leading to the church. In the demesne of Carriglea is an ancient rath.

KILLEEK, or KILLAUGH, a parish, in the barony of Nethercross, county of Dublin, and province of Leinster, 1½ Mile (W.) from Swords, on the road from Dublin to the Naul; containing 175 inhabitants, and 805 statute acres. It is a curacy, in the diocese of Dublin, forming part of the union of Swords. The rectory is appropriate to the economy estate of St. Patrick's cathedral, Dublin; the tithes amount to £168. 3. 5½. In the R. C. divisions it is part of the union or district of Finglas and St. Margaret's. Near New Place are the extensive ruins of a magnificent mansion; and there are some remains of the church.

KILLESTER, a parish, in the barony of Coolock, county of Dublin, and province of Leinster, 3 miles (N.E.) from Dublin; containing 113 inhabitants, and 228 statute acres. This parish commands fine views of the Dublin and Wicklow mountains, and of the bay of Dublin, and contains several seats, the principal of which are Killester House, the property of Gen. Luscombe, in which are incorporated the remains of an old abbey, and in the demesne is a fine grove of lime trees; Maryville, the seat of A. Barlow, Esq., Woodville, of J. Bingham, Esq.; Hollybrook House, of W. McDougall, Esq.; Hollybrook Park, of G. Symes, Esq.; Killester Lodge, of G. Wilson, Esq.; Clontarf Strand. of J. Chambers, Esq.; and Oatley, of G. Farran, Esq. It is a rectory, in the diocese of Dublin, appropriate to the economy estate of Christ-Church cathedral, Dublin, the tithes of which amount to £21. In the R. C. divisions it forms part of the union or district of Clontarf. There are some remains of the church, which, from its circular arches, appears to be very ancient. About 35 children are educated in a public school, and there is also a Sunday school.

KILLINEY, a parish, in the half-barony of Rathdown, county of Dublin, and province of Leinster, 2½ miles (S. by E.) from Kingstown, on the road from Dublin to Bray; containing 495 inhabitants. This parish comprises 1269 statute acres, as applotted under the tithe act, and valued at £3118 per annum. The hills of Killiney command magnificent views of Howth, Kingstown, and Dublin bay; the groves of Merrion and Mount Anville, with part of Dublin, the Phoenix Park, and the river Liffey, Killiney bay, Bray Head, and the two Sugar-Loaf mountains. They are visited by many parties of pleasure in summer, at which season Killiney and its vicinity are favourite places of residence, and several pretty villas and rustic cottages have been erected for such as may take up their abode here. There are three hills, called "the Three Sisters," in one of which was procured the stone for constructing Kingstown harbour: the second is of considerable elevation; the village of Killiney, which is in the parish of Kill, occupies the south side of the third hill. The principal seats are Loftus Hill, formerly belonging to Mr. Henry, which is beautifully situated to the north of the Killiney hills; Laughlinstown House, the residence of the Hon. Judge Day; Ballinclea, of the Hon. Mrs. Mellefont; Killiney Park, of Sir N. W. Brady, Knt.; Saintbury, of Capt. Stritch; Kilmarnock, of Lieut. Baker, R. N.; Ballybrack Grove, of Japhet Alley, Esq.; Killiney House, of Capt. Gaynor; Marino, of Mrs. King; Martello Farm, of T. Oxley, Esq.; and Druid Cottage, of Mrs. Patten. It is a perpetual curacy, in the diocese of Dublin, forming part of the union of Monkstown; the rectory forms part of the corps of the deanery of Christ-Church, Dublin. The tithes amount to £117. 0. 11½, of which £78. 0. 7¼. is payable to the dean, and £39. 0. 4¼. to the incumbent of Monkstown. By a public act passed in the 9th of Geo. IV. it was enacted that a church, or chapel of ease to Monkstown, should be erected at Killiney, and endowed with houses and land in the village of Dalkey, which were taken from the deanery. For some years divine service was performed by the Rev. Chas. Sleater, the first chaplain (who was appointed by the incumbent of Monkstown) in a private house, but in 1834 a chapel of ease was erected on a site given by Sir Compton Domville, Bart., who also gave a portion of glebe. It is in the later English style, and is built of the white granite that is found in great abundance on the spot; at the west end is an embattled tower with pinnacles. In the R. C. divisions this parish forms part of the union or district of Kingstown. In the village is a public school, in which about 60 children are educated, and a school-house was erected in 1834, in connection with the church. A dispensary in the village is maintained in the customary manner. Near Killiney bay are two Martello towers and two batteries. The picturesque ruins of the old church, covered with ivy, are on she shore. In Killiney Park and the grounds of Druid Cottage are some interesting druidical remains. Stone coffins and urns of baked clay were found in the grounds of Killiney House, about the year 1784; and ancient coins, ornaments and military weapons have been frequently found here. Near Dorset Lodge is a pyramidical monument of granite, erected to mark the spot where the fourth Duke of Dorset lost his life accidentally, while bunting, in 1815.

KILLOSSORY, a parish, partly in the baronies of Ballrothery, and Nethercross, but chiefly in the barony of Coolock, county of Dublin, and province of Leinster, 3 miles (N.W. by N.) from Swords, on the road from Dublin to Drogheda; containing 380 inhabitants. It comprises 2483 statute acres, as applotted under the tithe act; the land is of good quality, and the system of agriculture improving. The principal seats are Rathbeale, the residence of E. T. Corbally, Esq., a spacious mansion, situated in an improved demesne commanding some fine views; Rawlestown, of J. W. Stubbs, Esq.; Lays, of P. Aungier, Esq.; and Lispopple, of M. O'Reilly, Esq. Here is a station of the constabulary police. The parish is in the diocese of Dublin; the rectory is appropriate to the economy fund of the cathedral of St. Patrick's, Dublin, and the curacy forms part of the union of Swords: the tithes amount to: £161. 19. 4½., payable to the economy fund. The church is in ruins. In the R. C. divisions it is the head of a union or district called Rolleston, comprising also the parishes of Clonmethan, Kilsallaghan, and Palmerstown, and containing two chapels, situated respectively at Rolleston in this parish, and at Oldtown in Clonmethan. The font of the old church was removed to that of Swords, on the demolition of which it was removed to the R. C. chapel of this parish, where it is still preserved. Near the ruins of the old church a school-house was erected in 1823. There are some remains of the ancient castle of Bragil, which with the manor was granted by Jas. I. to Sir Richard Bolton, chancellor of Ireland, in whose family it still remains. It was defended, during the absence of her husband, by Lady Bolton, against Ruah O'Neill, by whom it was burnt, and Lady Bolton perished in the flames: considerable portions of the interior walls are yet standing, but the outworks have been long levelled.

KILMACTALWAY, a parish, in the barony of Newcastle, county of Dublin and province of Leinster, 7 miles (W.S.W.) from Dublin; containing 472 inhabitants and 1575 statute acres. Here are Castle Bagot, the seat of J. J. Bagot, Esq., a spacious mansion in a well-wooded demesne of about 500 statute acres; and Ballybane, of A. Graydon, Esq. It is a rectory, in the diocese of Dublin, and in the patronage of the Archbishop, forming the corps of the prebend of Kilmactalway in Christ-Church cathedral, Dublin, and is held with the union of Clondalkin: the tithes amount to £184. 12. 4. In the R. C. divisions it is part of the union or district of Lucan.

KILMACUD, a parish, in the half-barony of Rathdown, county of Dublin and province of Leinster, 4 miles (S.E.) from Dublin; containing 145 inhabitants. It comprises about 260 acres, which are in a high state of cultivation; and from the salubrity of its air and the beauty of its marine and mountain views, it is a favourite spot for country residences. Among these are Ribblesdale, the seat of His Grace the Archbishop of Dublin; Kilmacud House, of T. Mooney, Esq.; Merville, of W. J. McCausland, Esq.; Lakelands, of S. Boileau, Esq.; Woodley, of P. A. Leslie, Esq.; Rockfield, of J. Hone, Esq.; Westbury, of E. O'Beirne, Esq.; Kilmacud Cottage, of W. Flood, Esq.; and Parson's Green, of W. S. Magee, Esq. It is a chapelry, in the diocese of Dublin, forming part of the union of Stillorgan; the tithes amount to £42. In the R. C. divisions it forms part of the union or district of Booter's-town. This is said to be the birth-place of St. Cuthbert, Bishop of Lindisfarne, from whom its name is derived.

KILMAHUDDRICK, a parish, in the barony of Uppercross, county of Dublin, and province of Leinster, 5 miles (S.W.) from Dublin. It is a chapelry, in the diocese of Dublin, forming part of the union of Clondalkin: the tithes amount to £16. 13. 4. In the R. C. divisions it forms part of the union or district of Lucan. There are some remains of the old church, and of a castle at Grange.

KILMAINHAM, a suburban village, of the city of Dublin, in the parish St. James, barony of Newcastle, county of Dublin, and province of Leinster; the population is returned with the parish. This place, formerly called Kilmaignend, derived that name from a monastery founded on the south side of the city, of which St. Maignend was abbot about the beginning of the 7th century. On or near the site of this monastery was erected the ancient priory of Kilmainham, founded in 1174 for Knights Templars by Richard Strongbow, Earl of Pembroke, and dedicated to St. John the Baptist. The endowments of the priory, which were ample, were confirmed by Hen. II., and the founder, after bestowing on it all the lands of Kilmainham, died in 1176 and was interred in Christ-Church, Dublin. Upon the suppression of this order, in 1307, the lands and possessions of the priory were assigned by the Pope to the Knights of St. John of Jerusalem, and confirmed to them by Edw. II.; and the priory, which had been previously an hospital for the sick and infirm, became an asylum for guests and strangers, and was held by persons of the highest rank; its priors sat as barons in the House of Lords, and some of them were chancellors and lords-deputies of Ireland. Prior Keating, in 1482, having seized the castle of Dublin and disposed of the property of the hospital, was removed from his office; but he made his appointed successor prisoner, and compelled him to resign; and having given his warmest support to the imposture of Lambert Simnel, it was enacted that none but a person of English descent should in future be appointed prior. In 1535, John Rawson, an Englishman, who had been elected prior in conformity to that enactment, surrendered the priory, with all its possessions, into the hands of the King, by whom he was created Viscount Clontarf, with an annual revenue of 500 marks out of the hospital estate. In 1557, Sir Oswald Massingberd was made prior by the authority of Cardinal Pole, the Pope's legate, and was confirmed in the former possessions of the priory by Queen Mary; but on the accession of Queen Elizabeth, he privately withdrew from the kingdom. The buildings of the priory were spacious and of very elegant design; it was frequently the residence of the lords-deputies, and after its dissolution was still regarded as one of the finest buildings in the country. About the year 1675 Arthur, Earl of Granard, suggested to the Earl of Essex then Lord-Lieutenant, the foundation of a military establishment for the reception of disabled and superannuated soldiers; and the Duke of Ormonde, by incessant applications to the King for the same purpose, received from Chas. II., in 1679, an order for carrying it into effect. For this purpose 64 Irish acres adjacent to the site of the priory, and other lands, then forming part of the Phoenix Park, were granted for the site of this institution. The first stone was laid by the Duke of Ormonde, in 1680, and the whole was completed in three years, after a design by Sir Christopher Wren, and at an expense of £23,559. It is a quadrangular structure, 306 feet long, 288 feet broad, and two stories high, enclosing an area of 210 feet square, laid down in grass and intersected by walks meeting in the centre; the exterior fronts, with the exception of the north or principal front, which is of stone, are of brick rough-cast. Over the northern entrance, which is of the Corinthian order, is a square tower lighted by arched windows, with a clock turret surmounted by an octagonal spire; and in the centre of the eastern front is a wide archway leading into the quadrangle, which on three sides and part of the fourth is surrounded by a piazza of Doric arches, affording a covered passage to the dining-hall in the centre of the north range. The dining-hall is 100 feet in length and 50 in width; the lower part of the walls is wainscoted with oak and ornamented with muskets, bayonets, and other military weapons fancifully arranged, and the upper part decorated with portraits of most of the sovereigns and other distinguished personages; the ceiling is flat and divided into compartments, and in the central compartment is a large clock dial. On the south side of the hall is a gallery, supported on brackets of carved oak, leading from the apartments of the master of the hospital, at the west end of the hall, to the chapel, which is at the east end. The chapel is 86 feet long and 40 wide, and has a venerable and imposing appearance; the east window, which formerly belonged to the priory, is embellished with stained glass; the altar is of Irish oak exquisitely carved, and of the order; the master's seat is under a canopy in the gallery at the west extremity of the chapel, and on each side of it are pews for the various officers of the hospital; the ceiling is most elaborately ornamented in stucco, and divided into coved compartments filled with elegant and finely executed designs. The remainder of the north range is occupied by the apartments of the master, who is always the commander of the forces for the time being; and the other parts of the building contain apartments for the inmates, opening on the ground floor into the piazzas, which are neatly flagged, or from the upper story into spacious galleries above. The deputy master's house occupies a detached situation near the master's garden; and in the north-east part of the grounds is the infirmary, which, with the late additions, contains 48 beds, and cells for 12 lunatics. The present establishment is for 5 captains, an adjutant, and 250 invalid soldiers, selected from the list of out-pensioners in Ireland, amounting to 20,000; they are supplied with residence, clothing, diet, medical attendance, and every necessary comfort and accommodation, similar to those of Chelsea. The institution is under the direction of a governor, who is generally an officer of high rank, and the management of a master, deputy-master, chaplain, secretary, registrar, pay-master, physician, surgeon, assistant-surgeon, apothecary, reader, providore, chamberlain, butler, and fueler, all of whom (except the physician and surgeon, who live near the infirmary,) have apartments in the house. The expenses of the establishment amount annually to something more than £10,000, and, together with the original cost of the building, were formerly defrayed by a deduction of sixpence in the pound from all military issues from the Irish treasury, till 1796, when, on the surrender to Government of a considerable portion of the estates, it was resolved to issue an annual grant of parliament for its support.

The village is connected with the metropolis on the eastern side by a range of buildings along the great western road, and is situated in a small valley watered by a stream which, a little below it, falls into the Liffey. The Hibernian mills, established in 1812 by Messrs. Willans, for the manufacture of the finest woollen cloths, which trade they have successfully pursued, and having greatly extended their establishment, it affords employment to nearly 500 persons, for whose residence the proprietors have erected suitable dwellings, and also a place of worship of the Independent denomination. The election of members for the county takes place here; and by an act of council, issued on the 10th of Jan., 1837, under the act of the 6th and 7th of Wm. IV., for extending the jurisdiction and regulating the proceedings of the Civil Bill Court in Ireland, four general sessions of the peace are held annually at Kilmainham and two at Ballymore-Eustace, for one of the two districts into which the county has been divided, consisting of the baronies of Castleknock and Coolock, except the parts of the parishes of Swords, Killossory, and Malahide, which are in Coolock barony; also of the part of Finglas parish in the barony of Nethercross, and the baronies of Newcastle, Uppercross, and Rathdown: for the particulars of the other district, see Swords. The jurisdiction of the manor court, which is also held here, on alternate Mondays, embraces the whole of the barony of Newcastle: debts can be recovered in it to any amount, but the seneschal never takes cognizance of any above £10. The court-house, of recent erection, is a spacious and handsome building; and adjoining it is the county gaol, a well-arranged building enclosed by a lofty wall, including an area 283 feet long and 190 feet wide; the main building, 178 feet long and 102 feet wide, consists of two quadrangles, containing apartments for the keeper, a chapel, infirmary, work-room, common hall, 60 cells for criminals, and 8 for male and 2 for female debtors, with 10 spacious airing-yards, in one of which is a treadmill; the whole admirably adapted to classification, and to the employment and improvement of the prisoners; convicts from the north of Ireland are lodged in this prison previously to transportation. Adjoining the Royal hospital is an extensive cemetery, anciently the burial-place of the original monastery, subsequently of the Knights Templars and the Knights of St. John of Jerusalem, and still used by the inhabitants of Dublin. In it is an ancient tombstone of one entire block of coarse granite, nine feet above the surface of the ground, supposed to be a memorial of some of the Irish princes that fell in the battle of Clon-tarf. About 40 years since, having fallen down, it was again erected, on which occasion a number of Danish coins was found, and also a sword of the same period; the sword was placed by the master of the hospi-tal in the hall leading to his apartments, where it still remains.

KILSALLAGHAN, a parish, in the barony of Castleknock, county of Dublin, and province of Leinster 8 miles (N.) from Dublin, on the old mail road to Drogheda; containing 78 inhabitants. This parish, anciently called Kilsaughan, is bounded on the north by a small stream, called the Fieldstown river, which falls into the sea a little to the north of the town of Swords. It comprises about 2595 statute acres, of which about 190 are common, 1134 arable, and the remainder meadow and pasture: the system of agriculture is improving and tillage increasing; the chief and almost the only manure is a rich black marl, which is plentiful, and building stone of good quality is found in the parish. There are several good houses, of which the principal are the residence of — Smith, Esq., on the grounds of which are the ruins of Kilsal-laghan castle, forming a conspicuous feature for many miles round: New Barn, of J. Segrave, Esq., where is a rath or moat; and Dun-mickary, of J. T. Armstrong, Esq., near which is a rath surrounded by a deep ditch. Fairs for horses, cattle, and pigs, are held on Ascension-day, and Sept. 8th; and on the grounds of New Barn is a constabulary police station. The living is a rectory and vicarage, in the diocese of Dublin, the rectory appropriate to the incumbent for the time being, provided he be resident, at a reserved rent of £10. 7. to the Crown; and the vicarage united to that of Chapelmidway, and in the patronage of the Crown. The tithes, including those of Chapelmidway, amount to £170. The glebe-house was built in 1748, by a gift of £173 from the late Board of First Fruits; the glebe comprises 30, acres of well-cultivated land. The church, rebuilt in 1812, by a loan of £768 from the same Board, is a neat small edifice. In the R. C. divisions the parish forms part of the union of Rollestown. About 120 children are taught in two public schools, of which one is supported by subscription, and the other under the New Board of Education.

KILTERNAN, a parish, in the half-barony of Rathdown, county of Dublin, and province of Leinster, 6 miles (S. by E.) from Dublin, on the road to Enniskerry; containing 913 inhabitants. This parish, which joins the county of Wicklow at the remarkable pass called the Scalp, comprises 3190¾ statute acres, as applotted under the tithe act: the land is rocky and mountainous, abounding with heath, and there is a considerable quantity of waste, but the system of agriculture is improving; there is some good bog. It abounds with remarkably fine granite, which is quarried for building, flagging, and other uses; great numbers are employed in cutting the stone on the spot, which is afterwards sent to Dublin. The principal seats are Springfield, the residence of T. Thompson, Esq., a handsome modern mansion, commanding a fine view of the two Sugar Loaf mountains and the adjacent country; Glancullen, of C. Fitz-Simon, Esq., M. P. for the county, finely situated in a handsome demesne, surrounded with interesting scenery; Kingstown Lodge, of J. Brennan, Esq., a handsome villa with an Ionic portico, in tastefully disposed grounds; Kilternan House, formerly belonging to the monks of St. Mary's Abbey, Dublin, and now the property of R. Anderson, Esq., commanding a fine view of the hill of Howth and Killiney bay; Kilternan Cottage, of R. D. Dwyer, Esq.; Kingstown House, of the Rev. – McNamara; Jamestown, of J. Rorke, Esq.; and Fountain Hill, of B. Shaw, Esq. Part of the Three Rocks mountain is in this parish, which abounds with boldly diversified and strikingly majestic scenery. The mountains at

Glancullen abound with grouse. On the road to Enniskerry, and within two miles of that beautiful village, is the Scalp, a deep natural chasm in the mountain, forming a narrow defile with lofty and shelving ramparts on each side, from which large detached masses of granite of many tons weight have fallen; on each side large masses of detached rock are heaped together in the wildest confusion, apparently arrested in their descent, and threatening every moment to crush the traveller by their fall. On entering the ravine from Dublin, the Great Sugar Loaf mountain appears to close up the egress, but on advancing the view expands and becomes exceedingly beautiful, embracing the two mountains of that name, Bray Head, and the fine country in the neighbourhood. There are a cotton and a paper mill, each employing about 40 persons. A twopenny post has been established at the small village of Golden Ball, which is partly within the parish.

The living is a vicarage, in the diocese of Dublin, united to that of Kilgobbin, and in the patronage of the Archbishop and the Archdeacon, the former having one and the latter two presentations; the rectory is impropriate in Sir Compton Domville, Bart., C. Fitz-Simon, Esq., and Mrs. Anderson. The tithes amount to £186. 3. 8., of which £66. 1. 7. is payable to Sir C. Domville, £63. 11. 8. to Mr. Fitz-Simon, £9. 18. 11. to Mrs. Anderson, and £46.11. 6. to the vicar; the gross tithes of the benefice are £196. 11. 6. The glebe-house was built by a gift of £450 and a loan of £50 from the late Board of First Fruits, in 1816; the glebe comprises 14 acres of profitable land. The church, a handsome edifice in the later English style, was erected in 1826, at an expense of £1900, of which £900 was a gift from the late Board of First Fruits, £500 from the late Lord Powerscourt, and £500 raised by assessment; the Ecclesiastical Commissioners have recently granted £181 for its repair. In the R. C. divisions the parish forms part of the union of Sandyford and Glancullen, at which latter place is a neat chapel with a burial-ground. At Glancullen a monastery was founded in 1835, on a piece of ground given by Mr. Fitz-Simon. About 200 children are taught in two public schools, of which one at Glancullen is supported by the National Board, and one at the Scalp by subscription. There are some remains of the ancient parish church, a picturesque ruin of the earliest ages; there are several raths, and in the demesne of Kilternan House is a cromlech. The Rev. Father O'Leary composed several of his works while on a visit with the Fitz-Simon family, at Glancullen, in this parish.

KINGSTOWN, formerly DUNLEARY, a sea-port and market-town, in the parish of Monkstown, half-barony of Rathdown, county of Dublin and province of Leinster, 5 miles (E.S.E.) from Dublin; containing 5736 inhabitants. This town, which is situated on the southern shore of the bay of Dublin, derived its former name *Dunleary,* signifying "the fort of Leary," from *Laeghaire* or *Leary,* son of "Nial of the nine hostages," monarch of Ireland, who reigned from the year 429 to 458, and had his residence at this place. Its present appellation, Kingstown, was given to it by permission of his late Majesty Geo. IV., on his embarkation at this port for England after his visit to Ireland, in 1821; in commemoration of which a handsome obelisk of granite, with an appropriate inscription and surmounted by a crown of the same material, was erected. Previously to the construction of the present magnificent harbour, Dunleary was merely a small village inhabited only by a few fishermen; but since the completion of that important undertaking it has become an extensive, and flourishing place of fashionable resort, and the immediate neighbourhood is thickly studded with elegant villas and handsome residences of the wealthy citizens of Dublin. The bay of Dublin had, from time immemorial, been regarded as extremely dangerous for shipping, from a bar of moveable sand which obstructed the entrance into the harbour, and rendered the western passage to the port impracticable during certain periods of the tide; and from the vast rocks that project along the eastern shore to the small town of Dunleary. The frequent wrecks that occurred, and the great loss of life and property, had powerfully shown the want of an asylum harbour for the protection of vessels during adverse winds; and application from the Dublin merchants had been made to Capt. Toucher, a gentleman of great nautical skill and experience, who resided among them, to select a proper station for that purpose. The loss of His Majesty's packet, the Prince of Wales, and of the Rochdale transport between Dublin and Dunleary, on the 17th Nov., 1807, when 380 persons perished, prompted fresh efforts to obtain this desirable object, and the merchants of Dublin and the Rathdown association again applied to Capt. Toucher, who selected the port of Dunleary as the fittest for the purpose, from its commanding a sufficient depth of water, soundness of bottom, and other requisites for the anchorage of large vessels; but nothing further was done at that time. A petition, signed by all the magistrates and gentry on the southern shore of the bay, was, in 1809, presented to the Duke of Richmond, then Lord-Lientenant; and a small pier, 500 feet in length, was constructed to the cast of the Chicken rocks, which, though accessible only at particular periods of the tide, contributed much to the preservation of life and property. The great want of accommodation for the port of Dublin and the channel trade, induced the citizens to make further efforts to obtain the sanction of the legislature for the construction of an asylum harbour more adequate to the safety of vessels frequenting the Irish channel, and bound to other ports; and in 1815 an act was passed for "the erection of an asylum harbour and place of refuge at Dunleary." Commissioners were appointed to carry the provisions of this act into effect, in which they were greatly assisted by the exertions and experience of Capt. Toucher; surveys were made and the works were commenced in 1816, under the direction and after the design of the late Mr. Rennie: the first stone of the eastern pier was laid by Earl Whitworth, Lord-Lieutenant, and the work was successfully prosecuted under the superintendence of Mr. Rennie, till his decease in 1817: the pier is 3500 feet in length. Though at first it was thought to be of itself sufficient to afford the requisite security, it was found necessary, for the protection of vessels from the north-west winds, to construct a western pier, which was commenced in 1820, and has been extended to a length of 4950 feet from the shore. The piers, by an angular deviation from a right line, incline towards each other, leaving at the mouth of the harbour a distance of 850 feet, and enclose an area of 251 statute acres, affording anchorage in a depth of water varying from 27 to 15 feet at low spring tides. The foundation is laid at a depth of 20 feet at low water, and for 14 feet from the bottom the piers are formed of fine Runcorn sandstone, in blocks of 50 cubic feet perfectly square; and from 6 feet below water mark to the coping, of granite of excellent quality found in the neighbourhood. They are 310 feet broad at the base, and 53 feet on the summit; towards the harbour they are faced with a perpendicular wall of heavy rubble-stone, and towards the sea with huge blocks of granite sloping towards the top in an angle of 10 or 12 degrees. A quay, 40 feet wide, is continued along the piers, protected on the sea-side by a strong parapet nine feet high. The extreme point of the piers, which had been left unfinished for the decision of the Lords of the Admiralty with respect to the breadth of the entrance, are to be faced in their present position. A spacious wharf, 500 feet in length, has been erected along the breast of the harbour, opposite the entrance, where merchant vessels of any burthen may deliver or receive their cargoes at all times of the tide. At the extremity of the eastern pier is a revolving light, which becomes eclipsed every two minutes. The old pier, which is now enclosed within the present harbour, affords good shelter for small vessels. More than half a million sterling has been already expended upon the construction of this noble harbour, and it is calculated that, to render it complete, about £200,000 more will be requisite. The materials for the piers, wharf, and quays, are granite of remarkably compact texture, brought from the quarries of Dalkey hill, about two miles distant, by means of railroads laid down for the purpose; the number of men daily employed was about 600 on the average. The Royal Harbour of Kingstown is now exclusively the station for the Holyhead and Liverpool mail packets; and from the great accommodation it affords to steam-vessels of every class, and the protection and security to all vessels navigating the Irish channel, it has fully realized all the benefits contemplated in its construction. The number of vessels that entered, during the year 1835, was 2000, of the aggregate burden of 244,282 tons, exclusively of 57 men of war and cruisers, and of the regular post-office steam-packets from Holyhead and Liverpool, of which there are six employed daily in conveying the mails and passengers. About 20 yawls belong to the port, of which the chief trade is the exportation of cattle, corn, granite, and lead ore, and the importation of coal, timber, and iron. The intercourse with the metropolis is greatly facilitated by the Dublin and Kingstown railway, which has been lately extended, by the Board of Works from the old harbour of Dunleary to the new wharf, which is very large and commodious. It was opened to the public on the 17th of Dec., 1834, and the number of passengers has since been on the average about 4000 daily; the number from Dublin and its environs to Kingstown, during the races, was, on the first day 8900, and on the second, 9700. The line, which is 5½ miles in length, was completed to the old harbour at an expense of more than, £200,000, of which £74,000 was advanced on loan by the Board of Public Works, and during its progress employed from 1500 to 1800 men daily.

It commences at Westlandrow, Dublin, where the company have erected a handsome and spacious building for passengers, and is carried over several streets, and across the dock of the Grand Canal by handsome and substantial arches of granite. At Merrion, about 2 miles from the city, it passes through the sea on an elevated embankment to Blackrock. Thence it passes through extensive excavations, and intersecting the demesnes of Lord Cloncurry and Sir Harcourt Lees, passes under a tunnel about 70 feet in length, and extends along the sea shore to the Martello tower at Seapoint, continuing along the base of the Monkstown cliffs to Salthill, and thence to the old harbour of Dunleary, where commences the extensive line to the new packet wharf. Six locomotive engines of the most approved construction are employed on the road, and there are three classes of carriages for passengers, the fares of which are respectively sixpence, eightpence, and a shilling. These carriages start every half hour, from both stations, from 6 in the morning till 10 o'clock at night, performing the journey in less than 15 minutes; the whole line is well lighted with gas.

The town consists of one spacious street, about half a mile in length, and of several smaller streets and avenues branching from it in various directions; there are also several ranges of handsome buildings, inhabited chiefly by the opulent citizens of Dublin, of which the principal are Gresham's Terrace, consisting of eight elegant houses, with a spacious hotel erected by Mr. Gresham, at an expense of £35,000, together forming one side of Victoria-square, so named at the request of the Princess Victoria; the ground in front of the terrace is tastefully laid out, and from the flat roofs of the houses, which are secured from the risk of accidents by iron railings, is a fine view of the bay, the hill of Howth, the Killiney hills, and the Dublin and Wicklow mountains. Haddington Terrace, consisting of eight houses in the Elizabethan style, was built in 1835; and there are many detached and handsome residences. The town, towards the improvement of which Mr. Gresham has contributed greatly at his own expense, is partly paved, and is lighted with gas by the Dublin Gas Company. From the purity of the air, the beauty of its situation, and convenience for sea-bathing, this place has become a favourite summer residence, and is greatly resorted to by visitors, for whose accommodation, besides the Gresham hotel, there is the Anglesey Arms on the quay; there are also several private lodging-houses on the western side of the harbour. The Dublin Railway Company have erected some elegant and spacious baths, and there are others also on the eastern side of the harbour, all commanding interesting and extensive views of the sea and of the surrounding scenery. Races are held annually, for which Mr. Gresham has purchased land near the town well adapted for a course, and on which he is about to erect a grand stand; and regattas annually take place in the harbour. In the town and neighbourhood are numerous handsome seats and pleasing villas, most of them commanding fine views of the bay of Dublin and of the richly diversified scenery on its shores. Of these, the principal are Fairyland, that of C. Halliday, Esq.; Granite Hall, of R. Garratt, Esq.; Stone View, of S. Smith, Esq.; Lodge Park, of the Rev. B. Sheridan; High Thorn, of J. Meara, Esq.; Glengarry, of R. Fletcher, Esq.; Prospect, of Assistant Commissioner Gen. Chalmers; Glengarry House, of J. Dillon, Esq.; Northumberland Lodge, of Sir William Lynar; Airhill House, of F. T. McCarthy, Esq.; Wellington Lodge, of M. McCaull, Esq.; Mount Irwin, of J. Smith, Esq.; Plunkett Lodge, of the Hon. Mrs. Plunkett; Carrig Castle, of C. N. Duff, Esq.; Marine Villa, of J. Duggan, Esq.; Eden Villa, of J. Sheridan, Esq.; Ashgrove Lodge, of B. McCulloch, Esq., Raven Lodge, of Lieut. Burniston; Leslie Cottage, of J. Twigg, Esq.; Echo Lodge, of Mrs. Leathley; and Valetta, of Capt. Drewe. The neighbourhood is remarkable for its quarries of fine granite, from which was raised the principal material for the bridge over the Menai straits, and for the harbours of Howth and Kingstown. A savings' bank has been opened, and a marketplace and court-house are in progress of erection. Kingstown is the head of a coast-guard district, comprising the stations of Dalkey, Bray, Graystones, Five-mile Point, and Wicklow Head, and including a force of 5 officers and 38 men, under an inspecting commander resident here; there is also a constabulary police force under a resident sub-inspector. Petty sessions are held every Monday; a court at which the Commissioners of Public Works preside, or a deputed magistrate, is held on Tuesday, to try harbour offences and the seneschal of the Glasnevin and Grangegorman manorial court, sits on alternate Fridays, for the recovery of debts to any amount within this district. An Episcopal chapel was built by subscription in 1836, in pursuance of a donation of £1000 late currency for its endowment; it is called the "Protestant Episcopal Mariners' Church at Kingstown Harbour." In the R. C. divisions the town is the head of a union or district, comprising the parishes of Dalkey, Killiney, Old Connaught, Rathmichael, Tully, and the greater part of Monkstown and Kill. The chapel is a handsome edifice, completed in 1835, at an expense of £4000; over the altar is a painting of the Crucifixion, presented by Mr. Gresham. There are chapels also at Cabinteely and Crinken. In the town are places of worship for Presbyterians in connection with the Synod of Ulster, of the third class, and Wesleyan Methodists; the former erected at an expense of £2000, and the latter of £1000, there is also a large lecture-room. A convent of the order of St. Clare, to which is attached a small chapel, was established here about 10 years since; but the community, having been much reduced in number, has been distributed among other religious houses, and the convent has been purchased by the nuns of Loretto House, Rathfarnham, who conduct a respectable boarding school. A convent of the order of Mercy was established in 1835, consisting of a superior and seven sisters from Baggot-street, Dublin, who have built a commodious school-room, in which 300 girls are gratuitously instructed; they also visit the sick in the neighbourhood, whom they supply with necessaries and religious instruction. About 120 children are taught in an infants' school and a school under the New Board of Education. A dispensary and fever hospital were established in 1825.

KINSEALY, a parish, in the barony of Coolock, county of Dublin, and province of Leinster, 1½ mile from Malahide; containing 650 inhabitants. It comprises 2105 statute acres, and is well cultivated. Feltrim Hill, on which are the remains of an encampment, commands magnificent sea and mountain views. Under this hill is a limestone quarry, in which fossils are frequently found, and near it is a holy well. Abbeville, a spacious mansion, was erected by the late Rt. Hon. J. C. Beresford, and is now occupied by H. and J. Batchelor, Esqrs.; in the gardens is a greenhouse more than 400 feet long. The other seats are Greenwood, the residence of W. Shaw, Esq.; Feltrim, of C. Farran, Esq., M.D.; Auburne, of J. Crawford, Esq.; Clairville, of Major St. Clair; and Kinsealy House, of J. Gorman, Esq. It is a vicarage, in the diocese of Dublin, forming part of the union of Swords; the rectory is appropriate to the economy estate of St. Patrick's cathedral, Dublin. The tithes amount to £224. 16. 1½ of which one-third is payable to the lessee of the economy estate, and two-thirds to the vicar. In the R. C. divisions it forms part of the union or district of Baldoyle and Howth; a small neat chapel with a spire was erected here by subscription in 1834. There is a public school, in which about 70 children are educated. The church, which was dedicated to St. Nicholas, is a picturesque ruin covered with ivy.

LAMBAY, an island, in the parish or Portrane, barony of Nethercross, county of Dublin, and province of Leinster, 3 miles (E.S.E.) from Rush; containing 100 inhabitants. This island, which is situated off the eastern coast, appears to have belonged at an early period to the cathedral establishment of Christ-Church, Dublin; by license from Edw. VI., in the 5th of his reign, it was, with the consent of the chapter, granted by the archbishop to John Chalenor and his heirs, at a fee-farm rent of £6. 13. 4., for the use of a colony which he had brought to inhabit it, on condition that within six years he should build a town for the habitation of fishermen, with a place of defence surrounded by a wall and ditch, and a convenient harbour for their boats. In the reign of Elizabeth the island was granted to Archbishop Ussher, who resided here for a considerable time, during which he is said to have written part of his works; after his decease it was purchased from his representatives by the family of Talbot, who are its present proprietors. It is about four miles in circumference, and forms an elevated ridge, with rocky knolls and cragged brows, strongly contrasting with the flat sandy shore of the mainland, appearing like the last offset of the Wicklow mountains in this direction, and corresponding with the detached heights of Ireland's Eye, Howth, and Dalkey, at the opposite extremity. It contains more than 650 plantation acres of land well watered with numerous streams and susceptible of cultivation, to which a portion of it has been subjected; it abounds with rabbits, sea parrots, puffins, and Cornish choughs. The rocky grounds surrounding the island form a plentiful lobster and crab fishery, and are much frequented by the Lough Shinny fishermen, who carry on a lucrative trade here. The channel between the island and the main land at Rush point and Portrane is about three miles wide; and about 200 yards from the west end is the Burrin rock, dry at half tide, and on which a perch is placed; between it and the island are four fathoms of water. About a quarter of a mile from the north-western extremity of the island, or Scotch point, is a cluster of rocks called "the Tailors," on which a beacon is placed; and between these rocks is a pier harbour, built by a grant of £591. 11.4. from the late Fishery Board, and of £451. 7. 8. from the proprietor, who afterwards obtained a grant from Government for its completion. It has four feet depth at the entrance at low water, and small vessels may find good anchorage and shelter from the north-east and south-east gales. On the northern side of the island is the Car-durris rock; the remainder of the shore is lofty and precipitous, with clear ground at a short distance; and vessels may anchor in safety to leeward; on the south-eastern side is a spacious cavern, called "Seal Hole," from the number of seals that breed there; and on the north side, between the Tailors and Cardurris rock, is a cavern about 150 feet in length, with stalagmites arising from the floor, and stalactites depending from the roof. Experienced pilots for the Dublin coast, and supplies of excellent spring water may always be obtained here, and on the island is a coast-guard station. The geological features are chiefly trap rock, greenstone in massive beds; greenstone porphyry alternat-ing with small strata of clay-slate, conglomerate sandstone well adapted for mill-stones; grauwacke, and grauwacke slate; the porphyry is found in abundance, and is susceptible of a very high polish, and indications of copper are found. The castle erected by Chalenor is of polygonal form, and is occasionally inhabited by the Rt. Hon. Lord Talbot de Malahide, proprietor of the island. In the R. C. divisions the island forms part of the union or district of Rush; the first stone of a chapel was laid in 1833 by the proprietor. There is an old burying-ground, also a well dedicated to the Holy Trinity.

LUCAN, a post-town and parish, in the barony of Newcastle, county of Dublin, and province of Leinster, 7 miles (W.) from Dublin, on the mail road to Galway and Sligo; containing 1755 inhabitants, of which number, 1229 are in the town. After the English settlement it appears to have been granted to Richard de Peche, one of the earliest English adventurers, and in 1220 was the property of Waryn de Peche, who founded the monastery of St. Catherine, near Leixlip. In the reign of Rich. II. it was in the possession of the Rokeby family, and in the 16th century it belonged to the Sarsfield family, of whom William, one of the ablest generals in the service of Jas. II., was by that monarch, after his abdication, created Earl of Lucan, from whom it descended by mar-riage to the ancestor of Col. G. Vesey, its late proprietor. The town is beautifully situated in a fertile vale on the eastern bank of the river Liffey, over which is a handsome stone bridge of one arch, built in 1794, and ornamented with balustrades of cast iron from the Phoenix iron-works, near Dublin. At the other side of the bridge, on the eastern bank of the river, is the picturesque glebe of the incumbent, the Rev. H. E. Prior. The total number of houses is 187, most of which are well built, and many of them are fitted up as lodging-houses for the reception of visitors, who, during the summer season, resort to this place to drink the waters, which are found efficacious in scorbutic, bilious, and rheumatic affections. A handsome Spa-house has been erected, consisting of a centre and two wings, in one of which is an assembly-room, 62 feet long and 22 feet wide, in which concerts and balls are given; the house affords excellent accommodation for families. The mineral spring, from its having a higher temperature than others in the neighbourhood, is called the "Boiling Spring;" the water, on an analysis made in 1822, was found to contain, in two gallons, 70 grains of crystallised carbonate of soda, 20 of carbonate of lime, $1\frac{1}{2}$ of carbonate of magnesia, 2 of silex, $6\frac{1}{2}$ of muriate of soda, and 14 of sulphur. The scenery of the neighbourhood is beautifully diversified, and its short distance from the metropolis renders the town a place of fashionable resort and of pleasant occasional residence. A chief constabulary police force is stationed in it, and petty sessions are held on Tuesdays. The parish, through a portion of which the Royal Canal passes, is in a high state of cultivation; the soil is fertile and the crops are abundant. Lucan, the interesting residence of Mrs. Vesey, is a spacious mansion, situated in a highly embellished demesne, comprising nearly 500 statute acres extending along the banks of the Liffey; within the grounds is a monument to one of the Sarsfield family, near which are an ancient oratory, dedicated to St. John, and thickly covered with ivy, and a holy well. Of the other seats the principal are St. Edmonsbury, that of T. R. Needham, Esq., a tasteful demesne beautifully situated and commanding some fine views; Weston Park, of J. Hamilton Reid, Esq., finely situated on the Liffey; Woodville, of Major-Gen. Sir H. S. Scott, K.C.B,; Hermitage, of Sir John Kingsmill, Knt.; Finstown House, of J. Rorke, Esq.; Lucan Abbey, or Canon Brook, of J. Gandon, Esq.; Primrose Hill, of A. Heron, Esq., M.D.; Glenwood, of J. Bingham, Esq.; Villa, of T. Smullen, Esq.; View Mount, of Major J. Wolfe; Lucan Lodge, of Capt. T. P. Poe; and Mount Pleasant, of E. Mac

Farland, Esq. On the river Liffey, and within the grounds of Weston Park, is a salmon leap, from the Latin name of which, "Saltus," the barony of Salt derives its name; it consists of a succession of rocky ledges, too extensive to be cleared at one bound, and in passing over it the fish consequently sustain great injury; it forms a beautiful cascade, the picturesque effect of which is greatly increased by the richly wooded banks of the river and the tastefully embellished demesne of Leixlip castle. An inquest was taken in the reign of Edw. II. to ascertain to whom the right to the fish taken here belonged; and another to enquire into the erection of certain weirs, "obstructions to the boats passing to our good city of Dublin with fish and timber." The latter is supposed to refer to a canal which at some very remote period must have been carried along the bank of the Liffey. In excavating the foundation for a mill, recently constructed at the salmon leap by Messrs. Reid and Co., the masonry which formed part of the lock of a canal was discovered; the sill of the lock is still to be seen, and more masonry for the same purpose has been found further down the river. At a later period a canal appears to have been formed along this line, as far as Castletown, two miles above the salmon leap, by which, according to tradition, coal was conveyed from Dublin to that place, and of which some remains are still to be seen. The flour-mills erected by Messrs. Reid and Co. are capable of producing from 700 to 800 barrels weekly; the water wheel is 28 feet in diameter, and in turning 5 pair of stones acts with a power equivalent to that of 60 or 70 horses.

The living is a rectory, in the diocese of Dublin, united to the vicarage of Leixlip, to the augmentation of which the rectorial tithes were appropriated by act of Wm. III.: the tithes are included in the amount given for Leixlip. A neat church with a tower and spire was erected in the town in 1822, towards which the late Board of First Fruits advanced £1100 on loan; and in the same year a perpetual curacy was instituted here, in the patronage of the Incumbent of Leixlip; the stipend of the curate has been augmented with £20 per ann. from Primate Boulter's fund. In the R. C. divisions the parish forms part of the union or district of Palmerstown, Clondalkin, and Lucan; the chapel, a very small edifice, is about to be rebuilt. There is a place of worship for Wesleyan Methodists, erected in 1832. About 250 children are taught in two public schools, of which the parochial school, with an infants' school attached, was built and is supported by subscription. The other is a national school. There are three private schools, in which are about 70 children. A poor-shop, with a lending library, and a loan fund have been established; and a dispensary is open to the poor of the neighbourhood. The vicinity affords some highly interesting specimens of irregular stratification of limestone, which occurs in parallel layers, separated by seams of decomposed calpe, dipping uniformly, at a small angle to the E.N.E. In a bank on the left side of the Liffey, a few yards only above the bridge, the strata become sinuous, forming curvatures of nearly two-thirds of their respective circumferences; and single slabs taken from the disturbed beds have an arched outline, conforming to the general curvature of the strata. At Canon Brook, for many years the residence of the late Mr. Gandon, architect, is a singular cave, discovered by that gentleman; it consists of one principal apartment and two side cells of smaller dimensions, curiously secured all round with stone, to prevent the walls from falling in; many curious relics of antiquity were found, consisting of celts, pieces of bone curiously inscribed and sculptured, military weapons of copper or bronze, and various others of more recent date. The hill in which these apartments am excavated is about 300 feet above the level of the vale, and is called the Fort Hill, from its being crowned with a fortification, the works of which are still in good preservation. The monastery of St. Catherine, founded by Waryn de Peche in 1220, though its endowment was augmented by subsequent benefactors, was, on account of its poverty, assigned, in 1323, to the abbey of St. Thomas, Dublin; there are no remains. Opposite to the gate of Col. Vesey's demesne was a very ancient and splendid cross, round the site of which it is still the custom at R. C. funerals to bear the corpse previous to interment. Above the modern bridge are some fragments of an older structure, said to have been built in the reign of John. Lucan gives the titles of baron and earl to the family of Bingham.

LUSK, a parish, partly in the barony of Nethercross, but chiefly in that of Balrothery, county of Archbishop; the vicarage is in the alternate patronage Dublin, and province of Leinster, 4 miles (N.) from Swords, on the road from Dublin to Skerries; containing, with the town of Rush (which is separately described), 5849 inhabitants, of which number, 924 are in the village of Lusk. This place was chiefly distinguished as the site of a monastery, over which St. Macculind, styled indifferently abbot, or bishop, presided till his death in 497. Cassan, a learned scribe, who is called the chronographer of Lusk, died abbot of this monastery in 695; and either in that or the following year, a grand synod was held here by St. Adamnanus, at which all the principal prelates of the kingdom were present. In 825 the abbey was plundered and destroyed, and in 854 it was, together with the whole town, consumed by fire; it also suffered a similar calamity in 1069; and in 1135 the town and abbey were burned and the whole country of Fingal wasted by Donel Mac Murrogh O'Melaghlin, in revenge for the murder of his brother Conor, prince of Meath. In 1190, a nunnery for sisters of the Aroasian order, which had been founded here at an early period and subsequently appropriated to the priory of All Saints, Dublin, was removed to Grace Dieu, in this parish, by John Comyn, Archbishop of Dublin, who placed in it a sisterhood following the rule of St. Augustine, and endowed it with ample possessions, which were confirmed to it by Pope Celestine in 1196. The parish is divided into three parts, called East, West, and Middle Lusk, of which the last is in the barony of Nethercross, and the two former in that of Balrothery. The land, with the exception of about 150 acres of sand hills is fertile and in good cultivation; 150½ acres are appropriated to the economy fund of the cathedral of St. Patrick, Dublin; and there are about 200 acres of common, which is good grazing land. There are some quarries of good limestone, in which are found beautiful crystals, and of stone of good quality for building; fullers' earth is also found in the parish, and at Loughshinny are veins of copper, but no mines have been worked. The principal seats are Corduff House, the residence of the Rev. F. Baker, at one time occupied by Stanihurst, the historian; Knock Ardmin, of J. Smith, Esq.; Rochestown, of J. Rochford, Esq.; Bettyville, of — Byrne, Esq.; the glebe-house, of the Rev. R. Macklin; and Kennure Park, of Sir W. H. Palmer, Bart., which last is described under the head of Rush. The village is pleasantly situated on the road from Dublin, and the surrounding scenery is agreeably diversified. At Rogerstown is a good quay for landing coal; and from a document dated 1175, prohibiting the illicit exportation of corn, and the departure of any of the retinue of William de Windsor from the port of Lusk, it appears that this place formerly possessed some maritime importance. Fairs are held on May 4th, June 24th, July 25th, and Nov.

25th, chiefly for cattle. A constabulary police force has been established here, and also a coast-guard station belonging to the district of Swords.

The living is a rectory and vicarage, in the diocese of Dublin; the rectory is divided into two portions, one united to the rectories of Ardrie, St. Andrew, and Burgage, together constituting the corps of the precentorship, and the other forming part of the union of Ballymore and corps of the treasurership, in the cathedral church of St. Patrick, Dublin, and both in the patronage of the Precentor and the Treasurer. The tithes amount to £985. 8. 6¾., of which £40 is payable to the vicar, and the remainder to the lessees of the precentor and treasurer. The lands belonging to the precentership comprise 986½ statute acres, of which 71 are in Lusk, 154 in Ardree, and 670¾ in Burgage, exclusively of the chanter's orchard and garden in the precincts of the cathedral church, three tenements in St. Patrick's close, and two houses in Bride-street, and four in Dame-street, Dublin; the whole let at an annual rent of £238. 11. 6½., and an annual renewal fine of £83. 1. 6½.: the gross value of the precentorship is £346. 8. 3¾., and of the vicarage, £120 per annum. The glebe-house was built in 1821; the late Board of First Fruits gave £400, and granted a loan of £400 towards its erection: there are two glebes, comprising together 22 acres. The church, built on the site and partly with the materials of the ancient abbey, is in the later English style of architecture, with a massive square embattled tower having at three of the angles a slender circular tower and at the fourth a similar tower of larger dimensions, which is roofless and without battlements. The interior consists of two long aisles separated by a series of seven pointed arches, now filled up with masonry; the eastern portion of the south aisle is the only part appropriated to divine service; the windows of the remaining portions are nearly all closed up, and the whole of the north aisle is almost in total darkness. There are numerous sepulchral monuments, some of which are very ancient and highly interesting; of these, one of various kinds of marble, in front of the altar in the south aisle, was erected about the close of the 16th century to Sir Christopher Barnewall and his lady, whose effigies in a recumbent porture are well sculptured and elaborately ornamented. In the north aisle is a monument of black marble to James Bermingham, of Ballogh, Esq., bearing his recumbent effigy in chain armour; there is also a tomb curiously sculptured in relief, with an inscription, to Walter Dermot and his lady, which from some obliteration has been by different antiquaries ascribed to the 6th and to the 16th centuries. Near the altar is a piscina, and there are two very ancient fonts; and near the church is the well of St. Macculin, the patron saint. In the R. C. divisions this place is a deanery, comprising the unions or districts of Lusk, Rush, Skerries, Ballybogbill, Garristown, Donaghbate, and Portrane. The chapel, a spacious edifice, was erected in 1809, at an expense of £2000, nearly half of which was given by James Dixon, Esq., of Kilmainham, and the remainder raised by subscription; attached to it is a burial-ground. About 300 children are taught in three public schools, of which two are under the new Board of Education, and one is supported by subscription; there are also four private schools, in which are about 80 children. There are some remains of an ancient church and castle in the demesne of Kennure, and also of the chapel of the convent at Grace Dieu, which, though never extensive, exhibits details of a superior character; and at Whitestown are also the ruins of an old church, dedicated to St. Maur. At Drummanagh and Rush are martello towers; and at the former place the remains of an extensive encampment, commanding a fine view of the surrounding country and of the sea. In digging the foundation for the glebe-house, several stone coffins were found, containing human bones.

MALAHIDE, a maritime post-town and a parish, in the barony of Coolock, county of Dublin, and province of Leinster 2½ miles (E.) from Swords, to which it has a sub-post-office, and 7 miles (N.) from Dublin Castle; containing 1223 inhabitants, of which number, 294 are in the town. The manor and castle were granted, in 1174, by Hen. II., to Richard Talbot, the common ancestor of the Earls of Shrewsbury and Lords of Malahide, who accompanied that monarch into Ireland; and have continued in the possession of his descendants from that period to the present day, through an uninterrupted succession of male heirs. This grant was subsequently confirmed to him by John, afterwards King of England, who also conferred on him various privileges and the advowson of the church of "Mullahide Beg", which he immediately assigned to the monks of St. Mary's abbey, Dublin. In 1372, Thomas Talbot was summoned to parliament by the title of Lord Talbot: and in 1375, the harbour of this place appears to have been of such importance that the exportation of unlicensed corn, and the departure of any of the retinue of William de Windsor, Chief Governor, from this port were prohibited under severe penalties. Edw. IV., in 1475, granted to the family a confirmation of the lordship, with courts leet and baron, and appointed the lord of Malahide high admiral of the seas with full power to hold a court of admiralty and to determine all pleas arising either on the high seas or elsewhere within the limits of the lordship. Sir Richard Edgecombe, who was sent by Hen. VII. into Ireland to administer the oath of allegiance to the nobility and chieftains there, after the suppression of Lambert Simnel's attempt to gain the crown, landed from England at this port, in 1488, and was entertained at the Castle, and afterwards conducted by the Bishop of Meath to Dublin; and in 1570, Malahide was enumerated by Hollinshed among the principal post-towns of Ireland. In the parliamentary war the castle was besieged and taken by Cromwell, who resided here for some time, during which he passed sentence of outlawry upon Thomas, Lord Talbot, and gave the castle and the manor to Miles Corbet, who retained possession of them for seven years, till, on the Restoration, the Talbot family regained possession of their estates.

The town is situated on a shallow inlet of the Irish Sea, between Lambay island, to the north, and Ireland's Eye and the promontory of Howth, to the south; it has a pleasing and sequestered character, and contains many handsome cottages, chiefly occupied by visitors during the bathing season and in some instances by permanent residents. In the centre is a well of excellent water, arched over and dedicated to the Blessed Virgin. The trade of the town, never very extensive, received a great check from the privileges granted to the port of Dublin in the 16th century. The cotton manufacture was introduced here on an extensive scale in the last century by Col. Talbot, father of the present proprietor; but, though the Irish parliament granted £2000 for the completion of the requisite machinery, it was ultimately abandoned. The same gentleman, in 1788, procured an act for the construction of a navigable canal at his own expense, for the conveyance of the imports of this place, through Swords to Fieldstown, for the supply of the surrounding districts, to which they were at that time sent wholly by land carriage; but this undertaking was also unsuccessful. The principal trade at present is the exportation of meal and flour, and the importation of coal from Whitehaven and Scotland, of which, on the average, about 15,000 tons are annually imported. There is a small silk-factory, and the inhabitants derive some advantages from the fishery off the coast, and from an exclusive property in a bed of oysters, which are sent to Dublin in considerable quantities, and are much esteemed. The inlet of Malahide is 4 miles north from Howth, and extends four miles up the country; it is dry at low water, but at high water, vessels drawing not more than 10 or 11 feet may enter the creek and lie afloat in the channel. At the entrance is a bar, having only one foot at low water, and the channel is divided by a gravel bank called Muldowney; both the channels are narrow and tortuous, and are of dangerous navigation without the assistance of a pilot. The town is one of the nine coast-guard stations constituting the district of Swords, and also a constabulary police station. Near it is the Castle, generally called the Court of Malahide, the seat of the Talbot family, a quadrangular building of irregular form and height, situated on a limestone rock of considerable elevation, and commanding a fine view of the town and bay. The original buildings have been much improved and enlarged by Richard, Lord Talbot de Malahide, the present proprietor; the principal front is embattled, and the entrance defended by two circular towers. The interior contains numerous superb apartments, of which the most curious is one called the oak chamber, wainscoted and ceiled with native oak richly carved in scriptural devices and lighted by a pointed window of stained glass. To the right of this chamber is the grand hall, a spacious and lofty room with a vaulted roof of richly carved oak, lighted by three large windows of elegant design, and having a gallery at the south end. To the left of the hall is the drawing-room, a stately apartment, richly embellished, and containing some very valuable paintings, among which is an altar-piece in three compartments, painted by Albert Durer, and originally placed in the oratory of Mary, Queen of Scots, at Holyrood House. There is in the castle a very large collection of portraits of royal and distinguished personages, among the latter of which are several members of the Talbot family, also paintings by the most celebrated masters of the Italian and Flemish schools. The demesne is extensive and richly embellished with groups of stately trees and plantations, and the gardens are tastefully laid out and kept in fine order.

The parish is of very small extent, comprising only 1070 statute acres: the soil is fertile and the system of agriculture improving. The

212

strand abounds with marine shells in great variety, and with sea-reeds, which, in conjunction with the carex arenaria, grow profusely. There are quarries of black, grey, and yellow limestone; and on the south of the high lands, towards the sea, lead ore has been found. There are several handsome seats and pleasing villas, of which the principal are La Mancha, the residence of M. M. O'Grady, Esq., M.D.; Sea Mount, of K. C. French, Esq., from which is a view of Lambay island, the hill of Howth, and the bay of Dublin, with the Dublin and Wicklow mountains; Sea Park Court, of W. Cosgrave, Jun., Esq., commanding a fine view of Malahide creek and bay; Gay-brook, of the Rev. F. Chamley; Mill View, of Capt. Ross, R. N.; and Auburn Cottage, of M. A. Dalton, Esq. The living is a perpetual curacy, in the diocese of Dublin, and in the patronage of the Dean and Chapter of St. Patrick's, Dublin, by whom it is endowed with the whole of the tithes of the rectory (which is appropriate to the economy fund), amounting to £120. The glebe, in the adjoining parish of Swords, comprises 8 acres of cultivated land. The church was erected in 1822, at an expense of £1300, of which £900 was a gift and £300 a loan from the late Board of First Fruits, and £100 a gift from Lord Talbot de Malahide; it is a neat edifice, in the later English style, and the Ecclesiastical Commissioners have recently granted £112 for its repair. In the R. C. divisions the parish forms part of the union or district of Swords; the chapel is a neat edifice. About 140 children are taught in two public schools. Contiguous to the castle are the remains of the ancient church, for ages the place of sepulture of the proprietors of the castle: it consists of a nave and choir, separated from each other by a lofty pointed arch nearly in the centre of the building; the east window is large and enriched with geometrical tracery, and over the western end is a small belfry thickly covered with ivy, beneath which is a window of two lights, ornamented with crocketed ogee canopies; the whole is shaded by chesnut trees, of which the branches bend over the roofless walls. Of the ancient monuments, only one decorated altar-tomb of the 15th century is remaining, bearing the effigy of Lady Matilda Plunkett, wife of Richard Talbot. Adjoining the church are the ruins of a chantry anciently attached to it; and on the lands of Sea Park is a martello tower. This place gives the title of Baron Talbot de Malahide to the family of Talbot.

MARGARET'S (ST.), a parish, in the barony of Coolock, county of Dublin, and province of Leinster, 5¾ miles (N.) from Dublin, on the old road to Naul, and about a mile from the mail coach road from Dublin to Ashbourne; containing 325 inhabitants, of which number, 96 are in the village. A fair is held on July 30th and 31st for the sale of horses and cattle. The principal seats are Dunbroe House, the residence of Miss Giles; Newtown, of Mrs. Stock; Newtown House, of B. Shew, Esq.; Harristown House, of P. Brennan, Esq.; Harristown, of J. Moore, Esq.; Kingstown House, of J. Shew, Esq.; and Barberstown House, of M. Brangan, Esq. In ecclesiastical arrangements it is a chapelry, in the diocese of Dublin, forming part of the benefice of Finglas and the corps of the chancellorship of St. Patrick's Dublin: the composition for tithes is included in the amount for Finglas. The church is in ruins. Over the door of a small adjoining chapel is a Latin inscription purporting that it was built by Sir John Plunkett, formerly chief justice of the king's bench in Ireland. In the R. C. divisions the parish also forms part of the union or district of Finglas and has a neat chapel in the village, in which is also a national school. About a mile distant are the ruins of Dunsoghly castle, consisting of a tower, still roofed, and the remains of a large hall, or diningroom, and kitchens: the tower is vaulted at the bottom, and it had three stories; the floors of the two upper stories have fallen in, but the room of the principal floor is in tolerable repair: the view from the top is very extensive. The ancient family of Plunkett originally owned this property, which now belongs to Mrs. Cavenagh, who inherits it through her grandfather. Adjoining the ruins are the remains of a private chapel, over the doorway of which is a tablet of freestone, exhibiting the emblems of the crucifixion, in high relief, with the letters and date I. P. M. O. 6. s. 1573, at the bottom. Mr. B. Shew, on planting an elevated spot in his grounds, a few years since, discovered a great quantity of human bones, supposed to be some of those who fell in the various skirmishes which at different periods have taken place in this district. Near the chapel is a tepid well, or bath, dedicated to St. Bridget, said to contain lime, muriate of soda, nitrate of kali and sulphur, but the last in only a small proportion.

MATTHEW'S (ST.), county of Dublin. —See RINGSEND.

MERRION (OLD), a village, in the parish of St. Mary's, Donny-brook, in the half-barony of Rathdown, county of Dublin, and province of Leinster, 3 miles (S.E. by S.) from the General Post-Office, Dublin: the population is returned with the parish. It is situated on the south side of the bay of Dublin, the strand of which is here crossed by the Dublin and Kingstown Railway. Here are several neat villas occupied during the summer months by visitors resorting hither for the benefit of sea-bathing, for which purpose the fine broad and firm strand at this place is well adapted; and in the immediate vicinity are several handsome seats, commanding fine views of the bay of Dublin. The principal are Elm Park, the residence of Joseph Watkins, Esq.; Bloomfield of Thos. Ord Lees, Esq.; Merrion Castle, of Fras. Low, Esq.; and Merrion Hall, of R. Davis, Esq. In the vicinity are also the extensive nursery grounds of Messrs. Simpson, from the dwelling-house in the centre of which is obtained a fine view of the hill of Howth and the sea, and there is a pleasing drive through the grounds from the Rock road to the road to Donnybrook. In the demesne of Merrion Castle are the ivied ruins of the old castle from which it derives its name; and at the village is an old burial-ground, still generally used.

MILLTOWN, a village, partly in the parish of Taney, but chiefly in that part of the united parishes of St. Peter's and St. Kevin's, which is in the barony of Uppercross, county of Dublin, and province of Leinster, 2½ miles (S.) from Dublin, on the road to Dundrum and Enniskerry; containing 673 inhabitants. It is situated on the river Dodder, and numerous dilapidated buildings testify that it was formerly an important place. A starch and glue mill is in operation, and the woollen mills, which were established 35 years since, for the manufacture of low-priced cloths, employ about 60 persons, under Mr. Morris Harnett. The Dodder, after heavy rains, being swelled by mountain torrents, overflows its banks and sometimes does considerable damage. The neighbourhood is adorned with many respectable residences, from several of which splendid views of the bay and city of Dublin are obtained, as well as of the Wicklow mountains: among them are Milltown Park, the residence of G. Russell, Esq.; Fairyland, of W. C. Hogan, Esq.; Nullamore, of W. H. Flemyng, Esq.; Rich View, of the Rev. S. W. Fox; Richmond House, of J. Somers, Esq.; South Hill, of J. Elliott, Esq.; Richmond Park, of W. McCann, Esq.; Brookfield, of J. Smith, Esq.; and the residence of the Misses Hunt, partly the repaired edifice of Milltown Castle. Here is a R. C. chapel, also a dissenting place of worship for Independents; and in that part of the village which is in Taney parish there is a school. Milltown gives the title of Earl to the family of Leeson.

MILLTOWN-DUNLAVAN, a parish, in the barony of Uppercross, county of Dublin, and province of Leinster, 2 miles (S. by W.) from Dunlavan; containing 712 inhabitants. This parish is in an isolated portion of the barony, south of Ballymore-Eustace, and whole enclosed within the counties of Kildare and Wicklow. In ecclesiastical concerns it is not known as a parish, dub is considered as forming part of the union of Dunlavan.

MONKSTOWN, a parish, in the half-barony of Rathdown, county of Dublin, and province of Leinster, 5 miles (S.E.) from Dublin, on the road to Bray by Kingstown; containing, with the town of Kingstown and the village of Blackrock (both of which are separately described), 9815 inhabitants. The parish probably derived its name from an ancient grange within its limits belonging to the priory of the Holy Trinity, Dublin. It is pleasantly situated on the bay of Dublin, and comprises 1214½ acres of land, of which a large portion is in demesnes and pleasure grounds. The scenery is beautifully diversified, and the neighbourhood thickly studded with handsome seats and pleasing villas, most of which command fine views of the bay and the adjacent country. Of these, the principal are Monkstown Castle, the residence of Linden Bolton, Esq., a modern house, in the grounds of which are the ruins of two ancient castles of unknown origin; Rockville, of S. Bewley, Esq.; Bloomsbury, of J. Pim, Esq.; Windsor, of M. Thunder, Esq.; Ashton Park, of A. Thunder, Esq.; Monkstown House, of Capt. Kirwan; Somerset, of W. Disney, Esq.; Rochford, of G. P. Wallace, Esq.; Ranelagh House, of Mrs. Molesworth; Rich View, of R. Jordan, Esq.; Richmond Villa, of E. Alexander, Esq.; Carrigbrennan, of J. Pim, jun., Esq.; Richmond Cottage, of R. Gray, Esq.; Glenville, of Mrs. Warburton; Glenville, of H. Rooke, Esq.; Easton Lodge, of Col. Burgoyne; Richview Priory, of R. Jordan, Esq.; Purbeck Lodge, of Capt. Rochfort Heathville, of J. M. Cheater, Esq.; Plantation, of W. Plant, Esq., M.D.;

De Vesci Lodge, of R. Allen Esq.; Hillsborough, of J. Pim, Esq.; Wood-park, of Mrs. Stepney; Avondale, of C. Hughes, Esq.; Albany House, of A. Williamson, Esq.; Millbeach, of J. Williamson, Esq.; Monkstown, of E. Maguire, Esq.; Thornhill, of B. Arthure, Esq.; Cromwell Lodge, of J. Price, Esq.; Lark Hill, of T. Allen, Esq.; Richmond Hill, of B. Grant, Esq.; Milfield, of P. Gogarty, Esq.; Monkstown Hill, of S. James, Esq.; and Seafield Cottage, of M. George, Esq. The Dublin and Kingstown railway passes from Blackrock to Kingstown along the coast of this parish. The living is a rectory and curacy, in the diocese of Dublin, the rectory united to those of Kill, Dalkey, Killiney, and Tully, together constituting the corps of the deanery of Christ-Church, Dublin, in the patronage of the Crown; and the curacy united to the curacies of the same parishes, forming the union of Monkstown, in the patronage of the Dean. The tithes amount to £204. 9., the whole payable to the curate; the dean receives only two-thirds of the tithes of the other parishes in the union, the remaining third being also paid to the curate. The glebe-house is a neat building, and there are two glebes, comprising together 14 acres. The church was rebuilt a few years since in the later English style, and the Ecclesiastical Commissioners have recently granted £216 towards its repair. There are chapels of ease at Blackrock, Killiney, and Kingstown. In the R. C. divisions the greater part of the parish is within the union or district of Kingstown. There is a place of worship for the Society of Friends. About 780 children are taught in five public schools, of which the parochial and infants' schools are supported by subscription, and two under the new Board of Education are aided by an annual donation from the R. C. clergyman; there is also a private school, in which are about 60 children. The Rathdown dispensary, in this parish, was established in 1812, and from that time till June, 1835, afforded relief to 28,424 patients. From an accumulation of its funds, amounting to £500, an hospital was erected in 1834, containing four wards with eight beds in each, and apartments for the requisite attendants; it is situated in a healthy spot, nearly in the centre of the barony, and is supported by subscription. There are some remains of the ancient church; and near the village of Glasthule is a curious rocking-stone of very large dimensions.

MULLAHIDDART, or MULLAHITHART, a parish, in the barony of Castleknock, county of Dublin and province of Leinster, 5¾ miles

(N.W. by N.) from Dublin, on the road to Navan; containing 478 inhabitants. "The guild or fraternity of the Blessed Virgin Mary," of Mullahiddart, was founded in the 23rd of Hen.VI. by act of parliament. The principal seats are Hollywood, the residence of Major Thompson; Tyrrelstown, of A. Rorke, Esq.; and Kilmartin, of J. Hoskins, Esq. The parish was formerly a northern portion of that of Castleknock. It is a rectory and curacy, in the diocese of Dublin: the rectory forms the corps of the prebend thereof in the cathedral of St. Patrick, Dublin, and in the patronage of the Archbishop; and the curacy forms part of the union of Castleknock. The tithes amount to £210, of which £70 is payable to the prebendary and the remainder to the incumbent of Castleknock. The church is in ruins, presenting, with its ivy-covered tower, a picturesque object. In the R. C. divisions the parish forms part of the union or district of Castleknock. A school under the National Board, aided by a collection at the R. C. chapel, affords instruction to 62 boys and 16 girls. A well not far from the church, dedicated to the Blessed Virgin, is frequented at certain periods by the peasantry. Ancient coins have been found near the church.

NAUL, formerly called The Naule, a parish, in the barony of Balrothery, county of Dublin, and province of Leinster, 14 miles (N.) from Dublin, on the road to Drogheda by Ballyboghill; containing 758 inhabitants, of which number, 216 are in the village. The parish comprises 1600 acres, of which two-thirds are arable, one-third pasture, and about 40 acres are woodland. The ancient castle, sometimes called the castle of Roches, is supposed to have been built by the family of De Geneville, from which it passed to the Cruises; and having passed through various hands since 1641, has become the property of Col. Tennison, of Castle Tennison, in the county of Roscommon. It is boldly situated on a rocky precipice on the brow of a chain of hills, commanding a fine view of the vale of Roches, above which it towers at a height of upwards of 150 feet. Through this vale, which is a romantic glen, bordered in many places with rocks of various size and form, and broken into caves, flows the winding Delvan rivulet, which separates the counties of Dublin and Meath, and after forming a waterfall of the same name as the glen, falls into the Irish sea at the village of Knockingin. A fine view of this picturesque glen is obtained from Westown House, the seat of Anthony Strong Hussey, Esq., a respectable mansion of antiquated character, apparently erected early in the last century, and standing in a highly improved demesne, embellished with some fine old timber, at a short distance from the village: in the demesne is a rath, which has been thickly planted. Reynoldstown, the residence of Wm. W. Yates, Esq., is the only other seat in the parish. By an act of the 1st of Geo. I, £2000 was granted to Arthur Mervyn to enable him to complete the mills at Naul, by the addition of granaries. Agriculture is not in a forward state: the principal crops are wheat, oats and potatoes; limestone is raised from quarries in the parish. In 1824, after several previous trials, a trial for coal was made by boring to the depth of 160 feet, but without success. There is a station of the constabulary police in the village. Fairs, established in 1832 and in which black cattle, horses, and pigs are sold, are held on March 16th, April 26th, Whit-Tuesday, and Oct. 2nd. It is a vicarage, in the diocese of Dublin, forming part of the union of Hollywood; the rectory is impropriate in W. Dutton Pollard, Esq. The church, which serves for the union, is a plain neat building, and adjoining it is a chapel in ruins, built, as is stated in an inscription on a stone over the western entrance, by the Hon. Col. E. Hussey, of Westown, in 1710. Mr. Pollard agreed, in 1833, to take £200 per ann. for his share of the tithes of this and the adjoining parishes of Hollywood and Grallagh. Naul forms part of the R. C. union or district of Naul or Damastown; a neat chapel was erected at the former of these places in 1822, by subscription, on a site given by A. S. Hussey, Esq. A commodious school-house was erected, in 1835, near the entrance to Westown demesne, on a site given by Col. Tennison, at an expense of £238, of which £138 was a grant from the Board of National Education and the remainder was defrayed by subscription; it is supported by an annual grant of £20 from the same Board, between £50 and £60 by subscriptions, and by the fees of the pupils. Here is a private school, in which 20 boys and 25 girls are educated.

NEWCASTLE, or NEWCASTLE-juxta-LYONS, a parish (formerly a parliamentary borough), in the barony of Newcastle, county of Dublin, and province of Leinster, 2 miles (N.W.) from Rathcoole; containing 1100 inhabitants, of which number, 397 are in the village. A charter, dated March 30th, 1613, was granted to this place by Jas. I. whereby it was erected into a corporation, consisting of a portreeve,

12 free burgesses, and a commonalty, with power to appoint inferior officers; to hold a court of record for pleas to the amount of five marks, and to be a guild mercatory and the portreeve to be clerk of the market. In 1608, a grant was made to Jas. Hamilton, Esq., to hold a market here on Thursdays, and fairs on the feasts of St. Swithin and All Saints, and the day after each; and in 1762 the portreeve and burgesses obtained a grant of a market on Mondays, and fairs on May 9th and Oct. 8th. All of these markets and fairs are discontinued. The borough also sent two members to the Irish parliament, but it was disfranchised at the Union. There is a dispensary in the village, and it is a constabulary police station. Agriculture is in a high state of improvement: the principal crops are wheat, oats, and potatoes. There are good quarries, the stone of which is used for building and repairing the roads. The Grand Canal passes through the parish. Part of the demesne of Lyons, the splendid seat of the Rt. Hon. Lord Cloncurry, is in the parish: the other seats are Athgoe Park, the residence of Mrs. Skerrett, one part of which is an old castle, erected at a very early period, and in the grounds is the tower or keep of Colmanstown, and an old burial-place; Newcastle House, the seat of Alex Graydon, Esq.; Newcastle, of the Very Rev. Archdeacon Langrishe; Peamount, of C. E. Kennedy, Esq.; Colganstown, of J. Andrews, Esq.; and Newcastle, of O. Moore, Esq. The living is a rectory, in the diocese of Dublin, and was made the corps of the archdeaconry of Glendalough by an act of the 8th of Edw. IV. (1467); it is in the patronage of the Archbishop. The tithes amount to £1250. A small plot of ground in Myler's Alley, Dublin, measuring 1r. 24p., on which some houses stand that are let on lease at £18. 9. 2. per ann., belongs to the archdeaconry: the gross annual value of the dignity is: £418. 9. 2. There is a glebe-house, and a glebe of 16 acres, to which 2a. 3r. 17p. were added on the enclosure of the common. The church was erected about the 15th century, and is chiefly remarkable for its fine eastern window, which was removed to it in 1724, when the building underwent a thorough repair; the ivy which covers the walls contributes also to its picturesque appearance: a grant of £180 has been lately made by the Ecclesiastical Commissioners towards its repairs. The church has an annual economy fund of £3. 8. 10. In the R. C. divisions the parish forms part of the union or district of Saggard; in the village is a neat chapel, with a belfry, erected in 1813 at a cost of about £1500. There is a school in connection with

the Bord of National Education. In the village are the ruins of three old castles.

OLD CONNAUGHT. —See CONNAUGHT, OLD.

PALMERSTOWN, a parish, in the barony of Balrothery, county of Dublin, and province of Leinster, 11 miles (N. by W.) from Dublin; containing 321 inhabitants. Good building stone is found in the parish. It is a rectory and vicarage, in the diocese of Dublin; the rectory is appropriate to the vicars choral of the cathedral of Dublin, and the vicarage forms part of the union and corps of the prebend of Clonmethan: of the tithes, amounting to £135, two-thirds are payable to the vicars choral, and the remainder to the vicar. In the R. C. divisions it is part of the union or district of Rollestown. Some remains of the church still exist.

PALMERSTOWN, a parish, in the barony of Newcastle, county of Dublin, and province of Leinster, 3 miles (W.) from Dublin, on the road to Lucan, and on the river Liffey; containing 1533 inhabitants. It comprises 1465 statute acres, as applotted under the tithe act, and valued at £3594 per annum. Near the village, which is irregularly built, and in which the dwellings are of a humble character, there was an hospital for lepers, previously to the Reformation. At the commencement of the present century here were extensive printing-works, large iron-works, oil and dye stuff mills, and wash-mills; lead and copper works have been established for 16 years; there are large cotton-mills, employing about 120 persons, and a flour-mill on the Liffey, which bounds the parish on the north. A fair for the sale of cattle and horses takes place on Aug. 21st. The city police have a station near Chapelizod bridge. Palmerstown House, erected by the late Rt. Hon. John Hely Hutchinson, Secretary of State for Ireland, and Provost of Trinity College, Dublin, now the seat of his grandson, the Earl of Donoughmore, is a spacious mansion on elevated ground, commanding most extensive and rich views; besides which there are several pleasing villas, including Riversdale, the seat of Gen. Sir Guy Campbell, Bart.; Brook Lawn, of M. Hackett, Esq.; Palmerstown, of Major Wilcox; and Bellgrove, of Major Watts. It is a rectory, in the diocese of Dublin, forming part of the union of Chapelizod: the tithes amount to £170. In the R. C. divisions it is part of the union of Lucan, Palmerstown, and Clondalkin, and contains a chapel; the parish priest is rural dean over his own union and those of Maynooth, Celbridge, and Saggard. There are two schools, in which about 150 children are taught. On the townland of Irishtown are the remains of an old castle, clothed with ivy, near which coins and bullets have been found; and at Cruise river a battle is said to have been fought between the Danes and the Irish. This place gives the title of Viscount Palmerston to the family of Temple.

PORTMARNOCK. —See PORT-ST.-MARNOCK.

PORTRANE, PORTRAHAN or PORTRAVEN (anciently called Portraehern), a parish, in the barony of Nethercross county of Dublin, and province of Leinster, 4¼ miles (N.E.) from Swords; containing 725 inhabitants. It comprises a great variety of substrata, including red sandstone, conglomerate, limestone, greenstone in rugged rocks, on the north side of the promontory; and grauwacke-slate, clay-slate, greenstone-slate, and a great variety of conglomerates, and minor minerals, on the coast, all curiously intermingled. The coast is remarkably grand and bold, and the sea has worked its way into the rocks, so as to form several excavations of large extent, in one of which is a curious well of fresh water, called Clink. Portrane House, the property and residence of Geo. Evans, Esq., M.P., is a spacious brick building nearly in the centre of a fine demesne of 420 acres, well stocked with deer, and commanding extensive and splendid views; some of the best land in the county is within this beautiful demesne, and its large plantations are more thriving than is usual in situations so much exposed to the sea blasts. It is a vicarage, in the diocese of Dublin, forming part of the union of Donabate; the rectory is impropriate in G. Evans, Esq., and W. Ward, Esq., who pay a small rent. The tithes amount to £137. 7. 7., of which £107. 3. 9. is payable to the impropriators, and £30. 3. 10. to the vicar. In the R. C. divisions the parish forms a portion of the union or district of Donabate: the chapel is in the form of a T, and was erected, about 12 years since, on land given for that purpose by the late Lord Trimleston; it has a burial-ground attached, and there is a residence for the priest. About 120 children are educated in two public schools, of which one for boys is supported by G. Evans, Esq., by whom the school-house, a neat rustic building, situated in a garden of about an acre in extent, was erected, and who gives the master a lodging and half an acre of land for a garden; the other school, for girls, is supported by Mrs. Evans, who built the school-house, with apartments for the mistress; at a proper age the children are taught embroidery, and several very elegant dresses and aprons have been worked here, one of which was for her Majesty Queen Dowager Adelaide: these schools are conducted on the Lancasterian system, and are open to all religious sects. Remains of the old castle exist, consisting of a small square tower, long since deserted as a habitation: the last occupant was Lady Acheson.

PORT-ST.-MARNOCK, a parish, in the barony of Coolock, county of Dublin, and province of Leinster 7½ miles (N.E.) from Dublin; containing 482 inhabitants. On a rock, close to the sea-shore, stands the small gloomy castle of Rob's-Wall, or Robuck's Wall, founded either in the 15th or early in the 16th century by Mac Robuck, descended from Robuck de Birmingham, and the head of a sept of this ancient family. The manor belonged, from a very early period, to the abbey of St. Mary, Dublin, and is now chiefly vested in a branch of the Plunkett family. The parish, which is bounded on the east by St. George's channel, comprises 1729 statute acres. The sea-reed, or bent, grows plentifully, in conjunction with *Carex arenaria*, on the sands near Rob's-Wall. There is a good limestone quarry, in which fossils are frequently found, and good potter's clay is procured within the parish. Here are several respectable seats, the principal of which are Broomfield, the residence of J. Frazier, Esq.; Beechwood, of N. J. Trumbull, Esq., in the grounds of which are some remarkably fine beech trees; Portmarnock House, of L. Plunkett, Esq.; Hazel Brook, of James Frazier, Esq.; St. Helen's, of T. Macartney, Esq.; the Grange, of F. Beggs, Esq.; and Drumnigh, of M. Farran, Esq. The living is a perpetual curacy, in the diocese of Dublin, and in the patronage of the Archbishop; the tithes amount to; £98. 1. 7., of which £23. 1. 7. is payable to Mr. Hudson, and £75 to the perpetual curate, who also receives £20 per ann. from Primate Boulter's augmentation fund. The glebe-house, situated in the parish of Cloghran, was erected in 1791, by aid of a gift of £150 and a loan from the late Board of First Fruits; the glebe comprises nine acres. The church, a small edifice with a tower and spire, was erected in 1788, by a gift of £500 from the same Board. In the R. C. divisions the parish forms part of the union or district of Baldoyle and Howth. A school, in which 23 children are educated, is supported by private subscriptions and an annual charity sermon. Here are two Martello towers, and remains of an old church, near Carrick-hill; from which elevation is obtained an extensive view of the surrounding country, with a vast expanse of sea.

RAHENY, a parish, in the barony of Coolock, county of Dublin, and province of Leinster, 4¼ miles (N.E.) from the Post-Office, Dublin, on the road to Howth; containing 612 inhabitants. This place, formerly called Rathenny, derived its name from an ancient rath or moat in the centre of the village, overhanging a small stream; and is supposed to have formed part of the district called Rechen, which, together with Baelduleek (Baldoyle) and Portrahern (Portrane), was granted by Anlave, King of Dublin, to the church of the Holy Trinity, in 1040. It is also noticed under the name of Rathena, by Archdall, as the birth-place or residence of a saint about the year 570, at which time probably there may have been a religious establishment. The celebrated battle of Clontarf took place in its immediate vicinity; and it may probably have been a post of some importance, as commanding the pass of the small river which flows beneath the rath in the village. The parish is bounded on the east by the sea: the land is in general of good quality, the greater portion is meadow and pasture, and the arable land produces excellent crops of wheat; the system of agriculture is in a very improved state, and there is neither waste land nor bog. Limestone of good quality is abundant and is quarried for building and for agricultural purposes. The chief seats are the Manor House, erected by a branch of the Grace family, and now the property of W. Sweetman, Esq.; Fox House, of J. A. Sweetman, Esq.; Fox Hill, of E. J. Irwin, Esq.; Edenmore (formerly Violet Hill), of J. Maconchy, Esq.; Raheny Cottage, of J. Ball, Esq.; Bettyville, of J. Classon, Esq.; Swan's Nest, of W. Craig, Esq.; Belmont, of Mrs. White; and Ballybay, of J. D'Arcey, Esq. A constabulary police force is stationed in the village; and petty sessions are held there on alternate Thursdays. The living, is a rectory, in the diocese of Dublin, and in the patronage of the Crown the tithes amount to £316. 10. 6.; the glebe-house is a good residence, and the glebe comprises about 30 acres of profitable land. The church, a small plain edifice, is supposed to have been rebuilt about the year 1609. In the R. C. divisions the parish forms part of the union of Clontarf. About 150 children are taught in two public schools, of which the parochial school is supported by the rents of eight houses forming the crescent of Raheny, bequeathed for that purpose by the late Samuel Dick, Esq., who, in 1787, built the school-house; the R. C. school is chiefly supported by the Sweetman family, of whom the late W. Sweetman, Esq., in 1820, built the school-house, with apartments for the master, at his own expense. There is a dispensary in the village; and the late Mrs. Preston, in 1831, bequeathed £100 for the poor of the parish.

RANELAGH, a village, in the parish of St. Peter, barony of Upper-cross, county of Dublin, and province of Leinster, 1½ mile (S. by E.) from the General Post-Office, Dublin, on the road to Enniskerry; containing 1988 inhabitants. Here is a nunnery of the Carmelite order, with a neat chapel attached: a school for poor girls is gratuitously conducted by the nuns. In the vicinity are several avenues in which are a number of neat villas; also the extensive nursery grounds of Messrs. Toole and Co. Adjoining the village is Cullenswood, noted for a dreadful massacre by the native Irish of upwards of 500 citizens (a colony from Bristol), who on Easter-Monday, 1209, went out to divert themselves near the wood, where they were surprised and slaughtered. The day was afterwards called "Black Monday," and the place is still known by the name of the "Bloody Fields."

RATHCOOLE, a post-town and parish, in the barony of Uppercross, county of Dublin, and province of Leinster, 8 miles (S.W.) from Dublin, on the road to Naas; containing 1409 inhabitants, of which number, 602 are in the town. This place, anciently called "Radcull," appears from various records to have been incorporated prior to the time of Hen. III., and to have had burgesses. In the 24th of that reign (1240), it is recorded that "Lucas, Archbishop of Dublin, grants to the burgesses of Radcull common of pasture and turbary in the mountain of Slescol with his men of Newcastle near Lyons, at 4s. per annum." The town, which is about a quarter of a mile in length, contains 112 houses irregularly built, and has a patent for holding fairs on April 23rd, June 18th, and Oct. 9th, but these fairs have not been held for some years. It is the head station of the constabulary police for the district of Uppercross, and the residence of the chief constable. The parish comprises 4005 statute acres, as applotted under the tithe act; the land is fertile, and generally under profitable cultivation; about 600 acres of common were enclosed in 1818. To the west of the town is a range of heights branching off from the chain of hills on the confines of the county of Wicklow, in a north-western direction, comprising the hills of Rathcoole, Windmill, Athgoe and Lyons, the formation of which is generally clay-slate loose and conglomerate, and grauwacke slate, with occasional alternations of granite, and some red conglomerate sandstone. The principal seat is Johnstown, the handsome residence of J. Kennedy, Esq., in a tastefully disposed and well-cultivated demesne of 200 acres. The living is a vicarage, in the diocese of Dublin, united to the rectory and vicarage of Calliaghstown, and in the patronage of the Archbishop; the rectory forms part of the corps of the deanery, of St. Patrick's, Dublin. The tithes amount to £310 of which £60 is payable to the dean, and the remainder to the vicar; the glebe-house is a good residence, and the glebe comprises 15 acres, of which 6 were allotted from the common on its enclosure in 1818. The church, for the repair of which the Ecclesiastical Commissioner have recently granted £111, is a neat plain edifice. In the R. C. divisions the parish forms part of the union of Saggard. A school, in which are about 70 children, is supported by J. D. La Touche, Esq., and there is a private school of about 40 children, also a dispensary. A school was endowed here for 50 Protestant girls by the late Mrs. Mary Mercer, which was removed some years since to the parish of Castleknock. This place formerly gave the title of Viscount to the family of Tracey, to which James Tracey, Esq., of Geashill, in King's county, is at present prosecuting his claim before the House of Lords.

RATHFARNHAM, a parish, in the barony of Newcastle, county of Dublin, and province of Leinster, 4 miles (S.) from Dublin, on the road to Rathdrum; containing 4573 inhabitants, of which number, 1572 are in the village. The castle of Rathfarnham was built by Archbishop Loftus, who was Lord Chancellor of Ireland in the reign of Elizabeth. On the breaking out of the war of 1641, Sir Adam Loftus held it with a garrison, as an outpost to protect the city of Dublin against the incursions of the septs of O'Toole and Byrne from the neighbouring mountains of Wicklow; in 1649 it was taken by the forces of the Duke of Ormonde. Adam Loftus, grandson of Sir Adam, was created baron of Rathfarnham in 1685. At the commencement of the insurrection of 1798, the village was the scene of a skirmish between a detachment of the King's troops and a party of the insurgents, in which several of the latter were killed and others taken prisoners. Near the village is a lofty bridge of a single arch over the river Dodder, the road from which is thickly shaded by the plantations of the demesnes on each side: the place itself is a long straggling street, with very little to attract attention. The country around is studded with numerous beautiful and richly planted seats, and presents a great variety of picturesque rural scenery. Petty sessions are held in the village every Wednesday: it is a metropolitan police station, and has a dispensary; a fair is held in it on the 10th of July. Near the bridge is a woollen factory, which employs about 100 persons; there are also paper and corn mills near it, which are worked by the waters of the Dodder and the Cruagh river, that form a junction here: at Rathgar are extensive calico print-works. The small villages of Roundtown and Templeogue are in the parish: in the latter are the ruins of a church with a small burial-ground still used as a cemetery attached to it. Archbishop Alan states, in his "Repertorium Viride," that the church was a chapel appendant to the church of Kilmesantan without the marches or pale, that it was built on the hither side of the Dodder, as being a safer place to hear divine service in during times of war, and that from its late erection it had the name of Templeogue, which signifies "New Church," given to it. The castle, now the property of the Marquess of Ely, is a large and stately mansion in the centre of a fine and thickly planted demesne, the principal entrance to which is a very beautiful gateway, built in the style of a Roman triumphal arch, besides which there is a very lofty pointed Gothic gateway leading to the village: the entrance to the house from the terrace on which it stands is by a portico of eight Doric columns which support a dome painted in fresco with the signs of the zodiac: the great hall is ornamented with a number of ancient and modern busts on pedestals of variegated marble, and has three windows of stained glass, in one of which are the arms of the Loftus family. The collection of family portraits and paintings by the old masters has been removed, in consequence of a determination to take the building down and to divide the demesne into a number of small plots for the erection of villas. The other more remarkable seats, besides those described in the articles on Roundtown and Rathgar, are Ashfield, the residence of Sir W. C. Smith, puisne baron of the Exchequer; Beaufort, of R. Hodgens, Esq.; Landscape, of H. O'Callaghan, Esq.; Whitehall, of W. P. Matthews, Esq.; Newtown, of John Kirby, Esq., LL.D., M.D., in the grounds of which there are some very fine evergreens; Rathfarnham House, of the Rev. H. McClean; Bolton Hall, of P. Jones, Esq.; Barton Lodge, of W. Conlan, Esq.; Sallymount, of J. Watson, Esq.; Edenbrook, of E. Coulan, Esq.; Ballyroan, of A. Reilly, Esq.; Brook Lodge, of R. Hutchinson, Esq.; Mount Browne, of Mrs. Johnson; Old Orchard, of P. Larkin, Esq.; Ballyhill, of the Rev. G. Browne; Butterfield House, of J. Wright, Esq.; Nutgrove, of P. Jones, Esq.; Washington Lodge, of the Rev. J. Burnett; Fairbrook, of Thos. Murphy, Esq.; Rusina, of B. Brunton, Esq.; Old Orchard House, of J. Sweeny, Esq., and Whitehall, of T. Laffan, Esq., an out-office of which is built in the shape of a pottery furnace, with a winding flight of steps on the outside to the top, whence there is a commanding prospect of the surrounding country.

The parish comprises 2724 statute acres. It is a rectory, in the diocese of Dublin, and one of the parishes which constitute the archdeaconry of Dublin: the tithes amount to £315. The church is a plain building of rough stone with hewn stone quoins, of very plain outward appearance, but fitted up within very neatly: in it is a mural tablet to the memory of Barry Yelverton, first Lord Avonmore, whose remains are in the cemetery, as are also those of the late Archbishop Magee. The church was enlarged and a tower and spire added to it, in 1821, at a cost of £900, being a loan from the Board of First Fruits, and the Ecclesiastical Commissioners have lately granted £270 for its repair. In the R. C. divisions this is the head of the union or district of Rathfarnham, Crumlin, and Bohernabreena, comprising the parishes of Rathfarnham, Crumlin, Tallaght, Cruagh, and Whitechurch. There are large chapels at Rathfarnham, Crumlin, and Bohernabreena, the last in the parish of Tallaght: near the first-named is a good house for the priest. Near the village is a convent of nuns of the order of Loretto: the building is a large brick mansion, which had been the seat of the late G. Grierson, Esq. The sisterhood have a boarding school for young ladies and also superintend a free school of upwards of 100 children, which is aided by the Board of National Education; the pupils receive a suit of clothes annually. Attached to the nunnery is a small chapel very elegantly fitted up: the sisterhood have lately purchased the convent of the nuns of St. Clare at Kingstown. The parochial school is aided by an annual donation from the archdeacon of Dublin; a school for boys in connection with the R. C. chapel is supported by subscriptions and a charity sermon; another school is in connection with the London Hibernian Society. Wilkes, the celebrated comedian, was a native of this parish.

RATHGAR, a district, partly in the united parishes of St. Peter and St. Kevin, barony of Uppercross, and partly in the parish of Rathfarnham, barony of Newcastle, county of Dublin, and province of Leinster 1½ mile (S.) from Dublin: the population is returned with the respective parishes. This place, which is on the road from Dublin, by way of Rathmines, to Roundtown, consists of several ranges of pleasant houses and numerous detached villas of which the. principal are Rathgar House, the residence of J. Farran, Esq.; Rathgar, of P. Waldron, Esq.; Rokeby, of C. Pickering, Esq.; Mote View, of J. Powell, Esq.; Mountain Prospect, of P. Nolan, Esq.; Roseville, of Miss Moore; Fair View, of Mrs. Fox; Prospect Villa, of J. Houston, Esq.; Maryville, of J. Jennings, Esq.; Prospect Lodge, of R. Clarke, Esq.; Primrose Cottage, of T. Alley, Esq.; and the handsome residences of G. Wall and W. Haughton, Esqrs. There is an extensive bleach-green, with printing-works belonging to Messrs. Waldron, Dodd, Carton, & Co., for muslin, calicoes, and silks; the works are set in motion by a steam engine of 30-horse power, and a water-wheel of equal force, and afford employment to 300 men. In the immediate vicinity are some quarries of good limestone, which are extensively worked; and strata of calp limestone have been discovered alternating with the limestone in several places, here, as well as in the quarries at Roundtown and Crumlin, inclined at a considerable angle and exhibiting other appearances of disturbance.

RATHMICHAEL, a parish, partly in the barony of Uppercross, and partly in that of Half-Rathdown, county of Dublin, and province of Leinster, 2 miles (N.W.) from Bray, on the road to Dublin; containing 1297 inhabitants. This place appears to have attained a considerable degree of importance at a very early period; the vicars choral of St. Patrick's, Dublin, claimed as their ancient inheritance the town of

Shanganagh, in this parish; and the whole of that extensive townland belonged, from the reign of Edw. I., to the family of Walsh, of Old Connaught, till the early part of the last century, when it was purchased by Lewis Roberts, Esq. It has since that time been divided into portions and let on leases in perpetuity by the heirs of that family, who hold the fee simple of the estate; the largest portion of the land, consisting of more than 100 plantation acres, has been for 40 years in the occupation of Gen. Sir George Cockburn, K. C. The parish, which is bounded on the east by the sea, comprises 2599 statute acres, as applotted under the tithe act, and valued at £4137 per annum. The soil is good and the system of agriculture improved; the only waste land is mountain, which affords rough pasturage, and there are about 8 acres of common. Granite is found in several places, and on the mountain of Shankill, near which there are mines of lead worked by the Mining Company of Ireland. Shanganagh, the seat of Sir G. Cockburn, is a spacious and handsome castellated mansion, almost wholly built by its proprietor: the interior contains many elegant apartments, an extensive and well-selected library, a fine collection of paintings by the best masters, a variety of marbles, antique casts, and bronzes, collected by Sir George while in Italy, and some fine specimens of Egyptian granite, mosaic work, and other articles of vertu. In front of the house is a handsome column of Grecian marble with a rich Corinthian antique capital, erected by the proprietor in commemoration of the passing of the Reform Bill. The views from the house are very rich and finely diversified, embracing woods, mountain, and sea; and the grounds are ornamented with a variety of statuary tastefully disposed. There are several other seats in the parish, which, from their elevated situation and proximity to the sea, command fine prospects. The principal are Shanganagh House, the residence of W. Hopper, Esq.; Clairmont, of J. Clarke, Esq.; Newbrighton, of W. Graves, Esq.; Newbrighton, of — Dillon, Esq.; Air Hill, of W. Hall, Esq.; Chantilly, of R. Tilly, Esq.; Shankill House, of J.V. Fowler, Esq.; Sylvan Mount, of G. Hillas, Esq.; Skerrington, of J. Harvey, Esq.; Ellerslie, of W. Bigger, Esq.; Ballybride House, of the Hon. R. Plunkett; Springfield, of Mrs. Morgan; Lordello, of P. Morgan, Esq.; Abington, of —Morigan, Esq.; Shanganagh, of —Carter, Esq.; Johnstown, of —Smith, Esq.; Cherrywood, of the Rev. J. Hunt; Emerald cottage, of Capt. J. S. Hore, R. N.; Shankill, of R. Maddock,

Esq.; and Clifton Cottage, of Mrs. Morgan. The eastern side of the Scalp, which abounds with features of the rudest magnificence, is within the parish. The lead-works of the Mining Company afford employment to many persons. The ore is chiefly galena, but carbonate is found in small portions; in the immediate vicinity of the mines is a tower for making shot, and at Ballycorus; are furnaces for smelting the ore not only of these but also of other mines in the neighbouring districts belonging to the same company; there are also works for rolling the lead and making pipes of all sizes. A patent exists for holding fairs near the present ruins of the ancient church, round which was formerly a considerable village, but none are now held.

The parish was separated from the union of Bray in 1826. The living is a rectory and vicarage, in the diocese of Dublin, constituting the prebend of Rathmichael in the cathedral of St. Patrick: the tithes amount to £250. The glebe-house is an inferior residence, built by Dr. John Lyon, the friend and cotemporary of Dean Swift; and there are a few acres of glebe. The church is in ruins; the Protestant parishioners attend the church of Bray. In the R. C. divisions the parish forms part of the union or district of Kingstown, and Cabinteely, and part of that of Sandyford and Glancullen. The parochial school, at Laughlinstown, in which are about 40 children, is supported by subscription; and there is a private school, in which are about 60 children. An estate was bequeathed by F. Adair, Esq., to the parish of Powerscourt and the unions of Delgany and Bray, of the proceeds of which this parish receives a portion. Near the ruins of the ancient church, which occupy an elevated site commanding a view of the sea and the adjoining country, are the remains of an ancient round tower, consisting of the foundation and about two feet of the wall above ground: it has a singular under-ground gallery, mostly choked up, which is said to be extensive. The remains of a line of castles and intrenchments may be traced, commencing on the lands of Shanganagh, near Laughlinstown, and continued over the mountain beyond Rathmichael to Ballyman; in such as yet exist, the vaults appear to have been centred with wicker-work. There are several Druidical relics in the neighbourhood; also the ruins of Puck's castle and that of Shankill, said to have been besieged by Cromwell, and near which have been frequently found human skeletons, and coins of the reigns of Chas. I. and Jas. I. In a field belonging to Mr. Hopper was discovered, in ploughing, a stone coffin containing human bones. The glebe-house was for several years the favourite retreat of Dr. Leland, author of the History of Ireland, who was rector of the union of Bray, and who planted the shrubbery which now surrounds it.

RATHMINES, a considerable village and suburb of Dublin, in that part of the united parishes of St. Peter, and St. Kevin which is in the barony of Uppercross, county of Dublin, and province of Leinster, on the old road to Milltown, 2 miles (S.) from the General Post-Office: containing 1600 inhabitants. This place is chiefly noted as the scene of the celebrated battle of Rathmines, which occurred Aug. 2nd, 1649: the marquess of Ormonde, with the royalist army, consisting of about 7000 foot and 4000 horse, had fixed his head-quarters at Old Rathmines Castle (now occupied by Mr. Jackson), on taking measures to invest the city of Dublin; but an action with the garrison being brought on by an attack upon the neighbouring castle of Baggotrath, the republican soldiers gained an advantage, which they pursued with vigour, and succeeded in putting to flight the whole of the forces under the Marquess of Ormonde, with the loss on the part of the latter of 600 slain and 1800 prisoners, among whom were 300 officers: the Marquess retired to Kilkenny. From the circumstance of cannon and musket-balls, and coins of the reign of Jas. I. being frequently ploughed up, it is conjectured that the conflict raged a considerable distance along the banks of the river Dodder. At the corner of the Rathgar road is a station of the city police: there is a small woollen factory belonging to Messrs. Wilans. Twelve years since Rathmines was only known as an obscure vil-lage; it now forms a fine suburb, commencing at Portobello bridge, and extending in a continued line of handsome houses, with some pretty detached villas, for about one mile and a half. Among the most conspicuous are Rathmines Castle, the residence of J. T. Purser, Esq., a castellated mansion in tastefully disposed grounds; Wood Park, of T. P. Hayes, Esq.; Fort-Royal Hall, of J. Rutherford, Esq., whence is obtained a splendid view of the bay of Dublin, and the Dublin and Wicklow mountains; Campobello, of M. Roache, Esq.; Fortfield, of P. Boylan, Esq.; Gortnasheelah, of the Rev. J. B. McCrea; Rathgar House, of the Hon. Capt. Coote Hely Hutchin-son; Bellwood House, of O. Willan, Esq.; Greenville, of J. Chadwick,

Esq.; Rookerick, of Mrs. Codd; Chapel View, of G. Taylor, Esq.; Somerville, of Roderick Connor, Esq.; and Ashgrove, of G. Watson, Esq. A handsome church was erected in 1828, at a cost of £2600, defrayed by the late Board of First Fruits; it is in the pointed style of architecture, with a square tower surmounted with a lofty spire: the design is an imitation of the ancient roofed crypts, the roof being a solid arch, and the walls and ceiling in the interior forming a continued vault: it is a chapel of ease to the united parishes of St. Peter and St. Kevin. In the vestry is a parochial library, presented by the Rev. S. W. Fox. On the Rathmines road is a neat R. C. chapel, which is the parochial chapel for the union or district of St. Mary and St. Peter, comprising parts of the Protestant parishes of St. Peter, St. Kevin, St. Catherine, and St. Mary Donnybrook in addition, there are R. C. chapels at Milltown, and at the nunneries at Harold's Cross and Ranelagh. Here is a female day school, partly supported by subscription; and a spacious school-house was erected in 1835, by subscription, near the Rathmines chapel, in connection with the new Board of Education.

RATHTOOLE, or BALLYCOR, a parish, in the barony of Newcastle, county of Dublin, though locally in the barony of Upper Talbotstown, county of Wicklow, and province of Leinster, 4 miles (N. W. by N.) from Baltinglass, on the road to Ballitore; containing 238 inhabitants. It comprises 687 statute acres, and is a vicarage, in the diocese of Dublin, forming part of the union of Timolin; the rectory is appropriate to the prebendaries and vicars choral of Christ-Church cathedral, Dublin. The tithes amount to £52. 10., of which £35 is payable to the appropriators, and the remainder to the vicar. At Ballycore is an ancient burial-place.

RINGSEND, a small town, in that part of the parish of St. Mary, Donnybrook, which is in the county of the city of Dublin, in the province of Leinster, 1½ mile (E.) from the General Post-Office: the population is returned with the parish. This place, according to O'Halloran, was originally called *Rin-Aun*, signifying, in the Irish language, "the point of the tide," from its situation at the confluence of the Dodder with the Liffey; its present name is either a singular corruption of the former, or may perhaps have arisen from the large blocks of stone into which rings of iron were inserted for mooring vessels, previously to the construction of the present mole. The town is built upon the eastern bank of the Dodder, and has a mean and dilapidated appearance, having fallen into decay since the discontinuance of its extensive salt-works: its southern portion, which is a few hundred yards detached, is called Irishtown, and is in a less ruinous condition; it is much frequented for sea-bathing, from its proximity to Dublin. There are also hot and cold sea-water baths; the Cranfield baths, which are here much frequented, are said to have been the first hot sea-water baths erected in Ireland. Iron-works were established here by the grandfather of the late proprietor, Mr. C. K. Clarke. by whom they have been recently disposed of: the articles manufactured are steam-engines and all kinds of machinery, iron boats and utensils of various kinds. There are also glass-works, a chymical laboratory, and a distillery. The Grand Canal Company have docks to the west of this place, opening a communication between the canal and the river Liffey. Ship-building is carried on, and many of the inhabitants are employed in the fishery. Along the whole of the shore are strong embankments to keep out the sea, which at high water is above the level of the town; and similar precautions are taken to prevent inundation from the river Dodder, which frequently overflows its banks. In 1649, Sir William Ussher, though attended by many of his friends, was drowned in crossing this dangerous stream, over which a bridge of stone was afterwards erected; but the river suddenly changed its course and rendered it useless, till the stream was again forced into its former channel. In 1796, the corporation for improving the port of Dublin diverted the stream into a new channel through the low grounds between Irishtown and Dublin; and in 1802 the bridge was destroyed by a flood, and a handsome bridge of granite, of one arch, was erected, over which the road by the docks to Dublin is carried. A church was built in Irishtown, in 1703, under an act of the 2nd of Queen Anne, on account of the distance from the parish church and the difficulty of access from the frequent inundation of the roads. It is an endowed chapelry, in the diocese of Dublin, and in the patronage of the Crown, and is designated, by the 10th of Geo. I., the "Royal chapel of St. Matthew, Ringsend." There is a R. C. chapel in Irishtown, in connection with which is a boys' school, and in the village of Ringsend is a place of worship for Wesleyan Methodists. A day school for boys, a Sunday school, an infants' school, a dispensary, and a shop for supplying the poor with necessaries at reduced prices, are all kept in one large and neat building, erected in Irishtown in 1832, at an expense of £800, defrayed by subscription.

ROEBUCK, a district, in the parish of Taney, half-barony of Rath-down, county of Dublin, and province of Leinster, 2½ miles (S.) from the General Post-Office, Dublin, on the road to Enniskerry, byway of Clonskea: the population is returned with the parish. Roebuck Cas-tle, the seat of A. B. Crofton, Esq., was originally erected at a remote period and strongly fortified. About the year 1534 it was the residence of Lord Trimleston, then Lord Chancellor of Ireland; and it was occu-pied by Jas. II. and the Duke of Berwick, when they encamped in this neighbourhood. It was subsequently suffered to fall into decay, until about the year 1790, when it was repaired by the then Lord Trimle-ston, who fitted up one of the apartments, a noble room, 50 feet in length, as a theatre. About 10 years after it was purchased by James Crofton, Esq., the father of the present proprietor, who pulled down a portion of the buildings, and modernised the remainder, of which the room before mentioned, now used as the drawing-room, is the only remaining part of the old castle. This district is chiefly occupied by handsome villas, situated in tastefully disposed grounds, many of which command magnificent views of the bay and city of Dublin, the Dublin and Wicklow mountains, and the beautiful adjacent country. Among these are Roebuck Lodge, the residence of J. E. Hyndman, Esq., formerly the manor-house, and about 50 years since the only house in the district with the exception of the castle; Rich View, the residence of M. Powell, Esq.; Springfield, of Sir John Franks, Knt.; Roebuck House, of J. Power, Esq.; Roebuck, of John Ennis, Esq.; Mount Dillon, of the Rev. Dr. Prior; Roebuck Hall, of the Rt. Hon. Fras. Blackburne; Moorefield, of P. Curtis, Esq.; Prospect House, of Lady Harty; Roebuck Park, of Geo. Kinahan, Esq.; Roebuck Villa of D. Kinahan, Esq.; Farm Hill, of Jas. Pratt, Esq.; Castle View, of A. Brew-ster, Esq.; Roebuck House, of J. D. Farrer, Esq.; Roebuck Grove, of Jno. Cumming, Esq.; Casino, of Geo. Stapleton, Esq.; Rosemount, of R. Corballis, Esq.; Rose Vale, of Geo. Thorpe, Esq.; Rose Villa, of L. E. Leipsett, Esq., M.D.; Roebuck, of R. Connor, Esq.; Bloom Villa, of Col. Thackeray; Bird Avenue, of F. Codd, Esq.; Hermitage, of W. C.

Quinn, Esq.; Friarsland, of C. Copland, Esq.; and Ivy Lodge, of Robt. Billing, Esq. Adjoining Roebuck Castle is a remarkable walnut tree, which grew out of an old wall, carrying in its trunk a large stone that is now upwards of four feet from the ground. Several coins of Elizabeth and Jas. I. have been found here.

ROUNDTOWN, a village, in the parish of Rathfarnham, barony of Newcastle, county of Dublin, and province of Leinster, 2½ miles (S.) from the General Post-Office; the population is returned with the parish. The place takes its name from the arrangement of its cottages in the form of a circle: it is neat and pleasantly situated, and forms a pleasing feature in the environs of the metropolis, to which it has a twopenny post. In the immediate vicinity are numerous handsome seats and elegant villas. Bushy Park, the seat of Sir Robt. Shaw, Bart., is a spacious mansion of brick, situated in an ample demesne tastefully embellished, and commanding some beautiful views of mountain scenery. Fortfield, the admired residence of the late Rt. Hon. Sir W. McMahon, Bart., Master of the Rolls, is pleasingly situated in grounds beautifully ornamented and comprehending much interesting scenery. Kimmage, the seat of the Rt. Hon. F. Shaw, Recorder of Dublin, is a handsome mansion in the ancient English style, in a demesne highly cultivated and embellished with great taste. Terenure, the handsome seat of F. Bourne, Esq., is remarkable for the picturesque beauty of its grounds, embellished with stately timber of many varieties, and its gardens laid out with great taste and comprehending a rich selection of choice plants and flowers. In the demesne and gardens are numerous varieties of orange trees, ash, elm, horse-chesnut, holly, and hawthorn, and more than 1750 different varieties of rose trees: the conservatories and hot-houses contain upwards of 12,000 square feet of glass, and the whole is arranged in the most perfect order and preserved with the greatest care. The other seats, all of which are more or less distinguished for beauty of situation and variety of scenery, are Fortfield Lodge, that of W. Crozier, Esq.; Fanny Ville, of Mrs. Reade; Elm Grove, of Mrs. Byrne; Wainsfort, of Capt. Theo. Norton; St. John's, of W. Darley, Esq.; Willow Mount, of W. Hodges, Esq.; Mount Tallant House, of P. Whelan, Esq.; Ashfield, of P. Cornwall, Esq.; Mount-Tallant Lodge, of B. H. Orpen, Esq.; Mountain View, of W. Deane, Esq.; Prospect, of J. Fagan, Esq.; Rathgar House, of G. McBride, Esq.;

Westbourne Lodge, of T. Dickson, Esq.; Meadowbank, of T. Copperthwaite, Esq.; Prospect House, of J. Halloway, Esq.; Mount Saville, of W. Shine, Esq.; Everton, of F. Burke, Esq.; Rose Villa, of C. Wood, Esq., Arbutus Lodge, of J. Walsh, Esq.; Elm Cottage, of R. F. Murphy, Esq., M. D.; and Rusina, of B. Brunton, Esq.

RUSH, a small sea-port and fishing town, in the parish of Lusk, barony of Balrothery, county of Dublin, and province of Leinster, 6 miles (N.E.) from Swords, and 13½ (N. by E.) from Dublin; containing 2144 inhabitants. This town, which is situated on the eastern coast, contains 442 houses, chiefly inhabited by fishermen; and has, since the 16th century, been celebrated for the great quantities of ling which are taken and cured by the inhabitants. Previously to the discontinuance of the fishing bounties, 22 boats were employed in this fishery, which number has since been reduced to 16 of about 40 tons each, carrying seven or eight men. The harbour is difficult of access and consequently adapted only for small vessels. The channel has from seven or eight feet depth at low water, and is much exposed to a heavy swell during the prevalence of winds from the north-east. A small pier has been erected on a ledge of rock extending into the sea, and covered on the north side by a reef of rocks, which affords good accommodation to the vessels employed in the fishery. The sands are celebrated for early potatoes, which are produced here in abundance. On the south side of the bay, and to the east of the pier, are beds of fine compact limestone and black slate clay and conglomerate limestone alternating. A coast-guard station has been established here, forming one of the nine which constitute the district of Swords; a constabulary police force is stationed in the town, and there is a martello tower on the beach. A patent exists for fairs on May 1st and Sept. 29th, but they are not held. The parish church is three miles distant, and therefore, for the accommodation of the town, divine service is performed once every Sunday in the parochial school-room, a large and commodious building, in which are a lending library and a depository of bibles. In the R. C. divisions the town forms the head of a union or district, including also Lambay island and part of the adjoining districts: there are chapels at Rush and on Lambay island; the former was built about 70 years since, and a tower, embattled and surmounted with a cross, was added to it in 1833, by subscription; the interior is well fitted up and has a carved altar-piece brought from France. Adjoining it is the residence of the parish priest, built in 1823 by subscription, to which the late Mrs. Palmer, of Rush House, largely contributed and also gave an acre and a half of land for a site. A dispensary in the town is supported in the usual manner. About half a mile from the town is Rush House, now called Kenure Park, formerly the residence of the great Duke of Ormonde, and subsequently of Sir Henry Echlin, Bart., from whom it was purchased by an ancestor of Sir W. H. Palmer, Bart., its present proprietor. The mansion is spacious and handsome, and contains many good apartments, a collection of valuable paintings by the first masters, and a selection of cases and other relics from the remains of Pompeii, collected by the late Mr. Palmer when in Italy. The demesne is richly embellished with stately timber, and commands some interesting views, embracing the town of Rush, Lambay island, and a great expanse of sea; and within the grounds are the picturesque ruins of Kenure church, in which is a large tomb inscribed to the memory of George, fourth Baron of Strabane, who died in 1668. Near these ruins are the remains of an ancient castle, a holy well dedicated to St. Catherine, and part of an ancient cross

SAGGARD, or TASSAGGARD, a parish, in the barony of Newcastle, county of Dublin, and province of Leinster, 1 mile (E. by S.) from Rathcoole, on the roads leading from Dublin to Blessington and Naas; containing 1673 inhabitants, of which number, 266 are in the village. This parish comprises 4260 statute acres, as applotted under the tithe act; the surface is mountainous, but the lower grounds are in good cultivation; limestone is quarried, and the mountains abound with peat. The principal seats are Saggard House, the residence of P. Smith, Esq.; Kingswood, of Mrs. Walsh; and Ashtree Cottage, of J. Wade, Esq., where the Saggard hounds are kept. The village is pleasantly situated near the Tallaght hills, and contains 71 houses, neatly built. The manufacture of paper is carried on in mills belonging to Mr. McDonnell, at Swift's Brook, where was formerly a residence of Dean Swift. Fairs are held on Corpus Christi day, Oct. 10th, and Nov. 8th. The living is a rectory, in the diocese of Dublin, and in the patronage of the Archbishop, partly appropriate to the deanery of St. Patrick's, Dublin, and partly constituting the corps of the prebend of Saggard in the cathedral of St. Patrick. The tithes amount to £250, of which £110 is payable to the dean, and the remainder to the prebendary. The church has long been in ruins, and the parishioners attend the church of Rathcoole; the churchyard is still used as a burial-place. In the R. C. divisions the parish is the head of a union or district, comprising also the parishes of Newcastle and Rathcoole, and part of the parish of Tallaght. There are chapels at Saggard and Newcastle; on the west side of the former is a monument of marble to the Rev. A. Hart, P. P., and dean of Maynooth, with his effigy in bass relief About 100 children are taught in a public school near the village. A monastery is said to have been founded here by St. Mosacre, who flourished about the middle of the 7th century, of which there is no further record; perhaps it was destroyed in 1131, when this place was ravaged by the septs of the Byrnes and O'Tooles.

SANDFORD, a village, in the parish of St. Peter, barony of Upper-cross, county of Dublin, and province of Leinster, 1½ mile (S.) from the General Post-Office, on the road to Enniskerry: the population is returned with the parish. The name of this place is derived from the circumstance of Lord Mount Sandford having, in 1896, erected and endowed an episcopal chapel, under the provisions of an act of the 11th and 12th of Geo. III. Though not possessed of any property in the neighbourhood, sympathising with a large population destitute of any place of worship for Protestants, his lordship liberally expended about £5000 in building a church, parsonage, and school-houses, besides securing an endowment of £50 per annum to the chaplain. These buildings occupy a very interesting site: the church is fitted up in a chaste and simple style, and is capable of accommodating 900 people; 300 sittings are free; the rent of the remainder, in addition to the endowment, forms the maintenance of the clergyman. The salaries of clerk, organist, school-master, &c., are paid by collections among the congregation; so that this chapelry has never been any charge on the parish. The founder vested the right of appointment to the chaplaincy in four clergymen and one layman, as trustees, with power to fill up vacancies in their number. Each school contains about 60 children of each sex, one-half of whom are Roman Catholics: there is a lending library attached to the establishment.

SANDYFORD, a village, in the parish of Tully, barony of Half-Rathdown, county of Dublin, and province of Leinster, 5 miles (S.) of

Dublin, on the old road to Enniskerry; the population is returned with the parish. This is the head of the R. C. union or district of Sandyford and Glancullen, comprising the parishes of Kilternan and Kilgobbin, and portions of those of Tullow, Rathmichael, Stillorgan, Kill, and Taney: the chapel is a spacious building, which, though commenced 20 years since, is not yet finished; attached is a good residence for the priest: another chapel is at Glancullen, in the parish of Kilternan. There is a school in connection with the new Board of Education.

SANDYMOUNT, a large and populous village, in that part of the parish of St. Mary, Donnybrook, which is within the county of the city of Dublin, and province of Leinster, 2 miles (S.E. by E.) from the General Post-Office, to which it has a twopenny post: the population is returned with the parish. It is on the southern coast of the bay of Dublin, and is much resorted to in summer for sea-bathing, for which its fine sandy beach presents every facility. The village is very pretty and contains many good houses forming a square, in the centre of which is an ornamental grass-plot surrounded by iron railings: there are numerous pretty villas on the strand, for the convenience of summer visitors, whence a new road to Merrion has lately been made along the shore. The principal seats are Lakelands, the residence of Mrs. Williamson, situated in grounds tastefully laid out and commanding fine sea and mountain views; Wilfield House, of N. Anderson, Esq.; Sandymount Castle, of R. Corbet, Esq.; and Sandymount Park, of Capt. W. Dillon, whence is obtained a fine view of the bay of Dublin, with the bill of Howth, Ireland's Eye, Lambay island, the South Wall and the Pigeon House. In the village there are a parochial school, erected in 1833, and supported by subscriptions, and a female school, built and supported by the Misses Hepenstall, aided by £100 from the Lord Lieutenant's fund. A loan fund and a Bible Association were established here in 1832; there are also a savings-bank and a lending library. A branch of the Sisters of Charity, from Stanhope-street, Dublin, established themselves in Sandymount Avenue about five years since; the inmates consist of a superioress and five nuns, who instruct about 80 children: a neat chapel attached is open to the public.

SANTRY, or SANTREFF, a parish, in the barony of Coolock, county of Dublin, and province of Leinster, 3 miles (N.) from Dublin, on the road to Swords; containing 1159 inhabitants, of which number, 125 are in the village. In 1641 the village was burnt, and great devastation committed in the parish, by a detachment from the parliamentarian forces stationed at Dublin, which had been sent against a party of royalists that had taken post here. The parish comprises 4525 statute acres, as applotted under the tithe act: the land is of good quality, chiefly in meadow and pasture; that which is under tillage is fertile, and the system of agriculture is improving. Nearly adjoining the village is Santry House, the seat of Sir Compton Domville, Bart., proprietor of the parish, a stately mansion of brick, containing many spacious apartments ornamented with numerous family portraits, a valuable collection of historical and scriptural paintings by the best masters, and many valuable specimens of the fine arts: the demesne, comprising more than 140 acres, is tastefully laid out in gardens and pleasure-grounds, richly embellished with timber, and commanding some beautiful scenery and some extensive mountain and sea views. There are numerous other seats and villas in the parish, of which the principal are Belcamp House, the residence of C. S. Hawthorne, Esq., a handsome mansion, situated in finely disposed grounds and commanding some rich views; Woodlands, of Col. A. Thomson, C. B., built by Dean Jackson, contemporary with Dean Swift, who was a frequent inmate here; Belcamp, of Sir H. M. J. W. Jervis, Bart., an elegant villa beautifully situated; Santry Lodge, of J. Martin, Esq.; Belcamp, of Mrs. Chamley; Woodford, of F. W. Edwards, Esq.; Woodlawn, of Capt. Logan; and Collinstown, of L. Brangan, Esq. The village is pleasantly situated on the road to Swords; it contains 25 houses, neatly built, and derives much interest from the adjoining demesne of Santry House: near it is a station of the city police. The living is a vicarage, in the diocese of Dublin, and in the patronage of the Crown, in which one-half of the rectorial tithes is impropriate; the other half is annexed to the vicarage. The tithes amount to £462, of which £200 is payable to the Crown, and £262 to the vicar. The glebe-house was built on a glebe of one acre in 1829, at an expense of £1300, towards which the late Board of First Fruits contributed a gift of £200 and a loan of £600; the remainder was defrayed by the Rev. Dennis Browne, the present incumbent. The church, towards the repair of which the Ecclesiastical Commissioners have granted £264, is a plain neat edifice, rebuilt in 1709, and contains the tombs of many of the Barry and Domville families, successive proprietors of the estate. In the R. C. divisions the parish forms part of the union of Clontarf; there is a chapel at Bally-man. The charter school under the Incorporated Society is endowed with land by R. H. L. Gardiner; the house, towards which Primate Boulter contributed £400, is a spacious building, situated on the road to Drogheda: in this school about 30 children are clothed, maintained, and educated, and when of age are placed out as apprentices; and about 30 children are taught in two other public schools.

SCALP, county of Dublin. —See KILTERNAN.

SKERRIES, a sea-port and fishing town, in the parish of Holmpatrick, barony of Balrothery, county of Dublin, and province of Leinster, 3¼ miles (S.E.) from Balbriggan; containing 2556 inhabitants. The town is situated on the eastern coast, and was the place at which Sir Henry Sydney landed, in 1575, when sent by Queen Elizabeth as Lord-Deputy of Ireland: it contains 528 houses, chiefly inhabited by persons employed in the fishery; and in the neighbourhood are several hand-some villas. Previously to the withdrawing of the fishery bounties, the trade of this place was very considerable; at present only 46 boats of 40 tons, and carrying 7 men each, are employed in the fishery. Off the coast are the islands called the Skerries, within which is a broad beach of sand, dry at low water, extending from Shenex island, the most southern, to Red island, the most northern, and connected with the mainland by a causeway which, with a small pier on the north side, forms the harbour of Skerries. This harbour is the best on this part of the coast, having a good roadstead which is safe in southerly winds; the channel between Red island and Colt island is only fit for boats; but within St. Patrick's isle are from 3 to 4 fathoms of water. Tambour-work is carried on to a very considerable extent, affording employment to more than 700 persons. Fairs for cattle and pigs are held on April 28th and Aug. 10th, a constabulary police force is stationed in the town, and it is also a coast-guard station, being one of the nine that constitute the district of Swords. The parish church, a neat edifice, to which an embat-tled tower crowned with pinnacles was added, in 1819, by Hans Hamil-ton, Esq., adjoins the town; and there is also a R. C. chapel, erected in 1823, a spacious and handsome edifice. There are circulating libraries in connection with both. The parochial school-house, with apartments for the master and mistress, was erected at the expense of J. H. Hamilton, Esq., and is near the church, and the national schools are situated in the town, in which there is also a dispensary. On the Red island and on that of Shenex are martello towers; and on St. Patrick's isle are some remains of an ancient church.

STILLORGAN, a parish, in the barony of Half-Rathdown, county of Dublin, and province of Leinster, 4 miles (S.E.) from Dublin, on the road by Donnybrook to Bray; containing 2001 inhabitants, of which number, 650 are in the village. This parish comprises only 648 statute acres, of which about three-fourths are meadow and pasture, chiefly demesne lands, and the remainder principally garden grounds. There are numerous handsome seats and pleasing villas beautifully situated and commanding some fine sea views and mountain scenery, with extensive prospects over Dublin bay. The principal are Stillorgan House, the residence of J. Verschoyle, Esq., anciently the property of the Allens, ancestors of the present Viscount and Baron Allen of Stillorgan; Carysford House, the seat of the Right Hon. W. Saurin, beautifully situated in grounds tastefully laid out; Stillorgan Abbey, of A. R. Blake, Esq., a handsome residence in the Elizabethan style, built in 1833 near the site of the old abbey; Mount Eagle, of H. D. Grady, Esq.; Obelisk Park, of H. Perry, Esq., so called from a lofty obelisk erected in the grounds by Lady Pierce, for the employment of the poor during the scarcity of 1741; Thornhill, of J. George, Esq.; Carysford Lodge, of T. Goold, Esq.; Stillorgan Park, of J. Busby, Esq.; Beaufield, of H. Darley, Esq; Oatlands, of M. Pollock, Esq.; the Grove, of J. Hughes, Esq.; Woodview, of G. W. Boileau, Esq.; Riversdale, of J. W. Barlow, Esq.; Stillorgan, of R. Guinness, Esq.; Dunstaffnage Lodge, of R. H. Sheehan, Esq.; Talbot Lodge, of Capt. Newenham; Limeville, of H. B. Reeves, Esq.; Rose Hill, of Mrs. Drevar; Maryville, of L. H. Thomas, Esq.; Oakley Park, of R. Everard, Esq.; Jane Villa, of Mrs. Wilson; Elm Grove, of Mrs. Richards; Littleton, of W. Wilson, Esq., M.D.; and Waltersland, of W. H. Smith, Esq. The village is within the delivery of the Dublin twopenny post, and is a constabulary police station; there is also a constabulary police station at the village of Newtown Park. Close to it is an ale and beer brewery, which has been carried on for more than 80 years by the family of Darley: it has been for more than 40 years in the possession of the present proprietors, who have also an extensive brewery and malting concern at Bray.

This parish, together with that of Kilmacud, constitutes the perpetual curacy of Stillorgan, in the diocese of Dublin, and in the patronage of the Dean of Christ-Church, Dublin: the tithes amount to £101. 10. 9¼., the whole payable to the incumbent; the glebe, which is situated in the parish of Kill, comprises 9 acres. The church, a neat edifice, was enlarged in 1812 and again in 1833, for which the late Board of First Fruits, in the former instance, granted a loan of £800, and in the latter a gift of £500. In the R. C. divisions the parish forms part of the union of Booterstown, and also part of that of Sandyford and Glancullen. About 150 children are taught in three public schools, and an infants' school is supported by Charles Doyne, Esq., of Newtown Park; there are also a dispensary in the village, and an institution for bettering the condition of the poor and suppressing mendicity. Adjoining the grounds of Waltersland is a field called Silver Park, from the great number of silver coins and ornaments found there. On clearing the rocky ground, more than 100 graves were discovered, together with numerous spear heads and other warlike instruments, confirming a tradition that a battle had been fought there; there were also discovered some urns of baked clay, containing ashes and burnt bones, and a small chamber, about a foot and a half square, formed of four upright stones, with one on the top and one at the bottom.

SWORDS, a market and post-town (formerly a parliamentary borough), and a parish, in the barony of Nethercross, county of Dublin, and province of Leinster, 7 miles (N.) from Dublin, on the road to Drogheda by Balbriggan; containing 3722 inhabitants, of which number, 2537 are in the town. The place appears to owe its origin to the foundation of a monastery here, in 512, by St. Columbkill, who presented to it a missal written by himself, appointed St. Finan Lobhair, or the Leper, its first abbot, and blessed the well there. The monastery continued long to increase in character and wealth, and the town in consequence rose to such a magnitude, that it had several additional places of worship, among which were chapels dedicated to St. Finan and St. Bridget, near the latter of which was an ancient cross, called "Pardon Crosse." It was repeatedly plundered and burnt by the Danes; and about the year 1035 it suffered in a similar manner from an attack by Conor O'Melaghlin, king of Meath, who was killed in the engagement, to revenge which his brother ravaged the whole district of Fingal with fire and sword. Notwithstanding these repeated injuries it still retained the character of a place of much importance: for when the bodies of Brian Boroimhe and his son Murrough, who fell in the arms of victory at the famous battle of Clontarf, were being conveyed to their final place of interment at Armagh, they were deposited for one night during the journey in the abbey of this town. On the foundation of the collegiate establishment of St. Patrick's, Dublin, by Archbishop Comyn in 1190, Swords was not only constituted a prebend of that church, but it is noticed by Archbishop Alan, in his *Repertorium Viride* as "the Golden Prebend, similar to that of Sarum in England;" and in the same work it is registered as giving name to one of the rural deaneries in the northern part of the diocese. King John granted to the same prelate the privilege of holding a fair there for eight days after the feast of St. Columbkill. It was incorporated by Queen Elizabeth in 1578. Jas. I., in 1603, granted to the Archbishop of Dublin a confirmation of the privileges of the town, together with a weekly market on Monday; in this document the place is called the Archbishop's manor of Swords. A grant of two additional fairs was made to it in 1699. On the breaking out of the war in 1641, the Irish army of the pale assembled for the first time at Swords, and on the 10th of the following January they were driven from it with the loss of 200 men, by Sir Chas. Coote, with scarcely any on his side except that of Sir Lorenzo Carey, a son of Lord Falkland, who was slain in the action.

The town occupies a pleasing situation on the steep banks of a small but rapid stream, which discharges itself northwards into the inner extremity of the creek or pill of Malahide: the creek, which comes within a mile of the town, is navigable for boats at high water. It consists chiefly of one wide street, a mile in length, formed of houses which, with but few exceptions, are of mean appearance. Fairs are held on March 17th and May 9th for cattle and pedlery; petty sessions on Wednesdays; and it is a constabulary police station. Its charter, already noticed, which bears date in the 20th year of the reign of Elizabeth, incorporates the place by the name of the "Bailiff and Burgesses within the Town of Swords." It was a potwalloping borough and sent two representatives to the Irish parliament, but was disfranchised at the union. By an order of the privy council of Ireland, dated

Jan. 10th, 1837, under the Act of the 6th and 7th of Wm. IV., for extending the jurisdiction and regulating the proceedings of the Civil Bill Court, the county of Dublin is divided into two districts: the northern, called the district of Balbriggan, consists of the barony of Balrothery, so much of the parishes of Swords, Killossory, and Malahide as are in the barony of Coolock, and the barony of Nether-cross, except the part of the parish of Finglass which is within that barony; the act of council directs that two general sessions of the peace are to be held annually at Balbriggan and two at Swords for this district: for the particulars of the southern district, named the district of Kilmainharn, see KILMAINHAM.

The parish, according to the county book in the custody of the treasurer, contains 3536 Irish acres, of which 1227 are in the town and its liberties. The soil is good and the system of agriculture rapidly improving there are several extensive corn-mills within the parish, and it is embellished with numerous seats and villas. Brackenstown, the seat of R. Manders, Esq., is a spacious mansion, situated in a demesne laid out with much taste, in which is a cemetery erected by the present proprietor's father, whose remains are interred there: this place was the residence of the Chief Baron Bysse in the time of Cromwell, who visited him here during his military expedition to Ireland, Balheary House, the residence of A. Baker, Esq., is a large square structure with several apartments of ample dimensions; in the saloon and dining-rooms are some fine pieces of tapestry, formerly the property of the Earl of Ormonde: the surrounding demesne, through which flow the small rivers of Fieldstown and Knocksedan, is well laid out, and commands a fine view of Howth and the Dublin mountains, with the town and environs of Swords, which, with its church, round tower, ruins of the monastery, and other interesting objects, presents a varied and picturesque scene in the foreground. Seafield is the residence of J. Arthure, Esq.; Little Lissenhall, of R. Smith, Esq.; Newport, of P. Wilson, Esq.; the Vicarage, of the Hon. and Rev. F. Howard; Swords House, of Jas. Taylor, Esq.; Prospect Point, of Capt Purcell; Cremona, of Lieut. Col. Gordon; and Mantua, of Mrs. Daly. The parish is a prebend, rectory, and vicarage. in the diocese of Dublin. In 1431 it was divided by Archbishop Talbot into three unequal portions, one of which was assigned to a prebendary of St. Patrick's, the second to the perpetual vicar, and the remainder to the Economy of the same cathedral, which was thereby bound to maintain six minor canons and six choristers, and to furnish lights and to keep the building in a proper state of repair. At present, the rectory in part constitutes the corps of the prebend of Swords; one of the other portions is appropriated to the Economy fund of St. Patrick's, Dublin; and the other, with the vicarage, is episcopally united to the rectory of Kinsealy, and the curacies of Killeek and Killossory, in the patronage of the Archbishop. The tithes amount to £273. 1. 2½ of which £112. 13½ is payable to the dean and chapter, and the remainder to the vicar. There is a glebe-house, and a glebe of 33a. 2r. 20p. The church, completed in 1818 by aid of a loan of £2500 from the late Board of First Fruits, is a handsome building of hewn stone in the pointed style of architecture: the interior is fitted up neatly but without any display of ornamental decoration; a gallery, in which is an organ, extends across the west end: the east window is of modern painted glass. The belfry tower is that of the former church, which was allowed to remain when the rest of the edifice was taken down; it stands a little detached from the main building. Near it, in the same direction, is an ancient round tower, 73 feet high, which is of a ruder construction than most of the others now existing, but has been kept in good repair; it also differs from all the others by having on the vertex of its conical roof a small cross: near the summit are four round-headed windows opening to the four cardinal points, and at different heights are four other small square windows; an opening of about four feet high, apparently intended for the doorway, is nearly 24 feet above the ground. In the R. C. divisions the parish is the head of a union or district, which comprises the parishes of Swords, Malahide, and Cloghran, and contains two chapels, one in the town, a spacious and neat edifice with a small tower and spire, the other at Balheary. The free school, which is situated in the town, owes its origin to circumstances connected with the Union. On the suppression of the elective franchise of the borough at that period, the claimants for shares of the £15,000 allowed as compensation for the loss of that right were very numerous: but all their claims were disallowed, and the sum was vested in the Lord Chancellor and several clergymen of high station, in trust to found a school here, for the daily education of the children of the place in reading, writing, arithmetic and such branches of manufacture as would be most likely to be useful to them during their future life; the surplus to be applied to apprentice fees for those pupils who had completed their school course, for premiums, and for the general encouragement of manufactures and agriculture in the district: upwards of 300 children receive instruction in the school, and 6 of each sex are apprenticed every May with a fee of £12 each: a dispensary attached to the institution is supported from the fund and also a coal yard for selling fuel to the poor at low prices in times of scarcity. The old R. C. chapel has been converted into a school, which is in connection with the Board of National Education: there are 87 boys and 52 girls in it. Another dispensary is supported by Grand Jury presentments and private subscriptions in equal proportions.

The principal relics of antiquity still in existence are the ancient round tower and the archbishop's palace; the latter was a fortified structure in the centre of a court surrounded by embattled walls flanked with towers; these walls compose the whole of the existing remains, the enclosed area having been converted into a garden. The only evidence of the former existence of a nunnery, founded here at an unknown period, is the record of a pension granted by parliament, in 1474, to the prioress and her successors. To the south of the town, near the sea-shore, are the ruins of Seatown castle, once a chief seat of the Russell family: about a mile from the town, in the same direction, is Drynam, built by the same family in 1627, and now the property of Robt. Russell Cruise, Esq. Lissenhall, an ancient seat in the vicinity of Swords, belonged to the de Lacey family in the reign of Edw. I.; Sir Wm. Fitzwilliam resided in it for some time, when he was Lord-Deputy of Ireland. Near Brackenstown House is a high rath, which commands a fine view of all the surrounding district: near Seafield is an old burial-ground, called Ballymadrouch.

TALLAGHT, a post-town and a parish, in the barony of Uppercross, county of Dublin, and province of Leinster, 5½ miles (S.W. by W.) from Dublin, on the road to Blessington; containing 4646 inhabitants, of which number, 359 are in the town. The name, which is also written Tavelagh, Tauelagh, Tamlact and Taimlacht, signifies a "place of burial," from a large cemetery attached to the church, which popular tradition states to be the place in which the whole race of Partholan, who formed a settlement in Ireland A. M. 1956, were interred after their destruction by a plague. An abbey was founded here, in the eighth century, of which St. Maelruane was first abbot; but no record remains concerning it after the year 1125. A castle was built here by Alexander de Bicknor, Archbishop of Dublin, as his residence, which continued to be the seat of his successors until a late period; in 1324, he obtained a remission of money in consideration of his expenses in its erection. In 1331, O'Toole, the chieftain of Imail, at the head of a numerous band, plundered the castle and demesne, slew many of the Archbishop's people, and defeated Sir Philip Britt and a body of Dublin men who had been sent against him. A very large mansion-house was subsequently erected, to which was attached an extensive and well-stocked garden, laid out in the Dutch style, and a demesne of upwards of 200 acres. Dr. Fowler, who died in 1803, was the last archbishop who resided here. Lord John G. Beresford, who was translated to the see of Dublin in 1819, obtained an act of parliament to sell the buildings and lands, and his successor, Dr. Magee, sold them to Major Palmer, who, after having taken down the buildings, with the materials of which he erected Tallaght House, a handsome modern residence, disposed of his interest in them to John Lentaigne, Esq., the present proprietor.

The parish contains 6604 acres, as applotted under the tithe act: the northern portion of it is generally flat, with a range of low hills, or escars, extending from Balrothery hill, on the Dodder, to the Greenhills at its western extremity; the southern and eastern parts rise into the range of Tallaght hills, which command a magnificent view of the vale of Dublin and are backed by the lofty range of Seechin, the summit of which is on the southern verge of the parish. The Dodder has its sources near Castlekelly, in the valley of Glennasmuil, or the "Thrushes' vale," in the south, and proceeding northward quits the parish at Templeogue near Rathfarnham: the Brittas river, a tributary of the Liffey, also rises in the parish. The hills consist of clay-slate, greenstone, and greenstone porphyry; the last-liamed formation is most abundant in the eastern part. There are several paper and flour-mills and a woollen-mill in the parish. In the town is a dispensary; it is a constabulary police station, and petty sessions are held in it on alternate Mondays. It has a patent for fairs but they are not held. Near Newlands is Belgarde Castle, originally the property of a branch of the Talbots of Malahide, from whom it passed by marriage to the Dillon family, and thence by purchase to the ancestors of the present proprietor, P. H. Cruise, Esq., who resides in it. The mansion is a large building in a demesne in which there are a number of very fine aged forest trees, and has at one of its angles a square tower of very antique appearance, that formed part of the original structure, which at some distance gives it the appearance of a church. The other more remarkable seats are Templeogue House, the residence of P. Gogarty, Esq.; Newlands, of J. Crotty, Esq., and at one time that of Viscount Kilwarden, chief justice of the King's Bench; Cypress Grove, of J. Duffy, Esq.; Friarstown, of Ponsonby Shaw, Esq.; Delaford, of B. Taylor Ottley, Esq.; Sally Park, of W. E. Handcock, Esq.; Kilvere, of J. Sealy Townsend, Esq.; Willington, of the Rev. Chas. McDonnell; Prospect, of the Rev. Dr. R. McDonnell; Allenton, of F. R. Cotton, Esq.; the Glebe House, of the Rev. W. Robinson; Kiltalown, of J. Robinson, Esq.; Fir House, of J. Armitage, Esq.; Orlagh, of N. Callwell, Esq.; Killymanagh, of J. Clancy, Esq.; Castlekelly, of J. Grierson, Esq.; Oldbawn, of M. McDonnell, Esq., an ancient mansion having in one of its apartments the date 1635; Ballyroan, of W. Poole, Esq.; Ellenborough, of N. Read, Esq.; Knocklyon, of W. Dunne, Esq.; Johnville, of N. Roe, Esq.; Annemount, of J. Gaham, Esq.; Newbawn, of S. P. Lea, Esq.; Newhall, of Edw. Manders, Esq.; Killininey, of W. Devine, Esq.; Mount Hastings, of R. Hastings, Esq.; and Cherryfield, of P. A. Lawless, Esq.

The living is a vicarage, in the diocese of Dublin, united to the rectory of Cruagh, and in the alternate patronage of the Archbishop of Dublin and W. Bryan, Esq.; the rectory forms part of the corps of the deanery of St. Patrick's. The chapel of Killahan, in the townland of Oldbawn, and dilapidated since 1532, and that of St. Bridget, near the Dodder, now in ruins, were appendant to the church of Tallaght. The Dean of St. Patrick's formerly had the right of presentation to the vicarage, by a grant from Pope Gregory IX., but the right afterwards lapsed by neglect. The tithes amount to £678. 18. 6., of which £369. 4. 7½. is payable to the dean, £221. 10. 9½. to the dean and chapter in their corporate capacity, and £88. 3. 1. to the vicar; the gross tithes of the vicarial union amount to £270. 0. 7. The glebe-house stands on a glebe of 17*a*. 0*r*. 20*p*. The church, dedicated to St. Maelruane, was built in 1829 on the site of the ancient structure, by a grant of nearly £3000 from the late Board of First Fruits; it is in the pointed style of architecture, with pinnacles at the angles and along the sides: the ancient belfry tower, which is of considerable height, is still preserved as part of the edifice: the Ecclesiastical Commissioiners have lately granted £107 towards its repairs. In the R. C. divisions the parish forms part of the union or district of Rathfarnham, and has a chapel at Bohernabreena. At Fir House, a convent of discalced Carmelites, consisting of a superioress and 13 professed and lay sisters, was founded about eight years since, with a small chapel attached. At Mount Anne is a small monastery of the order of Carmelites. A female parochial school is held near the church. Near the village is a neat school-house for boys and girls, erected in 1834 at an expense of £266, of which £130 was granted by the Board of National Education, on a site given by Mr. Lentaigne, and aided by subscription, to which W. D. Trant, Esq., contributed £25 and supplied the stone for its erection from his quarries: the last named gentleman has also erected and maintains a neat schoolhouse at Ballynascorney. A free school for girls is kept by the ladies of the Convent, and one for boys by the monks of St. Anne's. Near Fir House is a private school for the instruction of the deaf and dumb, and two others: the number of pupils in the free schools is about 430, and in the private schools, about 70. In 1789, Robert Murphy, Esq., bequeathed to the minister and churchwardens £10 Irish currency for the poor, and £10 Irish per ann. towards founding a Sunday school. In the garden of Tallaght House are the remains of the original castle, consisting of a large square tower with a lofty gateway. On a rising ground that commands a pass in the road leading from Crumlin and Drymnagh Castle to Fir House is the castle of Timon, or Timothan, which anciently was the chief place in the lordship or manor of Tymothan, granted by King John to Henry de Loundres, Archbishop of Dublin, in recompense for his losses in repairing the castle of Dublin and for other public services: in 1247 the manor was erected into a prebend in St. Patrick's Cathedral, which still exists but without any endowment. The building, which was in a ruinous condition in the reign of Hen. VIII., now consists of a square tower or keep with a few small windows in a very dilapidated state. At Aughfarrell are the remains of an old castle, and at Templeogue and beyond Friarstown are ruins of old churches; near the latter of which is a well, dedicated to St. Anne. At the Greenhills is a rath and a fort, apparently erected at an early period to curb the predatory incursions of the Wicklow septs: on the grounds of Fortville Lodge is a Danish rath, surrounded with a fosse.

TANEY, or TAWNEY, a parish, in the half-barony of Rathdown, county of Dublin, and province of Leinster, 3½ miles (S.) from Dublin, on the road to Enniskerry; containing 4020 inhabitants. It is beautifully situated on a sheltered declivity near the base of the Dublin and Wicklow mountains, and comprises 3691 statute acres, as applotted under the tithe act. The land, which is of good quality, is principally in demesne; the surrounding scenery is richly diversified, and the parish thickly studded with handsome seats and pleasing villas, most of them commanding interesting views of the city and bay of Dublin and the adjacent country. Of these the principal are Mount Merrion, the residence of Mrs. Verschoyle; Merville, formerly the residence of the late Judge Downes, who greatly improved the demesne, and now the seat of R. Manders, Esq.; Mount Anville, of the Hon. Chas. Burton, second justice of the Court of Queen's Bench, situated on elevated ground commanding fine mountain and sea views, and remarkable for its richly cultivated gardens and extensive conservatories; Taney Hill, of W. Bourne, Esq.; Seafield, of T. Beasley, Esq.; Bellefield, of T. Wallace, Esq.; Bellevue Lodge, of the Rev. C. Wolsley; Runnimede, of J. Fitzpatrick, Esq.; Moreen, of D. Mc Kay, Esq.; Drummartin Castle, of Mrs. Dawson; Campfield House, of S. Boxwell, Esq.; Anneville, of Sir Geo. Whitford, Bart.; Woodbine Lodge, of T. Sherlock, Esq.; Laurel Lodge, of G. Meyler, Esq.; Ludford Park, of G. Hatchell, Esq.; Priest House, of J. Robinson, Esq.; Greenmount, of J. Turbett, Esq.; Stonehouse, of J. Benton, Esq.; Drummartin House, of J. Curry, Esq.; the residence of the Rev. Dr. Singer; Holywell, of W. Walsh, Esq.; Bessmount, of T. M. Scully, Esq.; Farmley, of J. T. Underwood, Esq.; Rockmount, of T. Courtenay, Esq.; Dellbrook, of E. G. Mason, Esq.; Eden Park, of L. Finn, Esq.; Milltown, of Major Palmer; Mount Anville, of E. Butler, Esq.; Ballinteer Lodge, of Major W. St. Clair; Churchtown House, of J. Busby, Esq.; Duindrum House, of John Walshe, Esq.; Wickham, of Wm. Farran, Esq., who has here a museum containing a large collection of curious and rare articles; Sweetmount, of W. Nolan, Esq.; Churchtown, of N. Corbett, Esq.; Churchtown House, of D. Lynch, Esq.; Sweetmount Villa, of Jas. Burke, Esq.; Sweetmount House, of M. Ryan, Esq.; and Belleville, of W. A. H. Minchin, Esq. At Windy Harbour is a silk-throwing factory belonging to Mr John Sweeny, jun., employing about 80 persons; and in the village of Dundrum is an iron-foundry.

The living is a rectory, in the diocese of Dublin, forming part of the union of St. Peter's, and of the corps of the archdeaconry of Dublin: the tithes amount to £415. 7. 8½. The church, towards the erection of which the late Board of First Fruits granted a loan of £4300, in 1818, is a spacious and handsome cruciform structure, in the later English style, with a square embattled tower; the interior was thoroughly renovated in 1835, for which purpose the Ecclesiastical Commissioners granted £256. The old church is still remaining; one portion of it is used for reading the funeral service, and another is appropriated to the parochial school. In the cemetery are some interesting monumental inscriptions, among which is one to William Halliday, Jun., Esq., who died in 1812, aged 24; he was distinguished for his eminent proficiency in Irish literature and his critical knowledge of his native language. In the R. C. divisions the parish forms part of the unions of Booterstown, Sandyford, St. Mary Donnybrook, and St. Mary and St. Peter's Rathmines; there is a chapel at Dundrum, and a place of worship for Wesleyan Methodists. About 400 children are taught in four public schools, of which the parochial school is partly supported by the rector; there is an infants' school. —See DUNDRUM.

TAWNEY. —See TANEY.

TIPPERKEVIN, a parish, in the barony of Uppercross, county of Dublin, and province of Leinster, 3 miles (W.S.W.) from Blessington; containing 791 inhabitants. This parish comprises 1682 acres, as applotted under the tithe act; the state of agriculture is gradually improving, and a great number of calves are fattened here for the Dublin market. Slate exists, but it is not at present worked. It is a rectory, in the diocese of Dublin, constituting the corps of the prebend of Tipperkevin in the cathedral of St. Patrick, Dublin, and in the patronage of the Archbishop: the tithes amount to £117. 16. 8., and there is a glebe of 80 acres. The church is a neat edifice, in the later English style, erected about seven years since by aid of a grant of £900 from the late Board of First Fruits, and the Ecclesiastical Commissioners have lately granted £164 for its repair. In the R. C. divisions the parish forms part of the union or district of Ballymore-Eustace. At Barrettstown are the ruined castle of that name, and an ancient burial-ground; and at Slieve Ruagh, Dawdingstown, and Bishop's Hill, are moats or raths.

TUBBER, a parish, in the barony of Uppercross, county of Dublin, and province of Leinster, 1 mile (N.) from Dunlavan, on the road to Ballymore-Eustace, containing 104 inhabitants. The parish, which comprises only 900 acres, is situated at the point of junction of the counties of Kildare, Dublin, and Wicklow. It is a curacy, in the diocese of Dublin, annexed by act of council, in 1833, to the union of Dunlavan: the rectory is appropriate to the archbishop. The tithes amount to £88. 12. 3½. In the R. C. divisions it forms part of the union or district of Dunlavan. There are slight remains of the old church, situated in a burial-place near an old mansion, the property of the Leslie family, now occupied by the police.

TULLOW, county of Dublin. —See TULLY.

TULLY, or TULLOW, also called Bullock, a parish, in the barony of Half-Rathdown, county of Dublin, and province of Leinster; containing with the villages of Cabinteely and Carrickmines (each separately described), 1385 inhabitants. The former, which is the principal village, is situated 6½ miles (S.S.E.) from Dublin, on the road to Bray. At the village of Golden-Ball, the eastern side of which is in this parish, is a twopenny post-office. The parish comprises 2845 statute acres, chiefly in a high state of cultivation, and embellished with numerous seats and well-planted demesnes. Granite and firestone are procured at Murphystown. Near Rockville is a deep and romantic glen or dingle. The principal seats are Leopardstown, the handsome residence of Fenton Hort, Esq., situated in a demesne of about 1200 acres, the pleasure grounds of which are tastefully laid out, and command magnificent views of the bay of Dublin, Killiney hills, Bray Head and Wicklow and Dublin mountains; Brenanstown House, the handsome and substantial mansion of Geo. Pim, Esq., also situated in a fine demesne; Cherry-field, the residence of the Rev. J. Hunt; Rocklands, of J. H. Dunne, Esq.; Rockville, of C. W. Roche, Esq., commanding a fine view of the bay of Killiney; Glanamuck, of Jos. Strong, Esq.; Priorsland, of the Rev. L. H. Bolton; Kingstown House, of the Rev. M. McNamara; North Lodge, of John Gilbert, Esq.; Carrickmines Castle, of Robt. Taylor, Esq., in the grounds of which are the remains of the ancient castle of that name; Bellmont, of Thos. Smith, Esq., M. D., commanding a magnificent mountain view; and Glen Druid, of Mrs. Barrington, which derives its name from a very perfect cromlech or druidical altar situated in a picturesque and richly wooded glen watered by a mountain stream; from the summit of a lofty tower, erected by the late Mr. Barrington, is obtained a splendid view of the sea, with the hills of Howth and Killiney, Bray Head, the Sugar Loaves, Djouce, and the Three Rock and Shankill mountains, and the beautiful country in the foreground. It is a rectory and curacy, in the diocese of Dublin; the rectory forms part of the corps of the deanery of Christ-Church, and the curacy part of the union of Monkstown: the tithes amount to £291. 18., two-thirds of which are payable to the dean, and the remainder to the curate. In the R. C. divisions it is chiefly in the union or district of Kingstown, and has a chapel at Cabinteely. At Clonkeen is a school aided by subscription, in which about 70 children are educated, and about 40 are taught in a private school at Cabinteely. According to Ledwich, the church of Tully was founded by the Ostmen and dedicated to their favourite saint, Olave; its ruins, situated on an eminence, still form a picturesque object, and its circular arches bear evidence of its remote antiquity. Near the church are the remains of some ancient crosses with traces of rudely sculptured figures. The cromlech at Glen Druid consists of a large table stone, 14 feet long and 12 broad, supported by six upright stones: the former is supposed to weigh about 25 tons. Murphystown are the remains of an ancient castle.

WARD (THE), a chapelry, in the parish of Finglas, barony of Castleknock, county of Dublin, and province of Leinster, 6 miles (N.) from Dublin, on the mail road to Ashbourne; containing 251 inhabitants. Here is a station of the constabulary police, and petty sessions are held on alternate Mondays; there are quarries of good stone. It is a chapelry, in the diocese of Dublin, forming part of the union of Finglas and corps of the chancellorship of St. Patrick's cathedral, Dublin: the tithes are included with those of Finglas. In the R. C. divisions also it is part of the district of Finglas. The church is in ruins.

WESTPALSTOWN, a parish, in the barony of Balrothery, county of Dublin, and province of Leinster, 12 miles (N.) from Dublin, containing 280 inhabitants. It is a vicarage, in the diocese of Dublin, forming part of the union and corps of the prebend of Clonmethen in the cathedral of Christ-Church, Dublin; the rectory is appropriate to the vicars choral of that cathedral. The tithes amount to £150, of which two-thirds are payable to the vicars choral, and the remainder to the vicar. In the R. C. divisions it is in the union or district of Damastown. The ruins of the church still exist.

WHITECHURCH, a parish, in the barony of Half-Rathdown, county of Dublin, and province of Leinster, 5 miles (S.) from the General Post-Office; containing, with the villages of Whitechurch, Ballyboden, and Rockbrook, 1710 inhabitants. The parish comprises 2833 statute acres of very varied surface; the northern portion, though lying high with respect to the sea level of Dublin bay, is generally flat and of good quality, highly improved by continued cultivation; the southern rises into heights of considerable elevation, forming the base of the northern range of the Dublin and Wicklow mountains, whence the Cruagh river and another of smaller size, both carrying down a considerable volume of water during the rainy season, though nearly dry in summer, irrigate the whole district from south to north, and after uniting their streams join the Dodder at Rathfarnham. Each of these has several mill sites, on which are paper-mills at present little used, though capable of executing much work, and cotton-factories that employ about 120 hands in the aggregate: attached to the works of Mr. Bewley are bleaching grounds and an extensive laundry. The mountain land produces only pasturage, and about 550 acres of it are a barren waste, but they supply inexhaustible stores of granite, which is in great demand for the public buildings and the more ornamented dwelling-houses in Dublin and the surrounding country. The military road through the county of Wicklow passes by the villages of Ballyboden and Rockbrook. The greater portion of the cultivated part of the parish is enclosed in the demesnes and grounds of the gentry who reside here, all of which, from the situation of the land that forms a gentle declivity from the mountainous parts to the shores of Dublin bay, command fine views of the beautiful and highly cultivated valley of the Liffey and the basin of the bay itself, with its back-grounds of Howth, Lambay, and the Carlingford and Mourne mountains in the distance. Marlay, the residence of John David La Touche, Esq., took its name from Bishop Marlay, whose daughter was married to the Rt. Hon. David La Touche, by whom the place was built: the demesne contains about 400 acres, and enjoys all the advantages which fertility, high cultivation, variety of surface, copious supply of water, rich and varied printing and extent of prospect can bestow: the gardens, containing about four acres, are stocked with a large selection of native and exotic plants and have extensive ranges of glass. In a sequestered spot is a mausoleum with a monument to the memory of Elizabeth, Countess of Lanesborough, sister to the present proprietor. Among the other seats are Hollypark, the beautiful residence of the late Jeffrey Foote, Esq., situated at the base of Stagstown Hill, and tastefully laid out, with a well-planted deer-park attached to it; Glen-Southwall, better known by the name of the Little Dargle, as being a miniature resemblance of the celebrated valley of that name at Powerscourt, the seat of C. B. Ponsonby, Esq., by whom the grounds are thrown open for the inspection of visitors; Larch Hill, the residence of J. O'Neil, Esq.; Hermitage, of R. Moore, Esq.; the Priory, now of G. Hatchell, Esq., and previously that of the celebrated Rt. Hon. John Philpot Curran, who resided here during the latter part of his life; The Park, of John Davis, Esq.; Eden Park. of M. Harris, Esq.; Highfield, of John Whitcroft, Esq.; Sommerville, of Fras. Sommers, Esq.; Grange Cottage, of S. Whaley, Esq.; Elm Grove, of P. Morgan, Esq.; St. Thomas, of Mrs. Unthank; Kingston, of Mrs. Jones; Cloragh, of Chas. Davis, Esq.; Tibradden, of J. Jones, Esq.; and Harold's Grange, of C. Fottrell, Esq.

The living is a rectory and perpetual curacy, in the diocese of Dublin: the rectory is appropriate partly to the deanery of Christ-Church, Dublin, and partly to the incumbent of Tallaght: it was erected into a perpetual curacy in 1823, when it was separated from the union of Tallaght, and is in the alternate patronage of the Archbishop and W. Bryan, Esq. The tithes amount to £217. 11. 1., of which £52. 3. 10. is payable to the Dean of Christ-Church, and £165. 7. 3. to the incumbent of Tallaght, who allows the curate a stipend of £69. 7. 3.: 1089 acres of the parish are tithe-free. The new church was erected in 1826, at an expense of £2000, on a site in the grounds of Marlay, given by John David La Touche, Esq.; it is in the pointed style, with a tower and spire: the Ecclesiastical Commissioners have recently granted £283 towards its repairs. The old church, which has a burial-ground attached to it, and stands on an eminence about half a mile distant, forms a picturesque ruin. In the R. C. divisions the parish forms part of the union or district of Rathfarnham. There is a Moravian cemetery on the grounds of Marlay, not far from the church. Near it also is a school-house, with apartments for the master and mistress, erected in 1824: about 30 of the pupils are annually clothed. At the Little Dargle are the ruins of a cromlech, the three upright stones of which are still standing, but the table stone has been displaced and lies on the ground near them. At Larch Hill is a druidical circle, with an altar or cromlech in its centre; and on Kilmashogue mountain is a strong chalybeate spa.

WILLIAMSTOWN, a village, in the parish of Booterstown, barony of Half-Rathdown, county of Dublin, and province of Leinster, 3½ miles (S.E.) from Dublin, on the road to Kingstown and Bray: the population is returned with the parish. This village is situated upon the southern-shore of the bay of Dublin, close to the Dublin and Kingstown railway, with which it communicates for the purpose of taking up or setting down passengers. It is much frequented in the summer months as a bathing-place, from its fine, smooth, sandy beach and its bath; here is a station of the metropolitan police. The twopenny post has three deliveries daily from the city, and a constant communication is kept up with Kingstown. In the immediate vicinity are several neat villas, which embrace a fine prospect of the bay: the principal are Ruby Lodge, the residence of T. Bradley, Esq.; Belleview, of Hickman Kearney, Esq.; Seafort Lodge, of E. Tring, Esq.; Caroline Lodge, of R. Doyle, Esq.; Westfield, of M. Dunphy, Esq.; and Williamstown Castle, of J. Boyd, Esq. Here are two eminent boarding schools; Castledawson, conducted by the Rev. A. Leney; and Seafort, by the Rev. D. W. Cahill.

APPENDIX
Shewing the Boundaries of the Cities and Boroughs in Ireland, as adopted and defined by the Act passed in the 2nd and 3rd of William IV., cap. 89, intituled "An Act to settle and describe the Limits of Cities, Towns, and Boroughs in *Ireland,* in so far as respects the Election of Members to serve in Parliament."

DUBLIN

The County of the City of Dublin, and such parts of the County at large as lie within the Circular Road.